THE POLITICS OF COR

The Politics of Corruption

➤ • ⬅

THE ELECTION OF 1824 AND THE MAKING OF
PRESIDENTS IN JACKSONIAN AMERICA

David P. Callahan

UNIVERSITY OF VIRGINIA PRESS
Charlottesville and London

UNIVERSITY OF VIRGINIA PRESS
© 2022 by the Rector and Visitors of the University of Virginia
All rights reserved
Printed in the United States of America on acid-free paper

First published 2022

1 3 5 7 9 8 6 4 2

Library of Congress Cataloging-in-Publication Data

Names: Callahan, David P., author.
Title: The politics of corruption : the election of 1824 and the making
of presidents in Jacksonian America / David P. Callahan
Description: Charlottesville : University of Virginia Press, 2022.
| Includes bibliographical references and index.
Identifiers: LCCN 2022008337 (print) | LCCN 2022008338 (ebook) | ISBN 9780813948416 (hardcover) |
ISBN 9780813948423 (paperback) | ISBN 9780813948430 (ebook)
Subjects: LCSH: Presidents—United States—Election—1824. | United States—Politics and
government—1817-1825. | Political campaigns—United States—History—19th century. |
Adams, John Quincy, 1767-1848. | Crawford, William Harris, 1772-1834. | Calhoun, John C.
(John Caldwell), 1782-1850. | Clay, Henry, 1777-1852. | Jackson, Andrew, 1767-1845.
Classification: LCC E375 .C35 2022 (print) | LCC E375 (ebook) | DDC 324.973/54—dc23/eng/20220223
LC record available at https://lccn.loc.gov/2022008337
LC ebook record available at https://lccn.loc.gov/2022008338

Cover art: Golubovy/shutterstock.com; mikesj11/shutterstock.com; Here/shutterstock.com

For Debbie, who always believed

CONTENTS

LIST OF TABLES   ix

ACKNOWLEDGMENTS   xi

Introduction: The Transitional Election   1

1. The Big Five   9

2. Electioneering without Electioneering   34

3. One-Party Politics   60

4. The Perpetual Campaign   81

5. The Final Battles   106

6. The War within the States   157

7. Kingmaking behind Closed Doors   191

Epilogue: Winners and Losers   221

NOTES   233

BIBLIOGRAPHY   263

INDEX   273

TABLES

1. Election data by state in the presidential election of 1824   159
2. Vote totals for the presidential election of 1824   164
3. Vote totals for the House election of 1825   211

ACKNOWLEDGMENTS

ALL WORKS OF SCHOLARSHIP rest on the work of other scholars, and this book is no exception. I am profoundly indebted to the multitude of historians who collected, transcribed, organized, annotated, and published the correspondence and papers of John Quincy Adams, John C. Calhoun, Henry Clay, William Crawford, and Andrew Jackson. Without the work of these dedicated professionals, I simply would not have had the time and resources to create this book.

On a more personal level, I wish to thank Jessica Roney, Bryant Simon, and Michael G. Hagen, the members of my doctoral dissertation committee at Temple University, for their review of and input on the initial stages of this work. Andrew Isenberg, the committee chair, deserves special recognition; he was always there for me when I needed him the most. Two other scholars at Temple University, Elizabeth Varon and Robin Kolodny, also reviewed portions of this work and offered especially helpful commentary and criticism. As the book neared completion, the two anonymous readers secured by the University of Virginia Press provided many valuable suggestions that both enhanced my work and saved me from making several embarrassing errors.

Two individuals proved absolutely essential to the realization of this project. Nadine Zimmerli, my editor at the University of Virginia Press, was passionate and supportive from the start. She made many insightful suggestions that vastly improved this book. David Waldstreicher, my advisor at Temple University, guided my scholarly career, held my nervous hand when needed, and enthusiastically encouraged me to pursue this project. His unparalleled scholarship provides a model for his students and, if not for him, you would not be reading this book.

Finally, as with all things in my life, I could not have accomplished this work without the support and encouragement of my wife, Debbie. She has always been my untiring cheerleader, for which she has my eternal love and gratitude.

THE POLITICS OF CORRUPTION

INTRODUCTION

➜ • ⬅

The Transitional Election

I N AN 1820 ISSUE of the *Richmond Enquirer*, an anonymous editorialist named "Virginius" surveyed the prospective field of candidates for the next presidential election, still a long four years off, and declared that the voters would be treated to a "War of the Giants." There would indeed be a crowded field of well-known names, all of them Republican Party luminaries, seeking to succeed President James Monroe. Three cabinet secretaries—Treasury Secretary William Crawford, Secretary of State John Quincy Adams, and Secretary of War John C. Calhoun—would compete with House Speaker Henry Clay and renowned general Andrew Jackson to be elected the sixth president of the United States. The 1824 candidates had been key figures in American politics for at least a decade, and many would continue to dominate political history for the next twenty-five years.[1]

While the political personalities involved were certainly outsized giants, the presidential election of 1824 itself proved to be an important transitional moment in American political history, coming between the elite-centered elections in the Early Republic and the more democratically based contests of the Jacksonian era. The first presidential elections between the Federalists and the Republicans had been managed and dominated by high political figures, an elitists' game mostly played by insiders. Presidential electors had been most often selected by politicos in state legislative elections, rather than by ordinary voters in popular balloting. The candidates themselves had been handpicked by a caucus of elite congressmen in Washington, DC. Behind the scenes, heavyweights in Virginia and New York had cooperated to deliver the presidency to a Virginian and the vice presidency to a New Yorker. Since Jefferson, the new president had always served as secretary of state, the highest position in the cabinet. While these practices played a role in 1824, none would survive the election and into the Jacksonian era. Crawford was the last nominee designated by a congressional caucus, only two states used legislative elections to pick their electors in the next presidential contest in 1828, the Virginia/New York axis seemed as quaint as powdered wigs by the 1830s, and serving as secretary of state was no longer an automatic stepping-stone to the presidency.

Compared to the elitist Early Republic elections, the presidential contests between the Democrats and the Whigs were staged as showy outdoor spectacles. The vibrant elections of the Jacksonian era were governed by powerful partisan organizations that created newspaper networks, coordinated member meetings, and staged grandiose rallies and conventions. These developments were presaged by tools and methods employed by the 1824 candidates. They built robust organizations of elite politicians using correspondence, patronage, and social occasions to forge bonds with their supporters. They created newspaper networks in which a central media organ would disseminate candidate-approved content for reprinting in strings of regional and local newspapers. Each campaign also featured some public meetings of local supporters. Jackson's grassroots effort convened more gatherings, including the first delegate conventions ever to select presidential electors. In the 1824 contest, presidential politics had at least partially moved outdoors. Since it retained elements of Early Republic presidential elections but also pioneered new Jacksonian era aspects, the presidential election of 1824 served as a hinge between the two eras.

The transition from indoor to outdoor presidential elections had been sparked by popular demand for more participation in the process. As new states entered the union, most authorized the selection of their presidential electors in popular elections as their citizens desired. This pressured the older states to allow their voters a say in the process as well, and as a result, many changed from legislative to popular elections of electors. By 1824, only six of the twenty-four states retained legislative control over the electors. The popular election of electors helped democratize presidential politics, requiring elite indoor politicians to move outdoors and "election-eer" among the nonelite citizenry. If they hoped to win high office, can-didates would need to reach out and appeal to the ordinary people who were voting in the popular elections for electors. Unfortunately for the candidates, the voters' republican beliefs proscribed direct electioneering by presidential candidates. Much as they preferred less visible governance, especially at the federal level, voters frowned upon overt campaigning for the presidency. Presidential candidates appeared to be trapped between two conflicting currents in the political culture—republican belief for-bade electioneering among the voters, while democratized elections de-manded electioneering among the voters.[2]

To address this conundrum, the 1824 candidates and their campaigns adapted existing or pioneered new political tools and tactics. Presidential campaigns had always required organizations, newspapers, and correspon-dence. These tools would still be employed in 1824, but they would take on a popular patina. Candidates expected the elite politicos in their organiza-tions to serve as surrogate campaigners, carrying the candidate's message back to voters in his home state and locality. They widened the scope of their newspaper networks to reach more voters in more places, creating a sympathetic "public community" of followers. They carefully composed their correspondence, knowing that it would often be published for ordi-nary people to read. The candidates also introduced some truly novel meth-ods of campaigning. Materials aimed at informing, engaging, or involving regular voters, including candidate biographies, political buttons, sports-themed political cartoons, and straw polls, all debuted for the first time in presidential elections. Meanwhile, despite avidly participating in their own campaigns, the candidates maintained a discreet distance from these ef-forts. They situated their organization building and correspondence as nor-mal, acceptable political activity, while circumspectly financing newspaper networks. No candidate could afford to be directly connected to the new methods of popular campaigning. They at least attempted to electioneer among ordinary voters without appearing to electioneer among anyone.[3]

While presidential candidates had always been required to "election-eer without electioneering" to some degree, the 1824 campaigns faced circumstances unique to that election. The decline of the Federalist party meant that only Republicans would be running against each other. This one-party electoral environment, quite rare in American political history, compelled the candidates to pursue innovative strategies. To win a Republican-only contest, they sought state presidential nominations in addition to the traditional congressional caucus nomination. They proposed new axes of power to supplant the traditional Virginia/New York alliance that had dominated presidential politics. They increased political rumormongering to undermine rivals while dispensing patronage, assembling congressional factions, and throwing lavish parties to gain supporters within Republican ranks. The latter set of tactics—rumors, patronage, congressional factions, and throwing parties—would play an important role in future Jacksonian era presidential politics, further cementing 1824's role as a pivotal transitional election between early and later contests.

American politicians running for president in 1824 were forced to, or in some cases failed to, adapt to a new political culture in which popular votes increasingly mattered while simultaneously competing in a one-party environment. Crawford ran the most traditional campaign as the unabashed Republican party candidate. Adams emphasized the usual presidential credentials and his unmatched administrative experience, but he also assembled a vigorous organization and press network as he ran the broadest campaign in the cycle. Calhoun claimed to represent national—both northern and southern—interests; he assembled a strong congressional faction, but lacked much of a popular campaign. Clay championed protective tariffs and federally funded internal improvements, presaging the importance of national issues in future Jacksonian presidential campaigns, but he did so without using almost any of the old or new methods of electioneering. Only Jackson ran as a forthright populist, using many of the new political tools in a campaign against political corruption. Unsurprisingly, the Adams campaign, which best mixed traditional and novel elements, and the Jackson campaign, which best exploited the forward-looking political tools, proved the most successful in a transitional election like 1824.

The election battle intensified during Monroe's second term. Led by the cabinet secretaries, nearly every aspect of politics became enmeshed in a perpetual campaign for the succession. The candidates turned conventional political disputes in the cabinet, Congress, and the newspapers into covert methods of electioneering. They and their allies took opposing sides in debates over army reduction, government spending, Revolutionary War pensions, and the races for House Speaker. Under the cover of regular, acceptable political disputes, these clashes served a secondary purpose. The candidates exploited them to advance their presidential bids while undercutting the candidacies of their rivals. This sort of bruising, never-ending campaign became quite typical in future Jacksonian era presidential contests. While the 1824 contest is usually presumed to be much more sedate than its no-holds-barred successor election, this only holds true for Jackson. While the general faced far more scurrilous attacks in 1828 than he had in 1824, overall, both elections were equally ferocious. When comparing the front-runners in both elections—Crawford and Jackson—any difference in the level of negative campaigning disappears. Indeed, Crawford faced more serious, concerted, and voluminous attacks in 1824 than Jackson endured in 1828.

In 1824, Jackson cleverly ran as a populist outsider against the perpetual succession struggle the insiders were waging in Washington. While his rivals were simply practicing politics as usual, Jackson called their practices "corruption." Many citizens were still reeling from the divisiveness of the War of 1812, the economic ravages of the Panic of 1819, and the unsatisfying pro- and antislavery concessions of the Missouri Compromise. Jackson's message resonated with voters who felt that the nation had declined from the ideals of its revolutionary origins.

The 1824 election resolved itself into five regional contests. Adams overwhelmed Crawford in New England as the regional favorite. Popular with ordinary voters, Jackson proved a formidable challenge to Crawford's ascendency in the South. As a regional favorite and war hero, Jackson easily dominated Clay and Adams in the Southwest. With voters troubled by his stands on some issues, Clay barely eked out a victory over Jackson and Adams in the Northwest. The mid-Atlantic states lacked a "favorite son," as DeWitt Clinton, New York's popular governor and long expected to be a candidate, ultimately opted out of the race. The region proved to be the real showdown with all four candidates competing—Calhoun had already dropped out. In the mid-Atlantic states, the outsider Jackson dominated popular elections and the insider Adams captured electoral votes from state legislatures. The general's campaign against political corruption proved to be the decisive issue of the election, both in the region and nationwide. In a political culture transitioning between indoor and outdoor politics, a populist outsider inveighing against "corrupt" insiders proved successful. Jackson only achieved a plurality, not a majority, of electoral votes, however. The election was ultimately decided in Adams's favor by a subsequent election among the politicos in the House of Representatives. To win the vote in the House, Adams was obliged to bargain with the representatives. The deals that he cut, especially with Clay, seemed to validate Jackson's campaign message against corrupt political practice. The politically useful "corrupt bargain" charges were born, initiating the next perpetual campaign for the presidency and proving central to Jackson's 1828 victory.

As Michael Holt, the historian of the Whig Party, pithily observes, in political history, "events mattered." Indeed, four key developments largely determined the outcome of this transitional election. One, the collapse of the Federalist opposition at the level of the presidential election permitted the Republicans to factionalize into five competing presidential candidacies. Two, Calhoun executed a highly successful "Stop Crawford" strategy with unrelenting attacks on the treasury secretary's competence and character. Though he was widely regarded as the front-runner to succeed Monroe, scandal fatally undermined Crawford's candidacy. Three, Jackson focused his successful popular campaign on a broad, inclusive issue—political corruption. Rather than advocating specific policies, the general pilloried politicians as dishonesty personified and blasted their practices as scheming and intrigue. Jackson's promise to clean up Washington if elected helped him carry the popular vote. Four, once the election passed from the populace to the politicians, Adams's superb insider dealmaking abilities carried off the ultimate prize.[4]

Though historians have more frequently focused on the succeeding 1828 contest between Jackson and Adams, a few studies have recognized the importance of the 1824 election. M. J. Heale deems 1824 a significant "transitional election" between the elite-centered contests that preceded it to the more democratic ones that followed. He does not acknowledge the novel innovations to presidential campaigning undertaken, however, suggesting instead that the candidates were "mute tribunes" who contributed little to their own campaigns. Lynn Hudson Parsons correctly argues that a new, more republican political culture crystallized in 1824, but attributes the outcome of the election to regionalism rather than to any of the tools, tactics, and methods that were developed. Donald Ratcliffe accurately notes that the 1824 contest pioneered new advances in presidential campaigning and shaped the role of parties and ideology in future Jacksonian era politics. Focusing more on constituencies and ethnocultural identities, however, Ratcliffe does not offer a detailed analysis of high politics, which is crucial to understanding the election of 1824. Daniel Peart cogently maintains that, in 1824, political practices were largely driven by ambitious politicians seeking votes to win high office. He correctly recognizes the disenchantment felt by voters, but he attributes their feelings to antipartisanship. In fact, 1824's voters were disgusted with the corrupt practices of politicians and parties, rather than with the idea of parties themselves. This study will accept many of the conclusions of these historians, but it will also flesh out 1824's novel campaign innovations and high political maneuvering, as well as the vital role that perceived political corruption played in the outcome. It will demonstrate that the election of 1824 played a critical role in the transition from Early Republic to Jacksonian era presidential politics.[5]

1

→ • ←

The Big Five

SEVERAL POLITICIANS CONTEMPLATED A campaign for president in 1824, and many more were rumored to be running, but in the end only five men actually entered the contest to succeed James Monroe: from Georgia, Secretary of the Treasury William H. Crawford; from Massachusetts, Secretary of State John Quincy Adams; from South Carolina, Secretary of War John C. Calhoun; from Kentucky, Speaker of the House of Representatives Henry Clay; and from Tennessee, the soldier-turned-senator Andrew Jackson. The five shared one commonality; they were all Republicans, members of the party founded by Thomas Jefferson. The opposing Federalist party would not field a presidential candidate at all in 1824, so the Republicans would be running against each other.

While these Republicans all claimed fealty to Jeffersonian ideals, they used different strategies to achieve high office. Crawford ran as the traditional partisan Republican candidate favored by elite politicians. Adams emphasized his unparalleled administrative experience, which uniquely qualified him for high office. Calhoun trumpeted his national appeal, claiming to be the best candidate to represent both northern and southern interests. Clay campaigned on issues of national importance, alleging that the protective tariffs and federally funded internal improvements that he supported would benefit voters everywhere. Jackson ran as an unabashed populist; he insisted that the nation's problems were tied to a corrupt political class, including the very men he was running against. As we shall see in chapters 2 and 3, each strategy would mix traditional and novel approaches to campaigning to varying degrees—but given that presidential elections were becoming more democratized, as we shall see in chapter 6, the campaigns that most resonated with ordinary voters would prove the most successful.

More than Georgia on His Mind: William H. Crawford, the Party Candidate

To even desultory political observers in 1824, it probably seemed as if Crawford had been perpetually running for president. The treasury secretary had been Monroe's principal competition for the 1816 Republican nomination and had been angling to succeed him ever since, earning a reputation for political maneuvering in the process. Since Jefferson's candidacy in 1800, the Republican Party had designated its official nominee via a caucus of its senators and representatives in Washington. In 1816, Crawford's supporters tried several schemes to defeat the heavily favored Monroe, but their bids to convene an early caucus to catch Monroe's backers unaware, and then their plan to delay the nomination both failed. Monroe defeated Crawford, but only by an unexpectedly close eleven-vote margin. Crawford believed he might have taken the nomination from Monroe if he had pressed the issue, but his decision to cheerfully accede to his rival's victory displayed careful political calculation. While he might have prolonged the fight and possibly won the big prize, he was much younger than Monroe and could afford to wait another eight years for his almost-certain opportunity to be president. Meanwhile, he avoided unduly irritating Monroe's supporters, earned the goodwill of his fellow Republicans by not fracturing the party, and seemingly cemented his claim to the succession.[1]

While not as experienced as Adams, the youngish Crawford—he was fifty-two years old in 1824—had already amassed an impressive resume. Before his political career, Crawford had farmed, taught school, and practiced law. By his thirties, as a staunch Jeffersonian, he had become a fixture in Georgia's notoriously factionalized and occasionally violent state politics. Crawford himself had killed one political opponent in a duel and had his own wrist shattered by a bullet in another. He had emerged on the national scene in 1807, when the state legislature elected him as Georgia's junior senator in the Tenth Congress. Crawford, a sharp critic of wasteful public spending, rapidly rose to president pro tempore in 1811. President Madison picked Crawford, a committed supporter of the War of 1812, as minister to France in 1813, then secretary of war in 1815, and finally secretary of the treasury in 1816. Although the 1816 nomination fight had been quite bitter, surprisingly, Monroe asked his chief rival to remain at his post after Monroe became president in 1817. Throughout his tenure in various government positions, Crawford knew how to win friends and influence people. A persuasive debater, he never lost a case during his legal career when he personally delivered the closing argument. Rugged and brash, but also affable and humorous, Crawford always seemed popular with his fellow politicians and picked up a coterie of devoted followers as he ascended the political ladder.[2]

While many historians have dismissed the treasury secretary as a crass political schemer consumed by ambition, Crawford's contemporaries appreciated his managerial abilities, with some claiming that his knowledge of political economy and finance exceeded that of any previous president or cabinet secretary. Crawford administered the Treasury Department with competent efficiency, introducing significant improvements in both auditing and accountability. Upon taking office, he discovered that numerous accounts in every executive department had not been properly balanced, with a plethora of unpaid bills due the government. He instituted new collecting procedures that significantly reduced the financial arrearages plaguing the Treasury. When Crawford left his post, he had reduced his department's Washington staff and cut its payroll overall, despite adding significantly more government warehouses and customs facilities. Through his management of the turbulent postwar economy, he reduced the nation's debt and improved its credit. Even party founder Thomas Jefferson deemed Crawford the most qualified Republican presidential candidate in the 1824 field.[3]

Unfortunately for Crawford, the nation endured a severe economic downturn, the Panic of 1819, under his watch. During the panic, the United States faced runaway inflation, a collapse of the export market, a wave of bank failures, disintegrating real estate prices, a surge of business closures, an eye-popping national debt, and mass unemployment. While citizens from every stratum of society suffered, Crawford focused almost solely on saving the Bank of the United States (BUS) from failure. Exploiting his close relationship with BUS president Langdon Cheves, Crawford secured BUS loans for the government that helped stabilize both the BUS and the US Treasury. The recovery proved far less dynamic for many ordinary citizens. While the economy slowly improved in some areas, pockets of real misery filled with angry voters persisted into the 1824 election cycle.[4]

The panic had originated from a variety of sources. Imbalances in international trade, excessive speculation by state bankers, and the BUS's own hard money polices had triggered the downturn. Many citizens missed this complexity, however, and fingered one archvillain as the architect of their misfortune: the BUS. Unfortunately for a prospective presidential candidate, many voters linked Crawford indelibly with the domineering bank. He had championed the creation of the first BUS and now served as savior and principal cheerleader for the second. As we shall see in chapters 5 and 6, his work with the BUS severely compromised Crawford's candidacy. It virtually prevented him from competing in the northwestern states, those most ravaged in the panic, while providing excellent fodder for critiques of his administrative abilities by the other campaigns.[5]

Though ordinary people may have scorned Crawford's support for the BUS, his economic policies garnered him numerous allies among Republican elites. His most enthusiastic backers made up the so-called Radical faction. The Radicals, claiming to be the true heirs of Jefferson, advocated states' rights and weak federal government. The group contained many important political leaders in New York and Virginia, including the Albany Regency and the Richmond Junto. Its members wholeheartedly endorsed the Virginia/New York axis that had long controlled presidential politics, with an unspoken agreement that awarded the presidency to the Old Dominion and the vice presidency to the Empire State. Initially, Crawford seemed an unusual champion for this conservative group. He had supported the creation of the second BUS, favored mild tariff protection, and pragmatically backed some federally funded internal improvements, all policies the Radicals bitterly opposed. Crawford had ardently sought cuts in government spending, however, a central tenet of the Radical creed. Of all the candidates running in 1824, Crawford was clearly the most friendly to Radical ideals, so they ultimately joined his presidential campaign in droves. Most of Crawford's fellow Republicans loathed his Radical allies. "If permitted to triumph," one Jacksonian growled, the Radicals "would entail on this nation evils that would take a century to remove." Calhoun's supporters simply called them the "Powers of Darkness."[6]

Crawford's strategy for winning the election rested on his administrative, regional, and partisan identities. His executive department experience aligned his credentials with the last three presidents, as each had each claimed the highest office after serving in the cabinet. By ably performing his official departmental duties, Crawford appeared well qualified for advancement to voters across the nation irrespective of their opinions on any other issue. As a side benefit, the treasury secretary controlled numerous patronage positions that helped draw supporters to his campaign. Crawford had been born in Virginia, and as the most conservative southerner in the race, he appeared poised to take his place as the next member of the so-called Virginia Dynasty, since the last three presidents had also come from the Old Dominion. Crawford claimed to be the true proponent of Jeffersonian ideology and the most authentic Republican in the race. Irrespective of their regional identity, highly partisan Republicans, those most concerned with intraparty unity, gravitated toward Crawford. For voters outside his home region, Crawford hoped that his stance as the true Republican would overcome their reluctance to support a southern candidate.[7]

After his nearly successful challenge to Monroe's 1816 nomination, his widespread popularity within the party's leadership, his inheritance of the mantle of the Virginia Dynasty, and his dedicated backing from the Radical faction, Crawford emerged as the obvious front-runner to succeed Monroe. He positioned himself as more Republican than Adams, more Jeffersonian than Clay, more economy minded than Calhoun, and more experienced than Jackson. With his considerable support in Congress and from party elites, he planned from the beginning of his campaign to earn the next congressional caucus nomination. Anchored on his strong southern base, Crawford would build up his strength in Congress, claim the party's official benediction, and win the election with the support of traditionally minded, partisan Republicans nationwide.[8]

Unfortunately for the treasury secretary, his status as the front-runner engraved a gigantic target on his back. While Calhoun might deprecate Adams, and Adams might denigrate Clay, and Clay might disparage Jackson, *every* candidate denounced Crawford—early, often, and with vigor. Adams alleged that Crawford's "ethics are neither sound nor deep." Calhoun maintained that Crawford had "grossly duped" his fellow citizens and planned "not to serve, but to cheat them." Jackson called Crawford "desperately wicked" and insisted that "I would support the Devil first." Clay warned his prospective supporters, "Connect yourselves to the fortune of Mr. Crawford and lose this election." Each of his opponents concocted legitimate reasons for their unrelenting attacks on the party favorite. Adams and Calhoun insisted that he had deliberately opposed them in cabinet debates to further his presidential candidacy, Clay maintained that Crawford's parsimonious management of the Treasury threatened important government programs he supported, while Jackson remained furious that Crawford had criticized some of his more questionable military escapades. Regardless of the sincerity of their criticisms, however, each man realized that Crawford blocked his path to the White House. Unless his rivals acted, president-elect Crawford would be taking the oath of office in March 1825.[9]

Burdened with His Father's Legacy:
John Quincy Adams, the Experienced Candidate

While Crawford believed himself the logical successor to Monroe, the president did not reward him with the customary cabinet post given to the expected heir. Jefferson, Madison, and Monroe had each served as secretary of state; each had become president in turn, so the State Department had become increasingly considered the stepping-stone to the presidency. Monroe deliberately bypassed Crawford to bestow the honored position on Adams. The president insisted that the "country north & east" had begun to believe "that the citizens from Virga., holding the Presidency, have made appointments to that dep.ᵗ, to secure the succession, from it, to the Presidency, of a person who happens to be from that State." To counteract that notion, Monroe sought an "eastern" man to serve in the post. While Adams had been contemplating a run for the presidency while still on a diplomatic mission abroad in 1817, the president's selection effectively catapulted him into the 1824 presidential race. Monroe had also cleverly denied Crawford—the party's choice, but a man he personally disliked and distrusted—from receiving the traditional badge of succession.[10]

While Monroe appreciated Adams's "eastern" origins in balancing his cabinet, for the purposes of the presidential race, his new secretary of state deliberately distanced himself from his own roots. Adams claimed to be "unsure" that New England, let alone the North, "would unitedly offer me as a candidate." He argued that his regional identity might reduce his support from sectional-minded southerners or westerners. Referring to himself in the third person, Adams claimed that many men in his own section "professed a very high opinion of the Northern candidate, but always insisting there was no chance in his favor, no possibility of his being elected" over the opposition of southerners. When Robert Walsh coined the term "Universal Yankee Nation" in 1822 to signify New England and its émigrés throughout the union, Adams disputed Walsh's "prediction" that the voting bloc would support him as a group, insisting it "was much hazarded in point of fact, and perhaps questionably in point of principle." Despite Adams's self-effacing modesty, he surely realized that his northern and New England identity would translate into numerous votes in his own section. By downplaying his regionalism, however, he might siphon ballots from the other candidates in their home bases.[11]

Monroe's selection for the State Department also raised some hyperpartisan eyebrows. Not only was Adams the son of a famous Federalist president, he himself had been a member of the opposition party until he broke with his allies in 1808. While he had been a sitting Federalist senator from Massachusetts, Adams crossed the aisle to support Jefferson's Louisiana Purchase and Embargo Act. When his Federalist colleagues resisted joining him, Adams gradually switched sides and became a Republican. For

Monroe, who hoped to promote antipartisanship and dissolve parties entirely, Adams would serve as a visible, living symbol of his dream of party fusion—a man who had once been a steadfast Federalist, but now fit effortlessly into a Republican administration in the highest cabinet position of all. Unfortunately for Adams, many Republican voters in 1824 stridently objected to any "amalgamation" of the two parties. They had not forgiven the Federalists for opposing the War of 1812, while John Adams served as the villain in much of the party's celebratory Jeffersonian lore. "Recollection of the fathers [sic] deeds," one Jacksonian insisted, "[are] calculated to raise up irreconcileable [sic] prejudices against the son."[12]

The Monroe years had not been kind to the Federalists. Seen as too elitist, too monarchical, and much too Yankee-oriented, the opposition party had virtually collapsed as a national force. The Federalists had almost no presence in the South or West. In New England and the mid-Atlantic states, they remained a viable minority party, but served more as kingmakers rather than kings. In losing to Monroe in the 1816 presidential election, Federalist standard-bearer Rufus King received the lowest share of electoral votes of any of his party's nominees, ever. Deserted by the voters, denounced by the Republicans, and demoralized within their own ranks, the Federalists fielded no presidential candidate in 1820, so Monroe was reelected unopposed. By 1824, the Federalists ruled only tiny, inconsequential Delaware.[13]

Despite the ideological chasm that had separated Hamilton from Jefferson when the parties were founded, the Federalists smugly realized that the heirs of the latter had slowly adopted the policies of the former. A national bank, a larger peacetime army and navy, direct internal taxation, higher salaries for public officials—one by one, each plank of the Federalist platform had become Republican dogma since Jefferson defeated Adams. Other issues, including federally funded internal improvements and protective tariffs, counted supporters or opponents in both parties and offered no obvious electoral advantage to either side. Since the parties were no longer clearly divided ideologically, most Federalists became single-issue voters when choosing a president. Jefferson had purged every obvious Federalist from office, cleansing the government down to lowly army captains. Each

succeeding Republican administration had followed their leader and "proscribed" Federalists from civil service. No Republican president had ever
appointed any bona fide Federalist to any position whatsoever. Accordingly,
in every presidential election after 1816, most Federalists cast their ballot
for the Republican candidate they believed most likely to end proscription.
In turn, the candidates realized the important edge Federalist votes might
grant them in close contests, so almost every contender made a surreptitious play for their support.[14]

Adams proved the exception to that rule. Increased Republican factionalism, represented by the five presidential candidacies, only heightened
Republican fears that their own weakness might help revitalize Federalism
and led to demands that their next nominee "should be a decided Republican who would not sacrifice his old friends and old principles upon the
altars of 'good feelings.'" In this poisonous atmosphere, the politically savvy
Adams quickly realized that his checkered past had already tarnished his
Republican credentials and precluded even the slightest hint of Federalist
support for his candidacy. For the secretary of state, any Federalist votes
gained would never offset the Republican votes lost in their pursuit, so
both in public to voters and in private to supporters, Adams barred any
Federalist participation in his campaign for the presidency. Many Federalists returned Adams's disdain with equal ferocity. As his Federalist past
collided with his Republican present, Adams was practically exiled to a political no-man's-land. "The Old School Feds. regard him as an apostate &
the Repns. can't forget *the Family*," one Clay supporter colorfully observed.
"All parties disown me," Adams complained, "the Federalists as a deserter,
the Democrats [i.e., an alternate name for the Republican party] as an
apostate," and both sides criticized his "unsteadiness of principle." Every
other candidate had been a lifelong Republican, so Adams alone would
face an uphill battle in attracting voters concerned with his questionable
partisan purity.[15]

To win over voters uncomfortable with his Yankee and formerly Federalist identities, Adams offered his lengthy record of public service to the
entire nation as an inducement. Monroe had correctly noted Adams's experience as a recommendation for a cabinet post; indeed, not only was he

more than qualified to be secretary of state, but Adams was also probably the most experienced person to run for president up to that point. Aside from his stint as a US senator, Adams had served as a diplomat for every US administration. He had been minister to the Netherlands under Washington, minister to Prussia under Adams and Jefferson, and minister to Russia and the United Kingdom under Madison. He had also led the US delegation that negotiated—quite successfully, considering the Americans' position of weakness—the Treaty of Ghent that ended the War of 1812. As secretary of state, he continued accumulating an impressive number of diplomatic achievements, including the 1819 Adams-Onís Treaty with Spain that ceded Florida to the United States and set the western border of the Louisiana Purchase, the 1822 Commercial Treaty with France, and the Russo-American Treaty of 1824 that ceded Russia's claims in the Pacific Northwest south of Parallel 54° 40' north to the United States. While his rivals tried to undermine his candidacy by criticizing his treaties, Adams's unparalleled record of public service appealed to nationalists in every corner of the union. He could effectively win votes by simply performing his official duties with vigor.[16]

Adams's strategy for winning the election combined thoroughly repudiating his partisan past, discreetly capitalizing on his regional identity, and overwhelming any objections to his candidacy on those grounds with his extraordinary record of diplomatic public service. He expected to easily capture New England, with his position as the only nonslaveholder in the race also conferring an advantage across the North. Resting on his impressive diplomatic laurels, he would make inroads against his challengers in their home regions by attracting nationalist-minded voters everywhere. Meanwhile, he would scrub any taint of Federalism from his campaign. If events broke in his favor, he might even wrest the caucus nomination from Crawford's grip.[17]

Many politicos initially believed the contest to succeed Monroe would boil down to an Adams-versus-Crawford clash, and in the wily secretary of state, the cunning Crawford may indeed have met his match. Despite his frequent disavowals, incorrectly echoed by numerous historians, Adams displayed obvious skills at political infighting. His long service in the intrigue-filled world of international diplomacy had more than prepared him for combat in America's political trenches. Although pious, serious, and erudite, he excelled both at socializing with his political friends and eviscerating his political enemies. "He had an instinct for the jugular and carotid artery as unerring as that of any carnivorous animal," his own ally Rufus Choate observed. Adams's unmatched experience, coupled with his talents for political scheming, represented a formidable challenge to Crawford's ascendancy.[18]

The Heir Unapparent: John C. Calhoun, the National Candidate

Crawford and Adams were joined in the presidential race by their cabinet colleague Calhoun. The secretary of war's political rise had been truly meteoric. After Calhoun served a mere five years in the House as a representative from South Carolina, where he had vocally supported the War of 1812, Monroe plucked him from relative obscurity and dropped him into the high-profile War Department post as the successor to Crawford. Perhaps somewhat surprisingly, the youthful thirty-five-year-old Calhoun engineered immediate improvements in his administrative jurisdiction. Responding to an 1818 Senate resolution and, ironically, based on a plan Crawford had drafted, Calhoun established a much-needed bureau system for the War Department. Without a general staff in Washington, the army had lacked a proper chain of command and centralized control over ordinance, supplies, and medical care. The department's purchases varied in quality, but were almost always wastefully expensive. Calhoun established inspectors for each bureau, which helped reduce costs and increase efficiencies in one of the government's largest and most far-flung Departments. Like Crawford and Adams, Calhoun expected his adept job performance as a cabinet secretary to appeal to voters throughout the union.[19]

The secretary of war's candidacy soon acquired an unexpected ally, James Monroe, the president himself. In his choice of attire, Monroe appeared to have stepped out of another era. The president favored swallowtail coats, knee breeches with silver buckles, silk hose, and cocked hats that had not been popular menswear in nearly thirty years. While he may have dressed like some eighteenth-century relic, Monroe possessed a razor-sharp strategic mind, one well attuned to nineteenth-century politics. Though the president had welcomed Crawford into the cabinet, Monroe was still angered by Crawford's opposition to his 1816 nomination. With no intention of smoothing Crawford's path to the presidency, Monroe needed another candidate to block the imposing front-runner. As Calhoun rapidly gained the president's trust, the secretary of war seemed the ideal counterweight to the treasury secretary. Competent and compelling, the dynamic Calhoun was also, like Crawford, a southerner, which meant two native candidates would vie for, and perhaps split, the region's votes.[20]

Monroe began carefully, though furtively, aiding his protégé's presidential bid. He threatened to veto any bills reducing the size of the army while convincing the prickly Jackson to accept a position as Florida's territorial governor, which saved Calhoun from eliminating his position and facing the general's wrath. He also showered Calhoun's partisans with patronage positions while blocking allies of his rivals. Monroe's actions helped shield Calhoun from any unfavorable political fallout that might result from his departmental activities.[21]

Naturally, the president could never openly acknowledge his behind-the-scenes favoritism. "I declare most solemnly that I took no part in the election," Monroe intoned. "Nor did I ever express any preference to any one in favor of either of the candidates." While Monroe stoutly denied promoting Calhoun, the secretary of war's opponents were not fooled by the president's surreptitious activities. Martin Van Buren, a devoted Crawfordite, observed, "Altho' exercising his usual prudence in the matter, Mr. Monroe was notwithstanding well understood to prefer Mr. Calhoun." When one Adams follower suggested that Monroe would be supporting him for the succession, Adams curtly replied, "The President had enough to do to support the Secretary of War." Even Clay's allies possessed surreptitious intelligence that Monroe was actively backing Calhoun. Belying his historiographical reputation for passive conservatism, Monroe possessed a true aptitude for active, behind-the-scenes maneuvering.[22]

In turn, Calhoun entered the race expressly to support the principles of his secret backer. Dismissing his own personal interest, he insisted that he was running for the "welfare" of the administration, "identified as I am with it, and approving its policy." The two men shared more in common than current politics. Both had been vocal champions of American involvement in the War of 1812, and both shared a measure of personal guilt for its disastrous outcome. Aside from featuring a string of humiliating British military victories, the war had triggered an economic collapse and sparked disastrous interparty feuding and sectional bitterness.[23]

Monroe became convinced that wartime failures could be blamed on a lack of military preparedness. As president, he authorized the creation of a defensive ring around the nation's perimeter to address this shortcoming. His secretary of war enthusiastically supervised the construction of six new forts, with improvements to two others, effectively encircling the nation from the Canadian border to New Orleans. Though justifiably proud of their accomplishments, Monroe and Calhoun's defense buildup did not come cheap. The War Department spent almost $8,500,000 between 1816 and 1829 to achieve their vision. Politically, Calhoun's support for a muscular, expensive defense spending program placed him at odds with more traditional, parsimonious, Crawfordite Radicals. They would carefully scrutinize Calhoun's management of his far-flung fortifications program, looking for improprieties that might damage his presidential bid.[24]

Despite his Radical critics, Calhoun's nationalist defense buildup dovetailed nicely with his campaign strategy. Although a southerner, Calhoun planned to run as an overt nationalist. He had been born in South Carolina but educated at Yale University and Litchfield Law School in Connecticut, retaining numerous northern friends from his school days. As secretary of war, Calhoun also traveled extensively in the northern states, inspecting defense installations and earning the respect of the region's politicians. Trading on these experiences, he fancied himself a southerner with northern sensibilities, a man who could appeal to voters anywhere based on "the liberal and national character of my political views."[25]

Accordingly, Calhoun positioned himself between every conceivable political faction. He claimed the middle ground between Crawford and Adams. "My election would strengthen and invigorate the Rep[n] party," Calhoun boasted, "Mr. Cd's would distract it, and Mr. J Adams would endanger its existence by giving the occasion of rearing up a successful party against it." He straddled the middle region between North and South. "C-d stands no chance to the North. . . . I am the only man from the Southern States, that the North can be induced to support," he proclaimed. Calhoun even grabbed the middle position between Radicals and Federalists. "I stand on the great Republican cause, free alike from the charge of Federalism or Radicalism," he declared. As the race began, Calhoun believed he was at least every politician's second choice for the succession and could emerge victorious as Crawford and Adams attacked each other. Indeed, Calhoun's supporters generally loathed Crawford, but believed that Adams could not defeat him in the South or West, so they needed a candidate capable of uniting those regions.[26]

In running an in-between, nationalist campaign, Calhoun's strategy entailed a logical focus on capturing the nation's center region. He planned to devote most of his energies to securing two important mid-Atlantic states, Pennsylvania and Maryland. Appealing to voters of all stripes in those states, Calhoun promised to dispense patronage regardless of faction. "We shut the door against none," he insisted, "and much less will proscribe anyone." A focus on the middle was not without its risks, however. Calhoun had to beat back charges from the South that he was not states' rights enough and charges from the North that he was too prosouthern. Indeed, he had occasionally departed from the conservative orthodoxy popular in his home region, supporting the creation of the Second BUS, for instance. He insisted that he had been, like many others, simply following Jefferson and Madison. "Injustice is done, when I am opposed and others forgiven," Calhoun carped.[27]

There was another objection to his candidacy that Calhoun could not simply explain away. At forty-two, he was five years younger than the next oldest candidate, Clay, and fifteen years younger than Jackson and Adams, the oldest candidates. "Being a young man, he was not generally thought of for the Presidency," even one supporter conceded. To minimize any shortcomings, Calhoun offered voters his lifelong Republicanism, his support for the War of 1812 and the Monroe administration, his "habits of industry and business," and "the openness and candour which even my enemies concede to me." As the least experienced contender with the shortest tenure on the national stage, however, the secretary of war trailed every other candidate in both name recognition and popular following. With such long odds, Calhoun could only achieve victory if Adams and Crawford both underperformed.[28]

A Rising Star in the West: Henry Clay, the Issues Candidate

As the secretaries jockeyed to claim their position in the race, a candidate emerged who challenged the very notion of cabinet-based succession to the presidency. While he had never held any position in the executive branch, Clay had become a fixture in Congress. After two brief stretches as a US senator from Kentucky in 1806 and 1810, filling in unfinished terms of retiring predecessors, Clay truly found a home in the House of Representatives. Elected to office in 1811, by the time he ran for president, Clay had been serving almost continuously for thirteen years. More impressively, Clay's colleagues had picked the then-thirty-two-year-old as Speaker in his first term by a two-to-one margin over a more senior representative. Not only was Clay the youngest person to ever hold the position to that point, but he had also been elevated on his very first day in Congress, which had not occurred since the first speakership. Clay quickly set about refashioning the position into one with exceptional political power. Unlike past Speakers, Clay set the House agenda, carefully directed legislation to specific committees, worked behind the scenes to solicit votes, enforced rules to control debate, and both charmed and intimidated his colleagues to produce the majorities he desired. He even had an eye for the symbolic. In 1820, Clay supervised the redecoration of the House chamber, adding red damask settees, plush carpeting, gold curtains, and a silk canopy with gilt eagle placed over his own chair, the Speaker's dais. For maximum effect, Clay enlarged the public galleries, affording prospective voters a better view as he transfixed the chamber with his rhetorical flourishes. Clay changed the position of House Speaker from a sedate institutional custodian into a dynamic political manager. Droll, passionate, and with unrivaled oratorical skills, he exerted enormous influence over his fellow representatives. Clay seemed to always know precisely which backs to pat and which knees to break to achieve his legislative goals.[29]

Clay quickly learned the power that issues could play in campaigns for office. As a leading "War Hawk," his jingoistic demands for conflict with Great Britain not only helped pressure President Madison into declaring the War of 1812, but also brought him national renown, and some newspapers began touting him as a future president. However, he also supported the Compensation Act, which raised congressional salaries, and he nearly lost his seat in the ensuing public outcry against the bill. Clay's work as a Ghent Treaty negotiator—he had served in the US delegation under Adams—truly catapulted the Speaker into the upper ranks of potential presidents, and he expected to be rewarded with the State Department portfolio by president-elect Monroe, whom he had supported for the succession over Crawford. When Monroe passed over Clay in favor of Adams, the incensed Speaker petulantly retaliated by refusing to host the inauguration in the House chamber and boycotting the outdoor ceremony.[30]

The Speaker planned far more than a temper tantrum to undermine the new president and claim his right to be the next in line, however. Clay began using his speakership to raise issues that he believed would bring him national notoriety and burnish his presidential credentials. He tried to embarrass the Monroe administration at every turn. In highly publicized House speeches, Clay denounced Adams's prized Adams-Onís Treaty, pleaded for funds to repair poorly maintained roads, demanded support of the freedom-loving Spanish-American republics trying to overthrow their cruel European overlords, and excoriated General Jackson for his insubordinate, undemocratic actions during the Seminole War. In practical terms, Clay "lost" these debates; Adams's treaty was approved, no funds were appropriated for road repairs, no Spanish-American republics were recognized at that time, and Jackson was not censured by the House. Clay earned public credit to buttress a future presidential run as an administration outsider and critic, however. The Speaker was not acting completely cynically, of course. He truly believed in the causes he championed, but they served a dual purpose, conveniently satisfying both Clay's moral sensibilities and his political ambitions.[31]

Like Crawford, Clay had been born in Virginia, but his family moved west instead of south. As a twenty-year-old lawyer in Lexington, Kentucky, Clay soon became enmeshed in the state's volatile politics, including a duel in 1809. As a presidential candidate, Clay defined himself as western regional favorite. Although he had grown wealthy through marriage and his legal career, Clay also tried to appeal to the socioeconomic status of many voters. While his middle-class father had been a Baptist minister and a minor planter, Clay exaggerated the poverty of his upbringing to make himself appear to be more of a self-made man. While many ordinary people identified with his western and common man personas, Clay also had a reputation for immorality, and rumors swirled about his steamy adulterous affairs, wild gambling habits, and riotous drinking binges. Perhaps to counter his reputation for personal moral failures, Clay also cultivated his image as an activist legislator. Throughout his career in Washington, he had championed economic policies that he argued would benefit the entire nation. "The liberality and broadness of your views . . . are inestimably of value just now," editor Hezekiah Niles gushed. "The legislation or direction of public affairs seems to regard a quintal of codfish, a hhd. of tobacco or a bale of cotton, instead of keeping an eye to the whole." Building on what he learned about issues-based campaigning during his long tenure as Speaker, for his presidential run, Clay highlighted his support for federally funded internal improvements and protective tariffs. As we shall see in chapter 5, no prior presidential candidate had ever campaigned quite so overtly on a set of defined policy positions, so Clay became the first contender in US history to offer a sort of protoplatform to the voters.[32]

Unfortunately for Clay, promoting issues as an activist Speaker had required significant behind-the-scenes maneuvering. Perhaps no legislation better demonstrated the perils of an active speakership than the Missouri Compromise. When a bill addressing the Missouri Territory's preliminary admission to the union came before the House in 1819, New York representative James Tallmadge unexpectedly proposed amending it with antislavery provisions. Tallmadge's bombshell legislation sparked a fierce two-year political tussle, with Speaker Clay firmly in the center of the maelstrom. In addition to a series of emotional speeches supporting Missouri's admission without restrictions on slavery, Clay deployed every weapon in his political bag of tricks to bring the state into the union. Using secret backroom deals, obtuse language hiding real details, some not-so-subtle arm-twisting, and even the skirting of official House rules, Clay shepherded two pieces of compromise legislation through Congress, ensuring Missouri's admittance. Successfully legislating proved a double-edged sword, however. While there was celebration in Missouri and numerous sighs of relief across the nation that the divisive issue had been settled, many southerners now realized the precarious position that slavery occupied in a nation dominated by free states, and many northerners resented yielding anything to the slave state minority. The compromise may have saved the union, but it left a sour aftertaste in everyone's mouth, and Clay was the bartender who had mixed the drink. Clay's presidential rivals safely criticized aspects of the deal in private conversations with sympathetic supporters while publicly endorsing the compromise. None of them shared Clay's intimate connection with the deal, however. While some voters rewarded Clay for saving the union, he faced blame from others—those fearful for the future of slavery and those fearful that slavery had a future.[33]

With Missouri's admittance, Clay was heralded as the "Great Compromiser" and the "Savior of the Union"—at least by his friends and allies. Unfortunately for Clay, the unseemly political processes necessary to pass the compromise also helped forge his reputation as a political schemer. The Speaker's presidency would be "a perpetual succession of intrigue and management," Adams blustered. Such accusations forced candidate Clay to disavow the seamier side of politics. While running for office, he promised to "abstain from every species of compromitment; to reject every overture looking to arrangement or compromises; and to preserve my perfect freedom of action . . . neither giving or receiving promises from or to persons or parties." To make the voters aware of his pledge, Clay reprinted versions of this statement in numerous newspapers in 1823.[34]

In the presidential race, Clay insisted that his unanimous support in the West would give him an edge over his rivals. Indeed, no westerner had ever served in the cabinet, much less been considered for the highest office of all, and many in the restive region had begun to demand a president who understood their needs and problems. While Clay might carry the West, the states in his region would not yield enough electoral votes to win the election. To achieve that goal, the Speaker planned a turn from his home base to the mid-Atlantic states. Recognizing its ties to the West, the region should be quite receptive to his economic policies. With the West and Mid-Atlantic secured, the South, sensing Crawford's inevitable defeat, would fall in line behind Clay's candidacy. Given that he was popular in the House, Clay planned to compete for the congressional caucus nomination if possible, but his strategy for winning the election comprised sweeping the West based on his regional identity, adding the mid-Atlantic states based on his issues-focused campaign, then capturing the South based on his birth there. With so many states to consider, Clay would pragmatically concentrate on New York in the middle and Virginia in the South, the two states that had traditionally dominated presidential politics. Once he had three-quarters of the union behind him, Clay would easily defeat Adams even if the secretary of state carried New England.[35]

Many historians have incorrectly credited Clay with strategic fore-sight, insisting that he had always believed a House election inevitable and had planned to win one from the start of the election. In reality, the Speaker planned to win the election outright and would not refocus on a House election until 1824. Clay's reasonable strategy might actually have worked, but as often occurs in presidential elections, unforeseen circumstances intervened. A celebrity military hero with a popular national following and a novel approach to presidential campaigning entered the race and scrambled every contender's careful political calculations, especially the Speaker's.[36]

A Hero for His Times: Andrew Jackson, the Popular Candidate

There had never been a presidential candidate quite like Jackson. George Washington had been a military commander, of course, but he was also an educated Virginia gentleman and experienced politician. Jackson's schooling had been meager, and he possessed only trivial political quali-fications for high office. The general had endured a difficult, hardscrabble upbringing. He had been orphaned at age fourteen; his father died before he was born, and his mother succumbed to illness after tending to prisoners of war during the revolution. Jackson had himself been incarcerated by the British, contracting smallpox under the horrific conditions in their prison. After work in a saddlemaker's shop and teaching school, Jackson became a country lawyer and judge. Politically, he served as a delegate to Tennessee's constitutional convention in 1796. He spent less than a year as the state's congressional representative and then less than six months as US senator before he abruptly resigned. Unlike the men he would run against, Jackson had never served in the cabinet, had never received a diplomatic assignment, and had never visited Europe. When he arrived in Philadelphia to serve in the Fourth Congress, many capital politicians could barely conceal their disdain. "A tall, lank, uncouth looking personage, with long locks of hair hanging over his face, and a cue down his back tied in an eel skin . . . [with] manners and deportment that of a backwoodsman," Albert Gallatin noted disparagingly. By the standards of his rivals, the general was singularly unqualified to serve as president of the United States.[37]

Jackson dramatically burst into the nation's consciousness during the waning stages of the War of 1812. As commander of the US forces defending New Orleans, Jackson correctly predicted the route of British attack. To bar their advance, he ordered his soldiers to erect a mile-long, shoulder-high mud wall reinforced with picket fencing between the Mississippi River and an impenetrable cypress swamp. When 7,500 British troops arrived at Jackson's stoutly defended position on January 8, 1815, they foolishly attacked the 5,000 American soldiers safely secured behind the wall. The mauling ended in less than a half hour, with the British routed and in full retreat after suffering 2,037 casualties, including 291 dead—in contrast to the 71 US casualties, with only 13 dead.[38]

In a war in which nearly every American venture had failed, including bitterly divided politics on the home front, a string of battlefield defeats along the Canadian border, and the humiliating burning of the nation's capital, Jackson's overwhelming victory at New Orleans salved numerous psychic wounds. Ironically, his victory occurred after the peace treaty had already been signed in Europe about three weeks prior, but word of the general's defeat of the British spread before the news of Adams and Clay's diplomatic triumph reached North America. The newspapers blared exultant headlines, church bells tolled, congressional tributes poured in, and citizens partied in the streets. Politically, Jackson's triumph at New Orleans conferred both name recognition and popular appeal on the general. DeWitt Clinton, the much-admired governor of New York and former Federalist candidate for president, claimed that even he would lose to Jackson in an election in his home state. "The 8th of January and the battle of New Orleans was a thing that every man would understand," he maintained. Some newspapers began touting Jackson for the presidency shortly after his decisive victory.[39]

The general's succeeding ventures proved less acclaimed. After his battlefield triumph but before he received the certain news that the peace treaty had been signed, Jackson turned the city of New Orleans into a virtual police state. He became the first general in US history to impose martial law, suspending the writ of habeas corpus; abridging the freedoms of speech and press; arresting citizens, including a federal judge; and court-martialing a state senator. During the First Seminole War in 1818, Jackson and his troops, without the express (but perhaps with the intentionally ambiguous) approval of Monroe, invaded Spanish Florida to destroy Native American villages used as bases for raids into Georgia. Besides killing Seminoles, burning their homes and crops, and hanging their chiefs, he seized several Spanish forts, expelled their government, and summarily executed two British civilians accused of aiding the Seminoles. Ultimately, Jackson's actions helped deliver Florida to the Americans, but many politicians reproved the general's barbaric tactics. Crawford in the cabinet and Clay in Congress, in backhanded attacks on Monroe to further their identities as antiadministration candidates, had been especially outspoken against Jackson's activities. Though Congress ultimately rejected four separate resolutions censuring Jackson, the general never forgave the two prime movers behind these alleged assaults on his honor. Before he decided to run for president himself, Jackson favored Adams or Calhoun, as "great and enlightened statesmen," for the highest office.[40]

Despite the protests of some politicians, Monroe rewarded Jackson by naming him military governor of Florida. During his brief nine-month tenure, the general successfully established a functional government in the territory, but he also clashed vehemently with both Spanish and American officials serving there. Jackson justified his every action as militarily or administratively necessary, but the dual sides of his record created a mixed hero/despot image for the general. His supporters called him a courageous patriot who defended, protected, and avenged the country. His detractors labeled him a dangerous, insubordinate, and ruthless "Military Chieftain" without constitutional scruples. "I cannot believe," Clay wondered acerbically, "that killing 2500 Englishmen at N. Orleans qualifies for the various, difficult, and complicated duties of the Chief Magistracy." Perhaps surprisingly, his presidential rivals initially avoided attacking their fellow contender. Since Jackson's opponents considered him unqualified for high office and highly unlikely to win, they simply decided there was little upside to attacking a popular soldier. Jackson's dramatic victory in the Battle of New Orleans had transformed him into a "celebrity hero," granted him access to the 1824 contest, and served as his own personal shoulder-high mud wall insulating him from political criticism.[41]

For Jackson, it was a short mental leap from blasting the individual politicians who had criticized him to a blistering attack on the practice of politics itself. Throughout his career, the general had often conflated his desire for personal revenge with a larger mission to achieve justice for ordinary Americans. Jackson's first race for presidency would be no different. As he entered the campaign, he began accusing Washington insiders of committing a variety of insidious crimes against the republic. Politicians had misused government funds. "Scandalous defalcations in our public pecuniary agents, gross misapplications of public money, and an unprecedented laxity in official responsibilities occurred," he roared. Rapacious officeholders had subverted the Constitution, placing private interests ahead of the public good and exploiting lesser offices merely to obtain higher positions. "In our republican Government . . . you will find, hypocrisy, duplicity, and the lowest kind of intrigue, practiced by those in power to agrandise [sic] themselves," the general insisted. In Jackson's run for presidency, the capital itself would be in his crosshairs; few politicians—and certainly no presidential candidate—had ever run quite so overtly against the practice of politics itself. Jackson's focus on the "perfidious conduct" of the nation's political elite would not only undergird all of his campaigns for the presidency, it would become almost standard practice in future presidential elections.[42]

Unfortunately for his opponents, the times seemed ripe for Jackson's message. In a bit of soul-searching during a shared a carriage ride in early 1820, Calhoun and Adams agreed that "a vague but wide-spread discontent" gripped the body politic, with the "general impression that there was something radically wrong in the administration of Government." Voters were "ready to seize upon any event and looking out anywhere for a leader," Calhoun theorized. Though elite politicians, the secretaries had correctly gauged the mood of many ordinary Americans. The legacy of a disastrous war, a devastating financial panic, and discordant debates over slavery in Missouri had indeed left the nation in "deep distress." Wistful memories also added to the disaffection. With the fiftieth anniversary of the revolution looming and most of the founders dead or long retired, many Americans dwelled nostalgically on their allegedly heroic past. Though the actual revolution had been chaotic and challenging, memories shimmered with unambiguous glory. Many believed the small-r republicanism of the founders had triumphed over monarchy and aristocracy. Amid current political turmoil, many Americans felt with regret that the United States had abandoned its revolutionary virtue and lost its way. The nation had not only declined from its celebrated past, but political corruption threatened the republic itself.[43]

In this toxic political environment, Jackson's lack of traditional presidential credentials resonated with voters disgusted by national politics. "You have been your countrys [sic] Great Centinel," Samuel Houston proclaimed to Jackson, "at a time when her watchmen, had been caught slumbering on post—Her Capitol had been reduced to ashes. You have been her faithful guardian. . . . Will not the nation looke to you again?" Contrarily, the nation's political elite disdained him. "Jackson was not the choice of the politicians," Van Buren—who himself disliked Jackson in 1824—observed. They "had worked their minds into the strongest convictions . . . of his unfitness for the place." Since currying favor with elected politicians was an untenable option for a Washington outsider like Jackson, he and his allies instead planned a more popular campaign for the popular candidate. In 1822, they began plotting trips to regions outside the Southwest and assembling materials for a hagiographic biography that would be published in 1824. Jackson had little support from elected officials, so he waged a grassroots effort out of necessity; the customary routes to high office were largely closed to candidates without traditional qualifications.[44]

Despite his protestations against politics, Jackson's army service had unofficially trained him to succeed on this new type of battlefield. "His military career . . . had given him a spirit of watchfulness in regard to the movement of his enemies," Van Buren insisted. More practically, the officer appointment process was notoriously political, and Jackson's rise through the ranks proved his adeptness at this form of maneuvers. The general also displayed an intuitive sense for political strategies that might attract ordinary voters. As a westerner, he expected to receive numerous votes from his region, especially in the Southwest, but he would cultivate his personal popularity in waging his national campaign. Beyond his admired wartime exploits, he also emphasized his humble roots. His campaign literature incessantly reminded voters that Jackson was "coming directly from the people, and bearing with him an intimate acquaintance with their feelings, wishes, and wants." He claimed to be an honorable common man opposed to "treacherous and corrupt" politicians, a virtuous farmer amid the "courts, where courtiers dwell." Jackson's crusade against political corruption would overarch every other message he delivered to the voters. One Jacksonian argued that the general's supporters "thought him the only man in the Union who could successfully revise what they thought a corrupt system of government."[45]

While Adams and Calhoun ran as administration supporters and Clay and Crawford as administration critics, with Clay calling for a more activist government and Crawford less, Jackson ran against all capital politicians. His unusual campaign eschewed traditional political qualifications and emphasized popular over official support. If his unorthodox methods succeeded, Jackson's image as the heroic soldier fighting government corruption would overwhelm any public perception of his tyrannical barbarism. Accusing his competitors of corruptly administering the government was also a smart strategy, especially in light of the war, panic, and slavery debates that the nation had endured.

As we will see in chapter 6, his campaign proved well adapted to its turbulent times, as Jackson's legendary reputation as a wartime savior attracted many voters disturbed by the nation's problems. Jackson's decision to define his presidential bid as a fight against political corruption was a key development in the outcome of the election of 1824. The strategies that the big five candidates employed ensured that voters had clear choices for their next chief executive—a partisan Republican, a competent administrator, a broad-minded nationalist, an activist legislator, and a populist crusader.

2

→ • ←

Electioneering without Electioneering

T HE MONROE YEARS HAD hardly been an "Era of Good Feelings." The aftermath of the War of 1812, the Panic of 1819, and the debates about the Missouri Compromise left many ordinary Americans reeling. Voters, enduring the political, partisan, economic, and sectional tensions lingering from James Monroe's first term, demanded solutions to their problems from their elected officials. Fortunately for some citizens, their votes had become increasingly consequential in presidential electoral politics. Since the colonial era, deference had largely defined the relationship between the elected elite and the voting masses. The propertied, educated, and wealthy minority enjoyed the leisure time and social status seemingly necessary for officeholding, with the poorer and less-educated majority relegated to passing judgment on their "betters" via elections. Elite politicians dominated the system, choosing the candidates, building the coalitions, running the campaigns, and defining the issues.[1]

By the early 1820s, this deferential political culture had seriously eroded. As Federalists and Republicans waged increasingly fierce partisan warfare, they needed every weapon available to win elections—which included drawing more ordinary people into the process, even if it ultimately diminished party control over the system. Given that 1824 represented a transitional election, deference persisted in the newly democratized culture. The 1824 presidential aspirants were obliged to continue currying favor with political elites as presidential hopefuls had always done, but the candidates were also forced to navigate a far more democratized political landscape than their predecessors.[2]

Voting laws clearly telegraphed this democratization, as more ordinary people gained access to a ballot. When new states had entered the union, each almost invariably enfranchised all adult white males, but even the original thirteen had begrudgingly enlarged their voter rolls. By 1824, only five states—Rhode Island, Virginia, Louisiana, and the Carolinas—retained some combination of taxpaying or property-owning requirements that significantly restricted adult white male voting. As the electorate expanded, the number of offices it directly controlled, including the presidency, also increased. Because the Constitution had not specified a selection method for presidential electors, many state legislatures had initially managed this choice. In contrast to five of the sixteen states in 1800, eighteen of the twenty-four states had bowed to public pressure by 1824 and sanctioned popular elections to pick the electors. Only the six holdout legislatures of Vermont, Delaware, New York, South Carolina, Georgia, and Louisiana controlled their state's presidential choice in 1824. As we shall see in chapter 6, popular elections favored candidates with a greater following among ordinary voters, such as Andrew Jackson, while legislative elections favored candidates who appealed to elite politicians, such as William Crawford.[3]

Even the process of elections invited increased mass participation. Reductions in the size of election districts made voting more accessible in rural precincts while accommodating the increase in voters everywhere. Voters also faced less polling-place intimidation on election day as secret paper ballots continued steadily displacing viva voce voting. Enhanced citizen engagement in the process fed the growing allure of politics among ordinary people. Elite indoor debates spilled outdoors as public questions, including the presidency, were contested in barrooms, parlors, streets, and squares as much as in the halls of Congress. Though women and the enslaved remained unenfranchised and free black males suffered growing restrictions on their right to vote, democratization had given more adult white males a greater stake in the presidential derby.[4]

The 1824 contenders both realized and acknowledged the enhanced popular role in picking a president. "Candidates," Clay ostentatiously declared, "ought to be (as in name and fact I have endeavored honestly to be) Clay in the potter's hands. And that potter is the public." Winning in 1824 would require a greater engagement with the voters than any previous presidential candidate had practiced. Unfortunately for the hopefuls, the public's pesky republican beliefs seriously circumscribed any "electioneering" for the high office. Just like many Americans preferred unobtrusive governance to blatant displays of political authority, numerous voters rejected overt campaigning for the presidency by the candidates themselves. Many believed that the premier political office should be bestowed by the voters upon a high-minded, disinterested individual as a reward for superior public service. Already on alert for perceived corruption in the system, most voters deemed any candidate actively canvassing for votes as automatically disqualified from consideration. The 1824 election would challenge the candidates' political skills. Democratization required electioneering among the voters, but republicanism all but barred electioneering among the voters.[5]

The contenders' responses to this conundrum varied, but at the very least, every candidate paid lip service to the strictures against overt campaigning for the presidency. "I shall not degrade myself by importunity," Crawford insisted, "or suffer it to be done by others." The erudite Adams promised to follow the "Macbeth Policy," based on the Shakespeare quote, "If chance will have me king, why chance may crown me Without my stir." Clay claimed that he was "desirous to prevent an obtrusion of my name upon the public notice," even abjuring the use of the word "candidate." Calhoun joined this chorus. "I am much more attached to principle than promotion," he professed. "The result . . . is not to be unduly solicitous of my own advancement." Jackson offered the most direct pledge against electioneering. "I have no desire, nor do I expect ever to be called to fill the Presidential chair," he stated emphatically, "but should this be the case . . . it shall be without any exertion on my part . . . all that can be expected of me, is to obay [sic] the call of the people." The general ensured widespread public notice of his pious proclamation by repeating this pledge ad nauseam in his steady stream of correspondence.[6]

By conceding these constraints, the presidential candidates accepted 1824's tricky political landscape. Traditional methods of winning the presidency involving elite politicians remained crucial. American presidential candidates had always needed organizations, correspondence committees, and newspapers to win elections, and the campaign of 1824 would be no different. In this Republican-only election, each man would have to assemble his own components of a traditional campaign without relying on existing Republican apparatus.

In seeking the votes of regular citizens to win the highest office, however, they needed to look beyond their fellow elites. To reach the nonelite electorate, the campaigns employed new, innovative methods for carrying their message to the voters. They distributed pamphlets, published sports-themed cartoons, and, for the first time, issued candidate biographies and straw-polled ordinary people. Jackson's followers even minted the first political button ever used in a campaign for the presidency, a brass medallion bearing the likeness of the Hero of New Orleans that ordinary citizens could pin to their clothes. All of this electioneering, aimed at elites and nonelites alike, would have to occur without appearing to electioneer among anyone. The democratic facets of the political culture demanded, in essence, shouting, but in subdued republican tones. In the hinge election of 1824, both the old methods (organizations, correspondence, newspapers) and the new innovations (cartoons, biographies, straw polls) were required for victory.[7]

In through the Out-of-Doors: Popular Politics for a Democratized Electorate

In a nod to the increasing importance of ordinary voters, the presidential campaigns freely scattered electioneering literature to influence public opinion. Pamphlets, long a staple of American politics, were usually distributed unsigned or under an alias, so they could not be directly traced to the candidates themselves and therefore did not violate the republican limitations on electioneering. These documents either burnished a contender's image, sullied his opponents', or did both. Crawford's home-state enemy, Georgia governor John Clark, published one of the first pamphlets in the election. Distributed in 1819 and then reprinted in 1824, *Consideration on the Purity of Principles of W. H. Crawford, Esq.* brimmed with years-old charges against the treasury secretary. The booklet alleged that Crawford had slandered other Georgia politicians, improperly interfered in state legislative investigations, and—most explosively—secretly profited from an illegal slave-smuggling operation. Crawford's own allies retaliated with *An Address to the People of the United States, on the Presidential Election,* which soundly skewered both Jackson and Adams. Calhounites took an opposite tack. Their pamphlet, *Principles, Not Men,* chose not to slander his rivals, but instead praised Calhoun's *"Republican principles* and *enlightened national policy."*[8]

Jackson's publications both extolled and attacked. The most influential pamphlet of the entire election cycle may have been the nationally distributed *Letters of Wyoming.* Originally published as eleven pieces in Philadelphia's *Columbian Observer* during June and July 1823, the *Letters* were reissued as a pamphlet in 1824. Although penned under the alias "Wyoming," Jackson crony John Eaton had written them. He had based the letters on the "memorandoms" Jackson had recorded from his angry perusal of the newspapers, sometimes quoting exact phrases from the general's notes. The *Letters* focused squarely on political corruption emanating from the very center of power. "Look to the city of Washington," Wyoming screeched, "and let the virtuous patriots of the country weep at the spectacle. There corruption is . . . fast flourishing." The nation's "leading men" comprised an "ARISTOCRACY" that threatened to turn ordinary citizens into "mere instruments of the men in power." The solution to the mess in the capital rested on the "yeomanry" electing a new president, a man who was "never in *Europe*" and "never the HEAD OF A DEPARTMENT," which helpfully excluded every candidate running except Jackson. Only the general could end the corruption, because he was a "private citizen, committed to no party, pledged to no system, allied to no intrigue, free of all prejudices, but coming directly from the people." The popular 110-page booklet was widely disseminated throughout the union.[9]

While political pamphlets predated American independence, for the first time, three candidates published campaign biographies expressly as a positive image-making exercise for the voters. Calhoun's made the earliest appearance; it was serialized in nine installments in Philadelphia's *Franklin Gazette* during the spring and summer of 1822. Adams followed in 1824 as a series of letters from "Tell" in the *Baltimore American* that had actually been edited by the secretary of state himself. Calhoun's biography stressed his patriotism, intelligence, and independence, claiming he ignored both "personal consequences" and "the shiftings of the popular breeze" in making public decisions. Adams highlighted his patrician background, education, cosmopolitanism, and illustrious record of public service. Both backhandedly criticized Crawford, suggesting his presidential bid served to satisfy his personal ambitions. Meanwhile, in mid-June 1824, the always-busy Eaton updated and republished his hagiographic *Life of Andrew Jackson* for voters eager to read about the general's heroic military exploits.[10]

While campaign biographies or electioneering pamphlets might emphasize a candidate's traditional values, sports-themed political cartoons offered an alternative, more plebian image of the presidential contenders. Quite uncommon before 1820, these caricatures suddenly proliferated during the 1824 presidential election. A cartoon titled "A Foot Race" published in Boston depicted the candidates as horses vying for a $25,000 purse, an amount intentionally representing the president's salary. In this New England version, the Adams horse led the pack, of course, but in the "Political Horse Racing" cartoon that ran in the Nashville *Gazette*, the Jackson thoroughbred held a commanding lead. Meanwhile, Lexington's *Kentucky Reporter* featured a "Woodbee" cartoon that placed "Henry Woodbee" well ahead of "John Q. Woodbee" and "William H. Woodbee" in a footrace between the men who would be president. Sport-themed cartoons had been avoided in the past because horse racing, cockfighting, and gambling had been deemed antithetical to republican values, but increasing democratization encouraged the interpretation of elite politics using egalitarian metaphors. Ordinary voters might better identify with high-political president-making presented as a popular game. More important, most of these sports-themed cartoons appeared *before* the election and without picking a winner of the race, implying that the reader's vote was required for a contender to triumph.[11]

Alongside the increase in sports-themed cartoons, straw polls made their first appearance in the 1824 presidential election. "Prematurely collecting the opinion of the people," one newspaper editor observed, "was never resorted to, we believe, on any former occasion." This newly discovered interest in tabulating voter opinion before an election occurred represented yet another concession to the increasingly democratized political culture. The *Harrisburg Pennsylvanian* sponsored the first known opinion poll, with Jackson defeating Adams 335–169. Subsequent polls soon spread to nearly every state. Hoping to prove Crawford's unpopularity with ordinary voters, Calhoun supporters conducted many of the initial polls, but they soon abandoned the practice when he began losing most of his polls to Jackson. Candidate organizations often conducted their polls at campaign rallies or meetings called to endorse a certain candidate, but also at gatherings convened for other purposes, such as militia musters, grand juries, tax gatherings, and Fourth of July celebrations. Hotels and some public places maintained "poll books" open for several days for registering choices, while impromptu polls of barroom patrons or steamship passengers recorded the opinion of these random assemblies. Even elections were not sacrosanct; when voting for other offices, citizens might be asked to indicate their presidential preference by a show of hands or by writing it on the back of the ballot.[12]

While clearly unscientific from a modern standpoint, these polls also faced contemporaneous skepticism. Critics, usually the supporters of candidates who lost the poll, noted that these surveys sampled only a small sliver of citizens and contained numerous ineligible voters, including minors. They insisted that poll voting was bought, coerced, or inevitable, especially at venues favorable to certain candidates—naturally the soldier Jackson would win a straw poll of the militia. While most New England polls projected Adams as the winner, and Clay notched a few victories in the West, Jackson won an overwhelming majority of the nation's polls. With North Carolina's correctly pointing to a shocking upset of Crawford by Jackson in that state, these surveys should have cautioned the other campaigns against underestimating the general's electability.[13]

As the new straw polls clearly indicated, Jackson had made important headway in communicating with ordinary voters. The front-running

Crawford, as the candidate to beat, naturally suffered the most vicious of these popular attacks, while Adams and Calhoun used their forays into popular politics to burnish their traditional political credentials. Contrarily, Jackson's *Letters of Wyoming* focused on the central issue of his campaign: political corruption in Washington, DC. As we will see in chapter 6, the general's strident pamphleteering resonated with many ordinary voters.

A "Concert and Understanding between Them": Organizing Elite Politicians

While the techniques of popular politics represented some innovative additions to presidential campaigning in 1824, none of the hopefuls abandoned the more traditional methods of winning the White House. American presidential candidates had always relied upon some type of organization for election. Although less substantial than future political parties, groups of individuals had always acted together to wage their nominees' campaigns for the presidency. Ironically, the decline of the Federalist Party actually burdened the 1824 Republican aspirants, when compared to their predecessors. Since all of the candidates shared the same party affiliation, none could depend fully upon any existing partisan apparatus for winning the election. Each contender would have to build his own personal organization—a network of elite politicians and establishment supporters—if he hoped to occupy the presidential chair. Crawford's campaign drove the process. As the front-runner and establishment favorite, he immediately commanded the largest group of backers, and the other hopefuls would have to counter with equally powerful organizations if they hoped to upend the Georgian. As Calhoun succinctly informed one of his followers, "You must organize against organization." Despite its obvious violation of the rules against electioneering, candidates could justify the building of an organization of supporters as a means of countering the "illegitimate" organizations of the other contenders, especially Crawford's.[14]

Each presidential contender recruited a network of "active, enterprising, and influential men" throughout the country. Beyond drafting congressmen in Washington, the candidates sought to add state governors and legislators to their organization. In the United States' federal system, national politicians relied heavily on state and local politicos to gain and maintain their positions. Accordingly, Calhoun targeted each state's chief executive, arguing that voters "will be much under the influence of the messages of the respective governors." State legislators were important on two fronts: they could nominate favored candidates for president while providing crucial electoral votes in states without popularly elected electors. Members of an organization were expected to "hold" or "secure" their locality, state, or region for their favorite, and candidates might even gain control of a state's electoral machinery if they co-opted its key leaders as allies. In turn, state politicians assumed that a winning candidate would champion the issues they valued and funnel federal patronage their way, ensuring their preeminence in any Republican factional battles within states.[15]

While organizations in 1824 simply mirrored traditional political practice, they were also deployed to influence voters in the newly democratized political culture. With presidential candidates virtually barred from electioneering, members of an organization served as useful surrogates to circumvent the unspoken rules against campaigning. Jackson declined an invitation to visit states in the North. "At every Town & Village where I might alight, a suspicion could be indulged, that they considered me there expressly on a pilgrimage after their good opinion," the general noted cautiously. "Travel anywhere now would be improper." Facing less public scrutiny, however, allies could be conscripted for these electioneering trips. Calhoun sent one supporter from Maryland on a swing through the West "to make strong and lasting impressions" on "the publick mind." Meanwhile, Adams, conscious of the burden of his Federalist past, dispatched one backer into New York "to make friends by giving assurances" that the secretary of state would head a "*Republican* administration." Indiscreet followers proved a downside of campaigning via surrogates, however. One overenthusiastic Jackson supporter embarrassed the general with a gruesome public toast hoping that "the *skins* of the enemies of Jackson be converted into *carpeting,* for his friends to dance upon." Despite the potential pitfalls of irresponsible followers, the 1824 contenders still sought to assemble the largest, most robust, and most far-reaching organizations possible.[16]

If commanding a potent organization brimming with elite politicos ensured victory in 1824, then Crawford seemed certain to win the election. Building on the network of partisans he had enlisted for his 1816 nomination battle against Monroe, the treasury secretary aligned numerous senators and representatives behind his candidacy, a who's who of the nation's most influential power brokers. Outside the capital, the countless public servants he had worked with over his long career generally favored Crawford. He proved quite popular with elite Republicans in eastern states with long-standing party machinery, while his support was correspondingly weaker in the newer states in the West.[17]

Unsurprisingly, the treasury secretary towered over the political scene in his native Georgia, but his real advantage in the electoral sweepstakes derived from his supporters in the two most politically powerful states in the union. Traditional presidential politics had been virtually controlled by an unofficial alliance between Virginia and New York, with presidents drawn from the Old Dominion and vice presidents from the Empire State. This time around, the most prominent politicos in both states joined Crawford's team. In Virginia, tart-tongued ideologue Thomas Ritchie—editor of the influential *Richmond Enquirer* and leader of the shadowy Richmond Junto—and his numerous acolytes became early promoters of Crawford's cause. Meanwhile, New York's wily senator Martin Van Buren, after rejecting bids for his allegiance from both Adams and Calhoun, threw the considerable political weight of his formidable Albany Regency behind Crawford.[18]

The men had taken different routes to the Georgian's candidacy. Crawford's defense of the Radical agenda appealed to the conservative Virginian, while his role as party luminary attracted the partisan-minded New Yorker. Support from the key power brokers in the two most traditionally important states daunted Crawford's rivals. "However discordant," Calhoun grumbled, "cooperation . . . between the Constitutionists of Virginia and the political managers of New York" represented a real threat to rival campaigns.[19]

Still, astute observers might have detected some worrying warning signs of Crawford's chances. The treasury secretary never seemed quite as popular with the party's rank-and-file members as he did with its elite political leaders. Even more disquieting for Crawford, he faced outright hostility for his role in the Panic of 1819. As we have seen in chapter 1, many voters in the northwestern states blamed the panic on the BUS, which Crawford had ardently supported. Accordingly, he drew almost no organizational support from Republicans in that region, including electoral vote–rich Ohio. His rivals mostly overlooked Crawford's organizational deficiencies, however. "His party is so strong," Adams groused, "and they have such a ruffian-like manner of bearing down opposition that impartial and disinterested persons are intimidated." Crawford seemed unstoppable. He was the darling of the Radical faction, and Crawfordites dominated Congress and controlled several statehouses. Even two former presidents, Republican legends Jefferson and Madison, enthusiastically supported the treasury secretary.[20]

Organizationally, Crawford's only serious rival was Adams. The secretary of state assembled an impressive team of active supporters, a varied mix of port collectors, postmasters, state legislators, jurists, lawyers, and editors from around the union. His numerous allies honeycombed Washington's bureaucracy, including, in secret, an auditor in his rival's Treasury Department, and they kept him well-informed about political developments in the capital. Though exceeded in sheer numbers by the Crawfordites in Congress, Adams could rely on a panoply of representatives, mostly from New England and the mid-Atlantic states, to back his candidacy. While some supporters found that Adams's unparalleled record of public service rendered him more than qualified for the presidency, most were specifically attracted to the commercial aspects of his diplomatic career. The New Englander had long championed American trade interests internationally and continental expansion—and therefore market growth—domestically. Adams snared numerous allies from the nation's shipping, mercantile, and urban seaboard communities.[21]

Superficially, his organization appeared broad based, with supporters from Virginia, the Carolinas, Illinois, and Kentucky among his followers. Had his supporters delved deeper into the ranks, however, they would have uncovered real problems with Adams's viability outside his region. His most fervent support clearly originated above the Mason-Dixon line. Although he could depend on backing from emigrant Yankees throughout the union, New England was the secretary of state's power base, and even Adams understood his regional appeal. To expand his support beyond northern voters, Adams ultimately jettisoned his sanctified Macbeth Policy, admitting that "chance or merit" did not win presidencies. "Kings are made by politicians," the secretary of state acknowledged, "and the man who sits down waiting to be crowned, either by chance or just right, will go bareheaded all his life." As we will see in chapter 7, Adams would bargain extensively with politicos from outside his home region, especially those from the northwestern and mid-Atlantic states, in his pursuit of the presidency.[22]

The secretary of war also had no intention of remaining crownless, and he too assembled an organization to make certain of it. While clearly dwarfed by the Crawford and Adams contingents, Calhoun's backers in Congress included representatives from his home state and—consequentially, considering his campaign strategy—Maryland, New York, and Pennsylvania. Calhoun achieved greater success raising adherents outside the capital. Several state legislators in Maryland and Ohio joined his organization, while the politically well-connected Johnson family in Kentucky, inveterate enemies of Clay after he had successfully represented the BUS in a suit against them, adopted Calhoun's cause in the Bluegrass State. Despite the fact that the nation's most famous soldier was running against him, many military officers zealously championed the noncombatant Calhoun—so many, in fact, that dismissive Crawfordites disparagingly labeled him the "army candidate." Campaigning as a southern nationalist with hoped-for northern appeal, Calhoun pulled off his greatest coup in Pennsylvania. Philadelphia lawyer George M. Dallas, leader of the city's commanding Family Party and attracted to Calhoun's support for activist government, fell in line behind the South Carolinian and brought his own organization with him.[23]

Hinting at the president's secret support, Monroe's son-in-law and private secretary Samuel Gouverneur remained Calhoun's greatest confidante behind the scenes. Indeed, Calhoun's organization-building mirrored Monroe's attempted nonpartisan party amalgamation. Southern nationalists, defense-minded northerners, New York Clintonians, and Federalists figured prominently in both coalitions. However, the very nature of some of

Calhoun's supporters—Federalists who loathed Adams, Clintonians hostile to Van Buren, and anti-Radicals wary of Crawford—should have troubled the South Carolinian. Some of his allies seemed less pro-Calhoun than anti–other candidates, and they could easily switch their support from the secretary of war if some other, more popular contender emerged. Thomas Ritchie acerbically dismissed both Calhoun and his potentially brittle organization. "A regular system of puffing . . . cannot prevail upon the people to prefer Mr. Calhoun," he insisted.[24]

As individual congressmen aligned behind the three secretaries, they began working together as factions, which some even called "parties." While far more inchoate and ephemeral than true political parties, these congressional factions critically shaped the 1824 election. They could push legislation favorable to their candidate or chair committees responsible for investigating a rival's department. In turn, the secretaries could do favors for their party members, dispensing patronage or providing insider information on administration activities that benefited their supporters. As an added bonus, any dealings between the secretaries and their congressional parties looked like official business, so the republican rules against electioneering were seemingly not violated.[25]

Unlike the secretaries, Clay's efforts at organization-building proved underwhelming. With the unshakeable support of the entire Kentucky delegation, Clay relied on the power of his weighty speakership to buttress his presidential bid. Out in the states, unlike the other candidates who tried to build national campaigns, Clay focused myopically on those pillars of traditional presidential politics: Virginia and New York. Because it was already physically linked to the West via the Erie Canal, Clay argued that the Empire State should share political affinities with his home region as well. His most reliable ally in this fight was Peter Porter, a former New York congressman and gubernatorial contender. Porter had initially pledged to support the official Republican nominee, but disgusted with Van Buren's machinations in favor of Crawford, he began actively politicking for Clay.[26]

Although Clay stressed his deep roots in his birth state, the Speaker proved a much harder sell in tariff-averse Virginia. His campaign in the Old Dominion rested almost entirely on the shoulders of Francis Brooke, a

friend of nearly thirty years and now a state legislator. Though Brooke detested Clay's tariff policies as much as any Virginian, he agreed to back the
Kentuckian's bid after extensive cajoling from Clay himself. Beyond the New
York/Virginia axis, Clay's supporters in other states usually reflected the
ideological nature of his issues-oriented candidacy. Clay's men were often
locally prominent small businessmen attracted to his stand on internal
improvements and protective tariffs and included a confectioner, a liquor
dealer, a lottery office owner, a brick manufacturer, a wholesale grocer, a
bookseller, an auction house operator, a canal construction contractor, and
a papermaker. While Clay always described his organization optimistically,
even the most cursory analysis demonstrated its relative weakness compared to groups backing the other candidates. Its diminutive size hardly
threatened his opponents, prompting one Adams newspaper to airily dis-
miss the Speaker as a "junior candidate" and "more a nominal than a real
competitor."[27]

At its upper level, at least, Jackson fielded an even smaller organization
than Clay, which only reinforced his unlikely prospects for victory in the
minds of his opponents. Naturally suspicious, the general maintained a
narrow, close-knit group of intimates. His three most trusted advisors had
fought side by side with the general on the battlefield. Retired First Lieu-
tenant Richard Call had served as Jackson's personal aide in the Seminole
War, while current Tennessee senator—and *Letters of Wyoming* author—
Eaton had fought as a private soldier for him during the War of 1812. General John Coffee had commanded a militia brigade under Jackson during
the Battle of New Orleans; he had even been involved in Jackson's notorious 1813 barroom brawl with the Benton brothers, knocking Thomas Hart
Benton down a flight of stairs during the fight. "The friendships which were
formed in those times of difficulty and danger," as one ex-private phrased
it, linked many current and former soldiers to the Jackson campaign. Elite
politicians played a much less significant role for Jackson compared to
other candidates; his coterie consisted mostly of Tennessee politicos, including the powerful Nashville Junto.[28]

Jackson's meager band of high-profile allies struck little fear in the hearts
of his rivals, yet a closer analysis of his supporters might have given them

pause. The general effectively turned Crawford's problem upside down, as Jackson appeared *more* popular with ordinary Republican voters than with their elite leaders. "You are already secure with the multitude," one Pennsylvanian assured Jackson. While "the lower and middle classes of society" favored the general, he added, "the leading men . . . with very few exceptions, are opposed to you." Dissident Republican groups, for instance the "Quids" in New York or "Independent Republicans" in Pennsylvania and North Carolina, increasingly supported Jackson. Backing a political outsider appealed to these supporters, because they were outsiders themselves in local politics. Unfortunately for his rivals, the superficial weakness of Jackson's organization among elite politicians concealed its relative strength from the other presidential contenders.[29]

From a top-down perspective and judged by contemporaneous standards, the candidate organizations evidenced a predictable order of strength. Crawford's, followed by Adams's, were the most sizable; Calhoun's and Clay's trailed relatively far behind; and the outsider Jackson's proved the most miniscule. From a bottom-up perspective and assessed by numbers of ordinary followers, however, there were some important reversals of fortune. Jackson and Adams had the most devotees, readily leading Clay and Crawford, with Calhoun bringing up the rear. As we will see in chapter 3, however, in a one-party election, organization membership was not set in stone; continually shifting alliances and fickle elite politicians bedeviled the candidates, who were seeking organizational stability.

Say It (Carefully) in a Letter:
The Power and Perils of Correspondence

When possible, the candidates enlisted their allies face to face, but in a far-flung republic, the aspirants most often relied on correspondence to build their organizations, and they encouraged their followers to write to each other. Such committees of correspondence perpetuated a seemingly endless loop of letters between contenders and their allies. The candidates' committees resembled those that had evolved in the states since the 1790s.

Republican state legislators had often appointed members to manage intrastate campaigns centrally by corresponding with similar county committees. Because all the 1824 candidates hailed from the same party, they or their supporters formed their own new committees rather than using the preexisting apparatus. By election day, every candidate had one or more committees of correspondence operating in multiple states. While organizations might be made from men, it was the letters they wrote to each other that bound the group together.[30]

Letters proved central to electioneering without electioneering. They could generate positive buzz about a candidate by exploiting his strength in one area to buttress his campaign in another. For instance, Crawfordites dispatched sixty letters to North Carolina claiming that the treasury secretary would win New York. On the other hand, letters could also be employed to bludgeon one's opponents. In his own correspondence, Jackson quoted a letter from a "highly respectable" New Yorker to allege that Crawford and Clay were secretly working together. Old letters could also be dusted off to smear a rival. Some Crawfordites exploited Adams's tainted Federalist past by distributing the twenty-year-old correspondence between John Adams and William Cunningham, in which the senior Adams had acerbically and repeatedly denounced Republican icon Thomas Jefferson. Clay chuckled delightedly that "the public" would finally be exposed to the "egotism vanity & folly" that characterized both father and son.[31]

Even letters replete with overly rosy "panegyrics" about a candidate could become themselves fodder for attacking ones' competitors. Crawford ally Thomas Ritchie pilloried Calhoun's committee of correspondence. "They write from New York that she has turned in his favor," he sneered. "They write from Washington that Mr. Crawford is lost. . . . They write from Raleigh that Mr. Calhoun carries the day because the Speaker of the House of Representatives is his advocate . . . Quack medicines and lottery offices have not been more active."[32]

As Ritchie's attack on Calhoun's committee demonstrated, candidates needed to treat their correspondence carefully. Letters could never appear to be electioneering tools. Jackson claimed that he had "recd many letters from every quarter" about his candidacy, but "I have answered none, nor do

I intend to answer any." Yet, the general allowed "extracts" from his letters to be published in the press with the stipulation that "my name is not to be known." Meanwhile, one Calhoun backer told another, "If you ever publish any part of my letters omit everything that relates to the . . . members of Congress here, or give it such a general form of expression such as 'letters from New York to Washington state . . .' &c."[33]

Unsurprisingly, candidates warily regarded unsolicited letters from strangers as potential "gotcha" gambits from other campaigns. Adams observed that many unknown correspondents "professing good will" had asked for his opinions on the issues of the day. "I answer very few," he noted, "and perhaps ought to answer none." Calhoun asked a close ally to investigate one letter writer who had "connections" and was too important to ignore. "I am compelled to be very cautious in my correspondence," the secretary of war explained. Clay himself had been "deceived" by a covertly hostile correspondent, but such "unworthy" letter writers, he sighed, were "one of the misfortunes of public life. What can one do but answer civilly and kindly letters which breathe nothing but disinterested zeal and devotion?" In the election of 1824, both sending and receiving correspondence required careful circumspection.[34]

Still, for all the potential pitfalls, correspondence remained an essential means of campaigning for the presidency. While candidate organizations would have been severely weakened without the letters the members exchanged, correspondence also proved essential for bridging the gap between the politician and the public. When one ally asked Jackson if he could publish some of the general's letters, he carefully demurred. "Any thing from me on such a subject," Jackson balked, "probably would be interpreted as aiming at *electioneering*. That I was pressing my letters thro the country with a view to my own advancement." After this politically pious caveat, Jackson added that "this is only thrown out by way of suggestion to you, for I write no letter, the sentiments of which I would ever desire to conceal." His correspondent subsequently published Jackson's letters, of course. Candidates used correspondence to shape public opinion with their version of the facts. When one of Clay's letters "accidentally" found its way into the newspaper, it pleased the Speaker that voters could read his unadulterated opinion rather than "through the medium" of the opposition press. "All I feel anxious about," he added, "is that the public should not receive an impression that it was my intention that it should be published." In an age of increasing democratization, candidates needed correspondence to reach the voters, but could not appear to be foisting their correspondence on the public for electoral advantage.[35]

Read All about Them: The Candidates and Their Newspaper Networks

As Clay implied, even the most politically persuasive letters would have reached only a handful of voters without newspapers to bring them into the public sphere. Press coverage had long played an important role in presidential politics, but by 1824, newspapers had ballooned into an outsize factor in the race for the White House. The Post Office Act of 1792 had permitted any newspaper to be mailed for a nominal fee compared to other materials. Magazines and letters were 700 percent more expensive to transmit. The act also codified the long-standing printer's exchange policy; since the colonial era, editors had been authorized to swap one copy of their paper with each other for free as a means to obtain nonlocal news. Such favorable costs and conditions increased the sheer number of newspapers circulating throughout the country. Published broadsheets expanded at a greater rate than the population, and by the early 1820s, there were just over one subscription for every two US households. Nearly six million newspapers were being sent by mail, comprising one-third to one-half of the total weight of materials handled by the post office in a given year. Naturally, many elite politicians received multiple subscriptions, accounting for some of this growth, but ordinary voters also gained more access to the news. The candidates clearly recognized the importance of the press. "An able and active paper," Calhoun observed, "is almost everything in fact in the coming contest."[36]

The editors of these vital campaign tools maintained an uneasy relationship with the presidential candidates. Amos Kendall, editor of the *Argus of Western America,* called his profession a "vile business . . . [I] make great men who never thank me, new enmities which I neither wish nor deserve, get praised as a patriot, & cursed as a knave, with but a miserable compensation either for my favors or my labors." Politicians returned the disdain. Adams sourly denounced one editor's "great faculty and power as a slanderer [which] consists in mixing truth with falsehood in such proportions that with the ignorant, the malicious, and the interested, the compound is so like truth." Still, candidates needed favorable press coverage to propel their campaigns, and editors needed funding to keep their presses rolling; mutual interlocking interests ensured close cooperation between both sides in the 1824 campaign.[37]

While editors generally tried to support candidates they admired, many were forced to follow the money. One editor "hinted" to Adams "that he could not afford to be my friend for nothing." Newspapers relied upon government contracts, advertisements, loans from a "political sponsor," and subscriptions. The candidates best able to fund newspapers through these methods would receive the most favorable and widespread press coverage. When it came to financing newspapers, the cabinet secretaries possessed a distinct advantage over their nondepartmental rivals, with Adams holding the greatest influence of all. Since 1789, the secretary of state had been authorized to negotiate contracts with three newspapers in every state to print any laws that Congress had enacted. This power granted Adams unparalleled leverage over dozens of editors across the nation; he could fund those who covered his campaign favorably while cutting off any critical papers—with anything he did unassailably legal. When Adams switched printers in New York State, he explained his actions without a trace of irony. "The papers that printed the laws were perfectly at liberty to promulgate what political sentiments they pleased," he insisted tartly, "but I felt no obligation to countenance papers whose career was a succession of slanders and invectives upon the Government of the Union," which included the State Department, of course. Crawfordites in Congress demanded repeal of Adams's power over the press, but his allies blocked any changes to the law and the secretary of state maintained his enormous journalistic advantage.[38]

Crawford's backers hardly remained idle, however. Because they dominated the legislative branch, they effectively controlled Congress's own contracts for printing its journals, debates, and reports. In 1819, the treasury secretary's supporters tapped the *National Intelligencer*, edited by William Gales and Joseph Seaton, as the official printer of Congress. Considered "sentimental favorites" for the job after their establishment had been torched by the British during the attack on Washington, DC, in the War of 1812, their newspaper benefited handsomely from its relationship with the legislature. From 1817 through 1824, the *Intelligencer* reaped 55 percent of its profits from Congress's beneficence. While Gales and Seaton insisted—often hotly—that they remained scrupulously neutral in the presidential race, the other candidates discerned a distinct pro-Crawford slant in their pages. Calhoun and Adams both contended that their economic dependence on the Crawfordite Congress "palsied" their support for the pro-administration candidates. Similarly, one Jackson ally accused the *Intelligencer* of deliberately running shortened versions of the general's remarks, since full reportage "might show that he is not an *inferior statesman to any of them.*"[39]

Each secretary also had access to a variety of under-the-radar ways of subsidizing their pet news organs. Their department budgets contained ample funds for printing forms, directives, legal notices, job postings, and advertisements that the canny secretaries could funnel into the coffers of newspapers favorable to their cause. Cabinet secretaries also exploited their own staff of government-paid departmental clerks to supply campaign-related articles to supportive newspapers. Calhoun and Adams privately accused the treasury secretary's assistants of secretly editing one paper from within the department itself with the most vicious articles "coming almost directly from Mr. Crawford." However, Calhoun himself was embarrassed when his own adjutant-general was caught violating postal laws by using his department's official business franking privilege to mail out proposals for a new pro-Calhoun paper. Meanwhile, Adams denounced a former clerk, who had once "eulogized" him in the press, for writing critical articles after Adams fired him.[40]

Though Calhoun enjoyed some of the cabinet perks that allowed the secretaries to fund positive press coverage, he lacked control of the big-money government printing contracts that so benefited Adams and Crawford.

He and his minions compensated by deploying another funding stream that newspapers relied upon—the political loan. A group of the highest-level Calhounites, including Monroe's ever-active son-in-law Gouverneur, founded and funded the *Patriot*, a pro-Calhoun paper in New York City. Jackson, as the outsider in the race without access to any of Washington's funding tricks, also relied on a political loan to finance his favorable press coverage. Eaton, Jackson's closest confidante, loaned $15,000 to Stephen Simpson, editor of Jackson's principal paper, the Philadelphia *Columbian Observer*. Eaton had probably raised the money from Jackson's wealthy Tennessee patrons, and his cash infusion kept Simpson's presses busy churning out adulatory Jackson materials. Eaton's "loan" was never repaid, and his investment probably represented over $430,000 in 2022 dollars.[41]

Most of the candidates also pushed the members of their organization into subscribing to papers friendly to their cause. Again using his departmental franking privilege, the secretary of war mailed copies of a prospectus for a new pro-Calhoun newspaper to his most prominent backers in Maryland, South Carolina, Pennsylvania, Illinois, Kentucky, and Missouri, instructing them to pass it on to other Calhounites. Every ally who received a prospectus was expected to return it to Calhoun with a list of subscribers whom he had enrolled. Crawford dispatched his own department agents and clerks to some states to drum up subscribers for papers backing the treasury secretary. Even the candidates were expected to subscribe. After the election was over, Simpson billed Jackson $24.03 to cover his subscription to the *Columbian Observer* for 1822 to 1825, and the general readily paid up. Not all subscriptions were so costly. In a proto–direct mailing drive, editors apparently maintained address lists of elite power brokers, and these "leading men" received multiple free subscriptions to a wide array of papers representing every hue of the political spectrum. "Many newspapers have been sent to me, from every part of the Union, unsought," Monroe grumbled, "which having neither time nor curiosity to read, are in effect thrown away." The candidates themselves made these mailing lists; Jackson complained that "should I be called upon for the subscriptions of all news papers sent to me, for which I have never been a subscriber—it would require more funds to meet this demand, than all the neat [*sic*] proceeds of my estate." Despite these costly free subscriptions, reaching the political elite proved so essential to campaigning in 1824 that the candidate bank-rolling continued unabated.[42]

Despite all the money overtly and covertly exchanging hands between the candidates, their allies, and the editors, republican ideology demanded stark separation between the press and the politicians, so both sides tried vigorously to conceal any links between them from the voters. Though the editor of the *Nashville Republican* was "a private friend," Jackson stoutly insisted that he had "never been in his printing office in my life, nor on any occasion have I suggested, or attempted to regulate, the course pur-sued by him as a public printer." Privately, of course, the exact opposite was true—the general had personally selected editorials to be published in the *Nashville Republican*. His political loan to the *Columbian Observer* never became public knowledge, and despite Simpson's vociferous cheer-leading for the general, the two men never corresponded once during the long campaign. "It is prohibited to the conductor of a newspaper to Ad-dress a Candidate for the Presidency without subjecting him to evil impu-tations," Simpson noted when writing to Jackson only *after* the election had safely ended. Calhoun also disguised his personal efforts to build up positive press. "My name must not be used in connection with the paper," he stressed to supporters. Similarly, Adams claimed that "the mere sus-picion of my authorizing any one to tamper for the support [of one ed-itor] will do me more harm than he could do me good by a whole life of his friendship."[43]

Behind this soothing public charade of separation, candidates and ed-itors closely cooperated. The candidates personally composed pieces for publication or passed along notes that could be transformed into full-blown articles by an editor using his own words. Just as with Eaton's Wyoming letters, surrogates anonymously dispatched correspondence and articles to newspapers using innocuous aliases so they could not be connected back to a candidate's organization. The contenders and their supporters also passed on "extracts" from one supportive paper to be published in another. Despite their proper republican pronouncements, most of the candidates tried carefully to control their press coverage.[44]

The exchanging of "extracts" between press organs only demonstrated the interconnected nature of a candidate's editorial support. The presidential hopefuls purposely tried to link the newspapers backing them into a press network sympathetic to their candidacy. A central paper—in Washington for the cabinet secretaries and in Philadelphia for Jackson—produced candidate-approved content that could then be dispatched for reprinting in strings of regional and local newspapers. As with several other tactical measures, Crawford's camp had led the way. From the earliest moments of the election period, the other candidates observed "a signal of mutual intelligence" passing between the papers under his sway. To counter the treasury secretary, his opponents soon followed suit. "Would it not be advisable," Adams archly asked one supportive editor, "to observe the course of other newspapers, and endeavor to harmonize, or at least not to conflict, with those . . . disposed to support the same cause?"[45]

To craft their networks, campaigns exploited the law permitting the free exchange of newspapers by mail. They encouraged loyal editors to swap their papers with each other, which not only ensured consistent messaging, but also scrubbed a candidate's fingerprints from the process. Editors possessed unlimited reprint rights and could freely copy articles from other papers without payment, permission, or attribution, which proved a boon to the smaller and less well-funded newspapers supporting a candidate. Press networks proved a vital means of electioneering without electioneering, since most of the public probably remained unaware of the submerged but strong connections between what they were reading and for whom they were voting.[46]

Each of the secretaries employed a flagship publication based in Washington, which then passed on stories to network presses in at least six other states. With the advantage of his government contracts, Adams assembled the largest network, led by the *National Journal*. Crawford's presses closely rivaled Adams's. While the *National Intelligencer* could only surreptitiously support the Georgian, his Washington, DC, *City Gazette* openly headed Crawford's network. Calhoun counterattacked with *Republican and Congressional Examiner* directing his network. In a clever twist, Calhoun installed disgruntled former Crawford employees as editors for two of his papers.[47]

For an outsider given little chance to win the election by his cabinet opponents, Jackson nonetheless pieced together an impressive string of papers behind his candidacy. Eaton's loan to the Philadelphia *Columbian Observer* sealed a long-standing relationship between Simpson and Jackson; the editor had served under the general at the Battle of New Orleans. Simpson, son of a First BUS cashier and himself a former note clerk for the Second, shared Jackson's noted antipathy for banks. Simpson's newspaper headed a pack of presses in Pennsylvania, Tennessee, Ohio, New York, and Maryland. Much like the candidate they backed, Jackson's editors were often political outsiders in their own locality.[48]

The other noncabinet candidate pursued a strategy entirely opposite from Jackson's. Clay alone among the contenders made the fateful decision to try and win the presidency without any newspaper network at all. "I adhere to my purpose of spending no money on printers for two reasons." Clay informed one ally. "One of which is that I think it is wrong, and the other is that I have none to spare on such an object." While the first part of his justification fittingly acknowledged the republican restrictions against electioneering, the second part probably reflected the actual grim reality of Clay's situation. Without the funding perks available to the cabinet candidates and seemingly unable to attract the wealthy backers who propped up Jackson, Clay simply lacked the resources to assemble a vigorous press network. His lack of a true newspaper network troubled many of his allies. "We have been considerably dispirited to find the Western papers so obstinately silent," one lamented to Clay. Their silence was hardly "obstinate" however; it simply reflected the financial necessities of presidential press coverage in 1824.[49]

Still, there was some electioneering method to Clay's political madness. By the 1820s, congressmen used their congressional speeches more to influence the constituents back home than their fellow politicos in Washington. Clay, as the only true "issues candidate" in the race, undoubtedly calculated that the free press coverage of his speechifying antics in the House might compensate for his lack of a newspaper network. As an added bonus, the Speaker's reprinted speeches were official congressional business, so none could accuse him of electioneering by having them published. Some voters openly admitted that they supported Clay after reading his speeches in the newspapers; in the end, it was these voters who would determine whether Clay's unusual press strategy would triumph over the other candidate's press networks.[50]

By using their press networks to educate and mobilize potential voters, the presidential hopefuls hoped to enlarge their networks of personal followers. Newspapers proved essential to keeping a candidate's campaign on message. With the constraints against overt electioneering, candidate-funded press coverage provided a covert method of molding public opinion. Endless repetition of a candidate's message, both within an individual newspaper in subsequent editions or across the network in multiple papers, powerfully reinforced what candidates wanted voters to believe. Without violating any republican rules, they could advocate or defend their own positions and perhaps even stoke turnout by voters inspired by what they had read.[51]

Newspapers also had a dark side, of course. Editors often devoted more coverage to attacking their candidate's opponents than they did to lauding their candidate. "Was I to notice the falsehoods and false insinuations of . . . unprincipled editors," Jackson bristled, "I could have time for nothing else." Adams testily concurred. "To answer newspaper accusations would be an endless task," he seethed. "The tongue of falsehood can never be silenced." Unfortunately for the candidates, as we will see in chapter 4, the "torrents of filth" emanating from their press networks risked inundating their positive messaging in the minds of readers.[52]

Not-So-Strange Bedfellows: Electioneering and the Politics of Corruption

The 1824 presidential campaigns exploited each electioneering technique—pamphlets, cartoons, polls, organizations, correspondence, and newspaper networks—to burnish a candidate's public image, even—or especially—at the expense of his rivals. Campaigns used these elements to emphasize their candidate's positive attributes, repel their adversaries' assaults, and mount their own attacks against rivals. Candidates sought cohesive messaging by

promoting coordination throughout all aspects of their campaigns, trying
to interweave the individual elements of their electoral efforts as much
as possible. "You must understand and act with each other," Calhoun told
his allies, "Concert is indispensible." Organization members wrote pamphlets and articles for the newspapers. Newspapers conducted polls,
published cartoons, and printed extracts from an organization's correspondence. Letter writers reported on press activity or compiled their press
submissions into pamphlets. Pamphlet writers extolled a candidate's newspaper and organizational support. Despite the electorate's republican aver-
sion to electioneering, the candidates electioneered, surreptitiously and
innovatively, when trying to garner votes from the electorate.[53]

The contenders risked the electorate's perception of their electioneering, however. Despite their attempts to conceal its nature, the very voters
whom they sought might recognize the electioneering through the vehe-
ment denials. Electioneering clearly harmed the reputations of politicians.
Readers must, one newspaper editorialized, "suppose that our Presidents,
Secretaries, Senators, and Representatives, are all traitors and pirates, and,
the government of this people, has been committed to the hands of public
robbers." Following the calamities of the Monroe era, many angry voters
deemed the practice of presidential politics itself as corrupt, which could
scarcely comfort the candidates aware of the increasing power of ordinary
people. As we will see in chapter 6, voters would reward or punish candidates based upon their perceived connection to corrupt political processes.[54]

Many of the electioneering techniques used in the 1824 election were
simply advances on traditional practice, but they also presaged their
enhanced development in future president-making. Pamphleteering, orga-
nizing, writing letters, and press reportage had always played a role in the
battle between Republicans and Federalists. Larger, more overt organizations and ever-expanding networks of newspapers—as well as cartooning
and polling—would characterize the conflict between the Whigs and the
Democrats. While the election of 1824 represented a transition between
old and new practices, no sharp line demarcated these developments. Presidents would be made in the Jacksonian era using some new political tools,
but also with the innovative use of conventional tools.

3

→ • ←

One-Party Politics

W HILE CANDIDATES INTRODUCED SOME popular-minded innovations into the 1824 election, the staples of an electioneering-
without-electioneering campaign—organizations, correspondence, and newspapers—had always been a part of American presidential
politics. Tactics for winning in 1824 would differ significantly from the preceding and succeeding presidential contests, however, for one important
reason. Because the Federalists had collapsed as competitors for the highest office, for the first time, the Republicans faced a nonincumbent campaign for the presidency without a challenger from the opposition party.
Ironically, rather than strengthening the party, the Federalists' decline had
weakened the Republicans. Without the opposition as a unifying threat, the
Republicans' ideological underpinnings and policy positions lost coherence,
while its organizational structure, especially at the state level, had badly
frayed. Republican infighting had also increased. These divisions in turn
virtually invited, perhaps even demanded, the five competing Republican
presidential candidacies. "We shall not be surprised if there be a candidate
for each letter in the alphabet," one humorist joked in the *Fredericktown
Political Examiner*.[1]

The multiple candidacies were hardly a laughing matter for the Republican elites. The party that had once carefully concealed its quarrels behind closed doors for the last five presidential elections—while presenting
a happy, united face to the public—would now openly air its dirty laun-
dry for every voter to see. The decline of the Federalist party was a key

development in the outcome of the 1824 election. As a one-party contest, 1824 was almost unique in American political history, and the candidates were forced to respond accordingly.

In this one-party environment, campaigns employed new strategies to achieve their goals. The candidates supplemented their pursuit of the customary Republican congressional caucus endorsement with state nominations. They also proposed new axes of power to replace the hoary Virginia/New York alliance that had long dominated presidential politics. Both of these changes helped fatally destabilize traditional political practice. In addition, the candidates dispensed patronage and assembled congressional factions that extended the reach of their personal organizations. They sponsored lavish parties meant to strengthen the bonds with their fellow politicians. They turned political rumormongering into an art form aimed at undermining rivals. The one-party presidential election required a complicated, delicate electoral dance from the 1824 candidates. The novel strategies introduced that year represented a necessary response to the factionalism splintering the Republican Party, but each of these innovations also furthered the transition to Jacksonian era president-making.

On Unfamiliar Terrain: The Factional Challenges to Conventional Campaigning

Amid the chaos created by political factionalism, even deciding when to enter the race challenged the candidates. Most of them had probably been aiming to succeed Monroe even during his first term, but avoided any public declarations on the subject. Coming out too soon would open the contender to attacks from opponents while inviting the public's criticism of a candidate's electioneering. Conversely, waiting too long to enter the race risked losing the support of both voters and elites to other candidacies. "The name of any individual ought not to be prematurely thrust on the public notice. . . . It is offensive and indiscreet," Clay claimed. "[But] one's friends ought not to delay bringing his pretensions into public view so long as to expose them to the danger of being forgotten or obscured." Other candidates played the waiting game as well. In early 1823, Adams and Calhoun both advised their restive followers to wait before openly announcing any campaign for the presidency. Only Crawford lacked the luxury of timing his entrance. In late 1821, the treasury secretary balked at the arduous campaign ahead. "Why should I suffer myself to be made a mark at which every unprincipled knave shall direct the shafts of calumny and detraction for years?" he sighed. "I am already weary and disgusted in anticipation." Regardless of his vacillation, Crawford's second-place finish in 1816, combined with his giant organization, had stamped him as the 1824 front-runner from the earliest days of Monroe's presidency.[2]

While the contenders maneuvered behind the scenes to build their campaigns, most selected a more public venue to declare their candidacies officially. The last three Republican presidents had each been nominated for the office behind closed doors by a caucus of the party's congressmen in Washington. With party candidate Crawford the odds-on favorite to win the congressional caucus endorsement this time around, the other aspirants needed to find another method of placing their names before the voters in the event they were unable to dislodge the Georgian from his perch. Jackson's innovative campaign led the way, as the general was nominated for president via resolutions passed in both branches of Tennessee's state legislature in late summer 1822. He received a second nomination from Alabama's legislators in January 1824.[3]

Necessity was the mother of invention for Jackson. As a political novice running an outsider's campaign, he generated little support from members of Congress. If the path to victory in 1824 required winning the traditional Republican congressional caucus nomination, Jackson simply would not be president of the United States, so a state nomination was essential. The general, echoing proper republican sentiments, disclaimed playing any role in his nomination. "Hearing accidentally that something of the kind was intended, I instantly declined going there [the capital]," Jackson reassured one correspondent. "I knew it would have been said that I was there electioneering—as I never have." In another unusual tactic, the general bucked orthodoxy by entering the race much earlier than any other candidate. This strategy entailed little risk, since Jackson's rivals underestimated his appeal. The general's Tennessee endorsement "can produce no effect whatsoever," Crawford noted airily. "There is no other State in the Union that will take him for President." Clay cavalierly dismissed Jackson's nomination "as a mere compliment to the Genl. from his own state, without an expectation that it would be seconded by any other." Calhoun was even more cocky. "I consider Jackson's strength as ours," the secretary of war brashly informed his followers. "All he gains will be gained to us." Jackson's unthreatening candidacy prompted almost no counterattack from his rivals. Few elite politicos, even several from Tennessee, took Jackson seriously, so there was little upside to attacking a beloved national hero with virtually no chance of winning.[4]

Tennessee's endorsement conferred greater acceptability on state nominations, so every other candidate eventually followed the general's example and secured many of his own. Jackson's bold, early entry into the race galvanized Clay's antsy supporters. They fretted about the slow pace of Clay's campaign, urging the Speaker not to wait any longer to declare his intensions publicly. Clay had intentionally delayed, however. He knew that the Kentucky legislature would eagerly nominate their home state star, but that endorsement might appear to be simply inflated pretensions for a favorite son. Accordingly, Clay set his sights on wresting a nomination from neighboring Ohio first. In the fall of 1822, he worked closely with Kentucky editor Amos Kendall on a secret plan to generate a seemingly spontaneous nomination from the state legislators in Columbus. Working together, the two men composed a series of four letters, titled "To the People of Ohio," from "Wayne." This correspondence stressed the importance of federally funded internal improvements to the state, concluding that Clay alone best represented Ohio's interests on the issue. Kendall dispatched the letters for publication in several of the state's newspapers, but first he carefully concealed any connection to himself, Clay, and Kentucky. He had them recopied by a local Ohio resident first, because "m[y] handwriting is known to many persons in those places and to some of the printers." Despite these efforts, the Ohio legislature hesitated. Many supported Clay, but others, echoing the growing democratic sentiments of the new political culture, objected to caucus nominations made behind closed doors on principle, even for a preferred candidate.[5]

Meanwhile, some legislators also hoped to delay Clay's nomination in case New York's former governor DeWitt Clinton entered the race. Like Clay, Clinton, a prime mover behind the construction of the Erie Canal, embodied support for internal improvements in the public's imagination. Unlike Clay, however, Clinton lacked any association with the extension of slavery. The Missouri debates had intensified antislavery sentiments among some Ohioans, and the architect of the compromise bore the brunt of their disgust. Ultimately, Clay gave up on his push for nomination in Ohio as his first achievement, letting less significant Missouri, rapidly followed by Kentucky, nominate him for president in November 1822. Despite his best efforts, he garnered only a less compelling nomination by a rump caucus of less than half of Ohio legislators in January 1823. His final endorsements came from Illinois shortly afterward and by Louisiana the following March.[6]

The Speaker's contretemps in Ohio should have served as a cautionary tale for all the candidates. While admitting a slave state to the union may have seemed both reasoned and reasonable to Clay, antislavery voters in Ohio felt otherwise. In addition, secret caucusing was simply politics as usual to a seasoned politico like Clay, but anticorruption voters in Ohio believed otherwise. In a democratizing political culture in which the ballots of ordinary citizens increasingly decided presidential elections, voters, and not politicians, would decide which issues mattered most and which political tactics were acceptable practices.[7]

Like Clay, Calhoun focused on wresting nominations from states where he believed he was popular, but also like the Speaker, his success was mixed. At the behest of some Pennsylvania congressmen, the secretary of war, allegedly with "some hesitation," decided to officially enter the race in December 1821. Unfortunately for Calhoun, his timing could not have been worse—the South Carolina legislature was nominating popular native son William Lowndes for president at the same time. Calhoun dubiously claimed that the legislature had not nominated him because the members believed he was supporting Adams. His luck turned, however, when Lowndes propitiously died in 1822 and South Carolina's legislature dutifully nominated the secretary of war as his replacement in November 1823. He hoped for a second such affirmation from Maryland, but instructed his followers there only to push for one if they were certain of victory. "Nothing ought to be put to hazard," Calhoun warned. Ultimately, he never received any nomination from the state.[8]

While Calhoun had been blocked from an early nomination, Adams actively discouraged his backers from granting him one. In early 1823, the legislatures of Massachusetts and Maine, probably spooked about the activities of other campaigns, passed nearly identically worded resolutions expressing "unlimited confidence" in Adams as the next president, but they did not "deem it expedient" to make a formal nomination at that time. Instead, Adams saved their enthusiasm for an impressive explosion of endorsements early in the election year. In January 1824, Connecticut, Maine, and Rhode Island nominated Adams for president, followed by New Hampshire and Massachusetts in June. With his home state nomination coming after his others, Adams easily achieved what Clay had struggled to deliver. Other states appeared to be enthusiastically spearheading his candidacy, rather than just blindly following Massachusetts's predictable endorsement of its native son.[9]

For their part, the Crawfordites, expecting to win the official Republican Party congressional nomination, routinely denounced the state nominations of the other candidates. In the end, though, even they succumbed to the trend. Georgia's legislature eventually nominated Crawford in December 1823, while the treasury secretary snared Virginia's coveted endorsement in February the next year. Unlike previous presidential elections, a one-party contest ultimately required state nominations to validate a candidate's participation.[10]

While Republican factionalism caused the candidates to delay entering the race, many state and national politicos were equally laggard in joining the fray in favor of a particular aspirant. One of Clay's Maryland backers informed the Speaker that many of his supporters in the state had refrained from openly backing him until he proved he could win the election. "In all political contests," Clay's ally noted, "there are a number of persons of a certain description who *always* go with what is considered the strong side." John Eaton agreed, telling Jackson that most politicians "governed by the principles of self, would rather stand aloof until he who shall be seen to be the strongest before the people may be pretty accurately ascertained." Backing the eventual winner presumably increased a politician's future political power, while supporting a loser might significantly diminish it. Selecting among the candidates proved easier for politicians in areas with an overwhelming popular favorite, such as Tennessee, Kentucky, or New England, but it required more arduous calculation in places without a clear majority choice. "Everybody appears more anxious to be on the *strong* side than the *right* side," one state politico complained.[11]

In factionalized presidential politics, however, picking a candidate was not necessarily a permanent decision. Some politicians switched sides as a candidate's fortunes ebbed and flowed during the long campaign. When one Adams ally noted hopefully that New York representative Henry Storrs had opposed Adams in the past but favored him today, Adams shot back, "I asked him how Storrs would be tomorrow." Candidates could only warily navigate between hesitant politicians and their shifting alliances. The best strategy was to maintain good relations with as many politicians as possible, even with the current supporters of other candidates, because they might eventually switch sides. "The election must then be decided by *secondary* strength," one Calhounite informed another. "The successful candidate must *principally* depend upon the votes he obtains from those who were compelled to abandon their first choice." Clay adopted this line of thinking as well, instructing his followers to "maintain at least respectful relations with the other gentlemen and their friends" so the Speaker could count on their support when his opponents' candidacies faltered. Politicians had always wavered to some degree between presidential aspirants, of course, but 1824's one-party contest increased this indecisiveness dramatically. In the factionalized political culture, candidates could never be sure if today's enemy would be tomorrow's friend—sometimes they were both.[12]

Just as politicians shifted alliances in a one-party presidential election, state-to-state linkages also proved to be in play. As Crawford and Clay's organization-building strategies had demonstrated, the unofficial alliance between Virginia and New York continued to factor into presidential politics. Politicians who supported the partnership hoped to maintain the power their large states had enjoyed or to help reunify the Republican party after the political dissensions of the Monroe years, but the multiple presidential candidacies considerably weakened its dominance. Contenders unlikely to be backed by the Virginia/New York axis—effectively meaning every candidate except Crawford—promoted other state-to-state linkages in its place. Some tried to push Virginia into a new coalition, but, more often than not, the candidates focused on New York. The Empire State had always been the junior partner in its coalition with the Old Dominion, so the presidential hopefuls massaged New Yorkers' egos. Clay insisted that the other mid-Atlantic states would go along with New York, obliging Virginia "to *follow* instead of *leading*." Similarly, Calhoun exhorted New Yorkers to abandon Virginia and "assume her just weight in the Union" in partnership with Pennsylvania.[13]

Some proposed alliances dispensed with Virginia and New York entirely. Calhoun and Jackson, building on their presumed strength in Pennsylvania, usually anchored the Keystone state in their refocused version of presidential politics. Both men most frequently linked Pennsylvania with North Carolina, creating a new North/South alliance to replace the antiquated New York/Virginia partnership. As with New York, the campaigns appealed to North Carolina's sense of honor. Crawfordites, Calhoun maintained, arrogantly assumed that North Carolina would take its customary path and follow Virginia. Instead, the state should reject this "degrading supposition" and "decide [for] the South including even Virginia itself." He even sold himself as "the Carolina candidate" deserving of support from both North Carolina and South Carolina. On various other occasions, Calhoun and Jackson proposed aligning Pennsylvania with Maryland, New Jersey, or the West. In the end, all of these proposed realignments lethally undermined the aging Virginia/New York axis. As we will see in chapter 5, the two states would go their separate ways in 1824, and their direct alliance would no longer factor into the making of presidents in the Jacksonian era.[14]

Many of these maneuvers—snagging state nominations, scooping up unaffiliated politicos, and forging new state alliances—were intended to "demonstrate" a candidate's broad popularity. Displays of support in one state "might have a good collateral effect," Clay contended. Similarly, one Calhounite told another, "Many of those who now count for Adams only want to be convinced that Calhoun is strong elsewhere to declare for him." It was problematic for the candidates, however, that these smart political tactics increasingly demonstrated something else—the unseemly side of politics. One newspaper editorial denounced the Republican Party's elites as "this small number who work the wires of the puppet show. [A]ll expect promotion and reward from the next President. . . . They won't be troubled about his qualifications. It becomes important . . . that they should be on the *right* side, that is the *successful* side." As much as the candidates might try to pull secret strings behind the scenes, the public appeared increasingly aware of the hands slyly guiding the wires.[15]

Carrots and Sticks: The Secretaries' Patronage Power

If any politicians fit the description of "this small number who work the wires of the puppet show," the three cabinet secretaries fit the bill. Their executive branch duties conferred enormous advantages in a contest to replace Monroe. As we have seen in chapter 2, their government-paid departmental staff doubled as campaign workers, their departmental franking privileges sometimes covered the costs of mailing campaign materials, and their departmental printing budgets and government newspaper contracts funded favorable press coverage. To outsiders, succession from within the cabinet seemed to turn the presidency into an insiders' prize.[16]

One of the greatest benefits of cabinet service for ensuring an insiders' succession was patronage. Clay maintained that he had just as many supporters as the other candidates, but that "the Secretaries are able to throw out, from their respective departments, a more intense & vivifying heat than I am capable of ejecting." Indeed, federal positions had grown explosively since Jefferson's victory. No other American enterprise, public or private, had the sheer size, geographic scope, or organizational capacity as the federal government. From the early 1800s through the late 1820s, the number of jobs in Washington nearly doubled. Including legislators, the federal government amounted to over six hundred posts in the capital, with 41 percent of the growth attributed to appointive positions in the

Treasury Department and Post Office. While significant, the real growth in patronage possibilities had occurred out in the states, including in nearly 8,000 local post offices, which made the US Post Office the largest public agency in the world. The executive branch controlled much of this growing army, with the department heads enjoying significant autonomy in patronage decisions. Citizens seeking jobs possessed a greater stake in the outcome of presidential elections, which dovetailed with their demands for more control over picking a chief executive. Because securing jobs for one's allies was another way to electioneer without electioneering, patronage developed into one of the most powerful weapons for winning a presidential campaign, and the cabinet secretaries owned the best-stocked arsenals.[17]

Adding to his hoard of front-runner advantages, Crawford controlled more patronage than any other candidate and more than anyone in government other than the postmaster general and the president. His opponents regarded Crawford's appointment powers and his large organization as intertwined evils. His supporters "regard not the good of their country, but only look to their individual agrandisement [sic]," one Jacksonian complained, "for there is no man who in any way contributes to his elevation that does not expect an equivalent in return." Calhoun and Adams both accused the treasury secretary of building a "patronage machine" with his departmental appointment duties.[18]

Land sales in the Alabama Territory showcased the clout and reach of Crawford's patronage. Georgia's politicians had long influenced state affairs in their neighboring territory. Before Monroe even took office, Crawford had pressured the president-elect to install many of his friends in key positions in Alabama's government. Since the Land Office was part of the Treasury Department, Crawford was also able to commandeer territorial surveys and maps, documents that were crucial to identifying the best parcels of land in Alabama. Crawford opened the land sale office in Milledgeville, Georgia, 150 miles from the actual land being sold, which allowed his wealthy home-state allies to scoop up the best tracts of land while the poorer settlers who actually lived in Alabama were mostly shut out.[19]

As a result of Crawford's tactics, his Georgia cronies dominated Alabama's constitutional convention and ultimately the political and economic leadership of the new state. Crawford himself became one of the largest landowners in Alabama, and most of the people his policies benefited climbed aboard his presidential bandwagon. Crawford could not dispense patronage unimpeded, of course. His cabinet opponents, their congressional allies, and President Monroe carefully dissected his every move. Still, his opponents had to admit sullenly that Crawford's activities, while possibly corrupt, were completely legal.[20]

Like Crawford, Calhoun generated influence by controlling his own War Department positions, including office clerkships, cadet commissions, and officer appointments. He "has a candidate always ready for everything," Adams griped, "in all his movements of every kind [he] has an eye to himself." Calhoun was also blessed with a friend in a high place, as the president manipulated his own patronage to promote Calhoun's candidacy. From the earliest stages of the campaign, the secretary of war had urged Monroe to make Calhoun-friendly appointments. Monroe often complied, naming one Calhounite as Florida's territorial governor and another as postmaster general. Without consulting Crawford, the president appointed a pro-Calhoun Land Office commissioner, a position that reported directly to the treasury secretary. "Provision was at once made for a favorite of the Secretary of War," Clay snidely observed.[21]

Though the secretary of state controlled some appointive positions, Adams invariably lost the cabinet's patronage wars because Crawford's cornucopia of posts far exceeded his own and because he did not have the president's ear like Calhoun. Still, he deftly attempted a novel maneuver by using patronage for attack. Adams urged Monroe to make diplomatic appointments that would have sidelined his rivals or their important supporters from the election. Over the course of the campaign, the secretary of state recommended Calhoun and Clay for various foreign legations. He even ludicrously touted Jackson as minister to Mexico or Colombia, despite the general's admitted "violence of temper." Adams targeted Crawford's closest advisors as well, pushing for the exile of John Holmes to the legation in Chile and the sequestering of Martin Van Buren on the Supreme Court, a move that would have immeasurably improved Adams's chances of capturing New York's all-important electoral votes. Adams recognized that sending rivals "on a mission abroad would be attributed by some, perhaps, to a wish to get [them] out of the way," but insisted that his patronage schemes were actually "generous policy" toward his opponents. His fellow contenders openly mocked Adams's transparent tactics. "Some Siberian missions may lessen the number of your Competitors," one Clay partisan joked. In the end, the secretary of state's scheming failed, as his adversaries adroitly rejected every one of his politically motivated offers.[22]

While patronage was a useful tool for a presidential candidate, the Republican Party's factions complicated its distribution enormously. Even the simple appointment of an Albany postmaster roiled the Washington establishment. Calhoun, probably as part of a bid to woo Federalists, pushed Monroe to appoint the former Federalist Solomon Van Rensselaer to the position. Senator Van Buren exploded—not only was Van Rensselaer a Federalist, he was a Clintonian, and therefore a bitter enemy of Van Buren's Albany Regency. Encouraged by Crawford, Van Buren pushed Joseph Lansing as postmaster. The Van Rensselaer-versus-Lansing controversy eventually embroiled the cabinet and the Congress, with Calhoun, Adams, Postmaster General Return J. Meigs, and half the New York congressional delegation backing Van Rensselaer; Van Buren, Crawford, Navy Secretary Smith Thompson, Attorney General William Wirt, New York Senator Rufus King, Vice President Daniel Tompkins, and the other half of the New York delegation were behind Lansing. The donnybrook consumed an entire cabinet meeting, with Monroe proclaiming an "inclination" not to interfere in what was legally Meigs' decision—which also helpfully reinforced Calhoun, of course. Wirt sputtered that "determination now not to interfere would itself be an interference," with Adams countering that Monroe was simply following Madison's precedent and Crawford countercountering that Monroe should then agree not to interfere with *any* future appointments. Ultimately Monroe remained "neutral," Meigs appointed Van Rensselaer, Calhoun's wishes prevailed, and bitterness consumed the losing side. The episode demonstrated that presidential candidates might exploit patronage to further their bids for high office, but that Republican factionalism meant crossing a minefield to do so.[23]

Clay and Jackson were mostly on the outside looking in as the secretaries squabbled over patronage, and they occupied the least enviable positions of all. As prominent national figures, they were inundated by office seekers just as much as the cabinet candidates, but they lacked the actual patronage power the secretaries enjoyed. At best, the noncabinet candidates could only promise to beg the secretaries for patronage scraps in the present or dangle their own future appointments. The general cleverly turned disadvantage to advantage by linking executive branch patronage to his case against corruption in the capital. Unable to help one office seeker, he blamed the "political Jugglers" in the executive departments. "All things here appear to bend to the approaching Presidential election," he explained testily.[24]

Of course, Jackson had profited handsomely—almost as much as Crawford—from his own insider information in Alabama. As treaty commissioner during Monroe's first term, the general both persuaded and bullied Native Americans into ceding large parts of Georgia, Mississippi, Tennessee, and practically all of Alabama to the United States. He then wangled an appointment for his nephew as head government surveyor for the ceded lands. Exploiting the government-owned surveys, the pair, along with other assorted relatives and friends, formed a land investment company that purchased prime real estate in the territory, sometimes at far below market value. Jackson, conveniently ignoring any similarity between himself and the secretaries, continued to bash the cabinet over their patronage appointments.[25]

Despite its advantages, in a factionalized party environment, patronage proved a double-edged sword. Appointees routinely switched allegiances, while disappointed office seekers often blamed the capital's elite for their frustrated hopes. In Crawford's Alabama, for instance, a few of his appointees ultimately supported other presidential candidates, and those nominees Monroe rejected despite Crawford's recommendations usually blamed the treasury secretary more than the president. Adams dourly complained that one patronage seeker "has friends to recommend for appointments and, in that sort of jest which has serious meaning, desired my wife to advise me not to break my own neck." Although Clay had jealously eyed the secretaries' patronage power, he acknowledged the risk involved. "I think it will rather injure the cause which it is intended to subserve," the Speaker noted smugly. Ironically, the cabinet candidates might dangle patronage as carrots, but supporters could just as easily use their disaffections as sticks to beat down the secretaries' presidential hopes.[26]

It's Their Party and They'll Electioneer If They Want To: The Social Campaign for the Presidency

As the three cabinet secretaries divisively dispensed patronage, they only widened the fissures in Republican Party cohesiveness. When they also organized social events to further their candidacies, they sharpened these divisions further. Ironically, Washington gatherings—balls, parties, dinners, visits, and receptions—had long been used to promote party unity. During the December-to-March society season in the capital, Republican socializing had helped establish and strengthen the bonds among party members. Building on that example, the cabinet candidates naturally turned to this traditional method of forging new coalitions in support of their personal presidential bids. Throwing a party helped candidates attract allies, Eaton wryly reported to Jackson, "for it is hard, very hard you know that any man's wine & cordials should be drank; & his Ice creams fed upon and still to say or think ought [sic] against him."[27]

Parties now helped split the party, however, since a politician openly committed to one candidate might not receive an invitation to his opponent's soiree. Regardless of the effect on Republican unity, the contenders believed that social campaigning was essential to winning the election. Candidates could wine and dine congressmen for their support, representatives and senators could solicit patronage favors in return, and all sides could stay informed about the state of the race. As the electioneering intensified during Monroe's second term, the secretaries stretched Washington's social season, extending it from November to May and staging a seemingly exhausting, nonstop series of festive events. As historian Catherine Allgor explains, "Everyone complained about going to the parties that everyone else complained about giving, but go and give they did." For the Republican candidates of a disintegrating party, social occasions offered one key to hosting their own future parties in the White House.[28]

Every candidate joined in the fun. Crawford sponsored one "grand party . . . so crowded that no one had more than six Inches to move on." Calhoun opened his elegant Georgetown mansion to his fellow politicians and "dazzled [them] with his brilliant conversation." Even a committed Crawfordite such as Van Buren, who spent numerous evenings there playing whist, acknowledged that the secretary of war "was a fascinating man and I enjoyed his society greatly." Clay held court with some political luminaries over dinner at Brown's Hotel, reveling in a "triple alliance of flattery, vanity, and egotism," Adams claimed acerbically. Even Jackson, a harsh critic of the supposed corruption inherent in the capital's social whirl, participated in the entertainment when he arrived to take up a Senate seat in late 1823. "There is nothing done here but *Vissitting* [sic] & *carding each other,*" he complained to Rachel Jackson, "you know how much I was disgusted with those scenes when you & I were here." His wife must have been thoroughly confused when Eaton simultaneously reported to her that the general "is constantly in motion to some Dinner party or other." Jackson attended gatherings thrown by his cabinet rivals, while hosting Adams, Calhoun, and Clay at his own birthday party organized by twenty-five of his friends. Even a self-styled outsider like Jackson realized the benefits of entertaining a host of insiders.[29]

Despite his reputation for social frostiness, Adams appears to have won the battle of the balls. Well-trained by his long experience attending diplomatic social functions in the glitzy courts of Europe, the secretary of state proved quite adept at party planning. In 1823, John Quincy Adams remodeled his F Street home and added a 28-by-29-foot entertainment room as a venue for his political galas. His wife, Louisa Adams, staged "Mrs. Adams's Tuesday Nights" every week during the winter, where the pair became one of the nation's true power couples. The Adamses extended an open invitation to the capital's political elite to a reliable—and expensive, for the hosts—evening of amusement, which included eating, drinking, dancing, and cards, all accompanied by Louisa Adams on the piano, harp, or voice. On a good night, John Qunicy Adams could electioneer in front of two hundred people at once—but, like a respectable republican, without overtly electioneering in the eyes of anyone. By Monroe's second term, the secretary of state had turned visiting into an art form, calling on every member of Congress during his 1824 run. Drafting Louisa Adams into the cause, John Qunicy Adams carefully organized her daily schedule of congressional visits "as if he was drawing up some very important article to negotiate in a commercial treaty," Louisa Adams opined sardonically. The secretary's wife made as many as forty-five calls per day, once logging six miles in travel.[30]

Some candidates expanded their social campaigns beyond the typical dinner, drinks, and dancing, and even moved their venue far outside the capital. For Adams and Jackson, attending church services became a more respectable way of soliciting support in a social setting. "We are so depraved," Eaton bellowed to the deeply religious Rachel Jackson, "as scarcely even to go to church, unless to the Capitol where visits are made rather for the purpose of shewing ones self, than any pious feeling prompts." Despite his assurances to Rachel that Jackson did not participate in such a profane social campaign, the general clearly made his rounds. He bragged about spending his Sundays with a diverse set of believers—the Methodists one week, the Presbyterians following, the Baptists next, and the Episcopalians after that. Not to be outdone, Adams attended three services *every* Sunday—like Jackson, generally in different houses of worship each week. Candidates also attended or hosted an array of gatherings out in the states, where they could surreptitiously electioneer among ordinary voters.[31]

Ultimately, social campaigning aimed to establish a favorable image of the candidate in the minds of ordinary citizens. While the immediate event might be staged as an organization-building exercise for only a small handful of elite politicians, a candidate's press network widely disseminated news about these festivities. A social event limited in time and scope—one night with a few political cronies in a small drawing room, for instance—could potentially influence hundreds of voters across a vast nation on an ongoing basis as endlessly reprinted reports about the party or dinner filtered out into the hinterlands. As the historian Jeffrey Pasley notes, events were sometimes held as pretexts to have some news to print. Compelling press coverage of a party helped juice a candidate's favorability ratings, while reporting on toasts amplified his campaign messaging. Social politicking helped candidates navigate through the Republican Party's factions toward actual voters in the increasingly democratized electorate. The demands of the emerging political culture necessitated that a supremely indoor aspect of politics be widely publicized outdoors.[32]

The Whisper Campaign: The Fine Art of Ruining a Rival with a Rumor

A common thread linked these social interactions between elite politicians. Any time or any place these men gathered, they gossiped, and the rumors they spread fueled the campaign for the presidency. With a party so heavily factionalized, the political situation continually shifted. Politicians could stay informed of these rapid changes by tapping into the unending stream of insider chitchat that dominated every kind of political communication—congressional sessions, impromptu meetings, parties, and the letters they exchanged. As with most aspects of the campaign, rumors served to generate both positive and negative buzz; they could inflate a candidate's support or deflate his rival's backing. While political rumors had always been a part of American presidential elections, the one-party nature of the 1824 election ultimately intensified their use.[33]

Rumors were sometimes spread to stoke support for a candidate. "One plan adopted . . . by Crawford's friends," a Maryland representative observed, "is to impress a belief that he is so strong that all opposition would be useless." Calhounites spread a similar rumor that exaggerated the secretary of war's support in Pennsylvania. Although several Keystone State congressmen backed Calhoun, a false story circulated that the entire delegation had caucused, officially endorsed him, and were planning to send emissaries on a "political mission" to convert Pennsylvania's state legislators to the Calhoun cause. Sometimes candidates spread their own favorable gossip. While acknowledging that it was only a "rumor," Jackson claimed that he was firmly supported by eight states.[34]

Far more often than supportive gossip, however, politicians usually spread negative rumors meant to undermine a rival's campaign. False rumors might fool a candidate's supporters into thinking that their man had no chance of winning, so they might stop working for his election or, better yet in the era's factionalized politics, join another candidate's campaign. The lies passed around fell into three general areas—that the candidate had been abandoned by his supporters, that he had withdrawn from the race, or that he had entered into a contemptible alliance with a hated rival. Abandonment rumors claimed that individuals, states, or even regions no longer supported a candidate. Rumors abounded that Van Buren, one of Crawford's key allies and critical to winning New York, had severed his alliance with the treasury secretary. Jackson's opponents in state politics tried "difusing [sic] the intelligence that the State of Tennessee will not ultimately support me," the general fumed. Meanwhile, striking at Clay's epicenter of support and playing off his decision intentionally to delay his nomination from Kentucky, gossip proliferated that the Speaker was "being abandoned in the West."[35]

Devastating withdrawal rumors bedeviled every candidate. Some of Clay's allies were "elated" when rumors reached them that Crawford was about to drop out of the race, given that the Speaker would probably inherit his support. Clay himself spread false tales about the demise of the secretary of war's campaign. "Mr. Calhoun is no longer regarded as a candidate," he confidently reported to one editor, "and is spoken of by all his friends here as withdrawn." Meanwhile, Crawford gossiped that Calhoun "is understood to be hors du combat [out of the fight]." On another occasion, Calhoun supposedly withdrew when Robert Hayne, his favored candidate, lost South Carolina's Senate race to Crawfordite William Smith; this rumor contained a double lie—Calhoun had not withdrawn, and Hayne actually defeated Smith. Meanwhile, the treasury secretary's partisans undercut Jackson. "Mr. Crawford's folks [are] seeking to convey the idea that you have not consented to be placed before the nation as a candidate," Eaton warned the general. As one of the weaker aspirants in the race, an unsurprising number of withdrawal rumors also plagued Clay, and the Speaker worked overtime stamping out "widespread . . . utterly idle and unfounded" gossip that he had abandoned his candidacy. These rumors took their toll on Clay's campaign. He had actually garnered much support in Delaware, one ally there disclosed, "but you was thought to be almost withdrawn & they went over to other Candidates." Some rumors even went the extra mile, with a few Adams men spreading the lie that not only had Clay withdrawn, but he had actually died. While rumors were often dismissed as nakedly partisan attacks, they could undercut a candidate's support, as Clay's campaign clearly demonstrated.[36]

The most repeated and most damaging rumors of the election by far were the false charges that two candidates were secretly working together. Rumors of an insidious coalition between philosophically dissimilar rivals who claimed to hate each other devalued each man's message and tarnished two campaigns with one lie. Since voters and supporters regarded coalitions as an especially odious form of electioneering, candidates repeatedly stressed their independence from other campaigns. Calhoun emphasized that his organization should "avoid giving any ground to suspect a coalition" with Adamsites against Crawford. "None has, or can exist," he underscored emphatically. For a man not even running for president, Clinton occupied a prominent spot in the rumor mill, which placed him in a secret alliance with Clay, Calhoun, Adams, or Jackson on various occasions. "This story is one of the common tricks of electioneering," Clay exploded when he heard the rumor. "[It] assails . . . my integrity, in supposing me capable of countenancing or concurring in such an understanding [and] my judgment, in supposing that I could lend myself to such an injurious, foolish, & ridiculous scheme." While admitting he had exchanged letters with Clinton, Jackson bristled at the coalition rumors. "It is the most ludicrous idea imaginable," the general bellowed, "that man is not on earth, that can with truth say I was ever engaged in a political combination of any kind." Despite the protests, candidates and their organizations continued to promote these false stories with abandon.[37]

Perhaps because the front-runner aroused such strong negative feelings in rival campaigns, Crawford figured prominently in many coalition rumors. Clay or Adams were often linked in secret combinations with the treasury secretary. In a formulation that their allies found especially irksome, they were the junior partner in the alliance. The Jackson camp luridly highlighted the "*direct and certain* understanding" between Clay and Crawford as a purposeful plot to frustrate western demands for a president from their region. Indignantly rejecting "a position of inferiority to the South," Adams crossly burst several trial balloons floated by Crawfordites suggesting he play second fiddle as the treasury secretary's vice president in exchange for his own promotion to chief executive following a Crawford presidency. At least Adams commanded enough respect to warrant the vice presidency; some rumors trivialized Clay as accepting a mere attorney generalship or the Department of State portfolio under Crawford or as vice president serving Calhoun (who was ten years his junior). The Speaker's weak campaign invited such marginalization. In the end, political rumors were unreliable and frequently proven absolutely incorrect, yet no one could stop exchanging them.[38]

Business as Usual: One-Party
Tactics and the Politics of Corruption

Rumors of behind-the-scenes alliances between competing candidates may have troubled a republican-minded citizenry, but politicians were not so squeamish. Supporters of two candidates sometimes surreptitiously collaborated, especially if they deemed it necessary to defeat a third, but they denounced others suspected of secretly working together. In a rare moment of candor, Adams admitted that alliance rumors were frequently true. "The friends of every one of the candidates have sought to gain strength for their favorite by coalition with the friends of others," he confessed, "nor is there anything in it unconstitutional, illegal, or dishonorable."[39]

Most voters probably would have disagreed with the esteemed secretary of state. Politicos readily dropping one beloved candidate to support another just as ardently proved to voters that their leaders lacked integrity. A candidate's parties in the capital, where the cream of nation's political elite danced with European diplomats in formal dress, ate the richest foods, and swilled copious amounts of alcohol, seemed the height of corruption to folks back home in the states. The back-and-forth patronage favors necessary to win the presidency seemed sleazy to regular citizens. Candidates believed they needed side-switching politicians, patronage, social activities, congressional parties, and slanderous rumors to win, especially in a novel one-party election, but their tactics in pursuit of the presidency disillusioned the very voters who would deliver the prize.[40]

If the voters failed to see that corruption was consuming the capital, Jackson and his allies would be sure to point it out to them. "Oh! it is too abominably bad," Eaton moaned to the general, "to see gentlemen electioneering for this high office." Jackson himself had participated in numerous subtle forms of electioneering, of course, but he was clearly disassociated from the most visible methods of canvassing for votes in a one-party presidential election. Only the secretaries pandered with patronage, threw the swankiest parties, and cut the Congress into warring presidential factions in the process. Jackson had led the way with nominations from out in the states, while the capital politicians continued courting the congressional caucus in the epicenter of political power. The people, Eaton insisted, would be "confronted with the sad, melancholy & deplorable picture of gentlemen intriguing." As we will see in chapter 6, Jackson's pamphlets, press, and the rumor mill would see to that.[41]

While Jackson's focus on corruption helped decide the election of 1824, the one-party contest changed presidential politics going forward. Compelled by the unique nature of the election, the candidates sought state nominations and abandoned the Virginia/New York axis. Though neither practice survived, their decline permitted the development of party conventions and ever-shifting state alliances as methods of nominating presidential candidates. While traditional campaigns had always featured patronage, congressional factions, socializing, and rumormongering, their enhancement in the election of 1824 led to their increased importance in future president making. While unique, the 1824 one-party contest engendered some far-reaching consequences for American presidential elections in general.

4

→ • ←

The Perpetual Campaign

O N JULY 4, 1821, JOHN Quincy Adams fired what most contemporary politicos and the British diplomatic corps regarded as the opening shot of the 1824 presidential election. Invited to deliver a routine Independence Day address in the capital, Adams chose "What has America done for Mankind?" as his theme. After extolling his country's accomplishments, the sitting secretary of state turned to flaying Great Britain. He sarcastically excoriated America's former colonial rulers as "ye chivalrous knights of chartered liberties and the rotten boroughs! Ye improvers upon the sculpture of the Elgin marbles! Ye spawners of fustian romance and lascivious lyrics!" Adams claimed to find it a "pleasant surprise" that many of his fellow Americans applauded his widely reprinted remarks. Despite this claim, the secretary had probably carefully planned the speech as a subtle electioneering tool. As a former Federalist subject to charges that he still favored his old party and harbored their pro-British proclivities, making a speech that attacked Great Britain distanced Adams from his Federalist past while burnishing his Republican bona fides.[1]

Not every American received Adams's nationalistic oration with enthusiasm; his rivals for the presidency remained singularly unimpressed. "Of its author," Clay sneered, "it furnishes further proof of his total want of judgment and discretion." Adams's speech and his opponent's reaction demonstrated that a mere four months after Monroe's near unanimous reelection, his would-be successors were already jockeying for position in the next election. Unable to campaign openly for votes, the presidential competitors turned to alternate means to advance their candidacies. From 1821 to 1823, they twisted conventional political disputes in the cabinet, Congress, and the newspapers into nasty, but still covert, methods of electioneering. The candidates and their allies took opposing sides in fierce debates over army reduction, government spending, Revolutionary War pensions, and the races for the Speaker of the House. These disputes, portrayed to the public as regular, acceptable political arguments, were in fact covert ways of promoting one's presidential candidacy while undercutting that of a rival. "This subject of the next Presidential election comes up in forms almost numberless," Adams observed with wry candor. "The whole system of our politics is inseparably linked with the views of the aspirants to the Presidential succession." As almost every action in ordinary national politics became enmeshed in the succession question, Monroe's second term seemed like one endless, perpetual campaign for the presidency to the candidates, their supporters, and the voters. This sort of ferocious, all-encompassing, permanent campaign became quite typical in future Jacksonian era presidential contests.[2]

Cabinet War: The Ultimate Insiders' Ultimate Inside Battle

Far more than Jackson's angry pamphleteering and Clay's unsatisfying legislative compromising, the antics of the cabinet secretaries fueled the perpetual campaign for the presidency. The executive departments had been created by the First Congress in the early 1790s, growing inexorably over the next thirty years in size, responsibility, and autonomy. By the 1820s, cabinet posts had become "nurseries for presidential aspirants," with the press and postal powers that the secretaries exerted giving them an edge in succession politics. With three competing campaigns all uncomfortably squeezed into one cabinet, the secretaries quite literally staged their battle to follow Monroe in each others' faces. The executive branch titans simply could not escape confrontation. Trying to forge—or force—consensus behind administration policies, Monroe convened cabinet meetings on several days each week, sometimes for up to twenty hours over that span. Each secretary could comment on any area of policy under discussion, not just those considered their area of direct responsibility. Many of these talk-athons degenerated into quarrels pitting the secretaries against each other.[3]

Crawford naturally stood at the epicenter of most cabinet disputes as his competitors tried to knock the formidable front-runner out of the race. The origins of conflict rested on his long-standing feud with Monroe. The president never truly forgave Crawford for challenging him in the 1816 Republican caucus, and the treasury secretary returned the enmity. His cabinet rivals twisted Crawford's politically prudent acquiescence to Monroe's eventual nomination into a devious intrigue. He only "ostensibly" declined to oppose Monroe, Adams insisted, "seeming to sacrifice his own pretensions in his favor, so as to secure a seat in the administration under him, during which he has been incessantly engaged in preparing the way to succeed him." As the Radical faction in Congress began openly criticizing administration policy, even claiming that Crawford was far more republican than the current Republican president, Monroe fingered the treasury secretary as the impetus behind their attacks. The Radicals, Monroe insisted, "assailed me . . . [and Crawford] did not separate himself from them, by any public act, so as to shew that he did not approve their attacks."[4]

Crawford reciprocated Monroe's hostility with his own studied undermining of the president. For Monroe's 1819 message, Crawford provided an interim summary statement of the nation's finances showing that revenues covered expenses. Once Monroe released his message with those numbers included, Crawford published his own finalized treasury report that revealed an actual $5 million deficit. The discrepancy thoroughly embarrassed Monroe, who appeared woefully unaware of his own administration's financial figures. Crawford probably acted deliberately, since he had privately predicted a shortfall some months prior. His finalized version also served his presidential bid. The report recommended eliminating the deficit through spending cuts that would have disproportionally affected Calhoun's War Department budget while rejecting internal taxes that could be blamed on Crawford's Treasury Department.[5]

Crawford's executive branch rivals took their cues from the president and treated him just as warily. The three candidates had known each other long before their forced collaboration in Monroe's cabinet. Adams and Crawford had served together as senators in the Tenth Congress during Jefferson's presidency. Crawford's ties to Calhoun went even further back. Both men had attended the Carmel Academy near Appling, Georgia. Crawford had been both a student and, by the age of twenty-two, an assistant teacher at the institution, and he probably instructed the thirteen-year-old Calhoun. Initially, Crawford's administration opponents handled their principal challenger gingerly. Because the candidates were carefully delaying their entry into the presidential race, they avoided provoking hostilities with the front-runner too soon. Openly opposing Crawford only invited blistering attacks from the treasury secretary, his organization, and his presses.[6]

Once the secretary of war officially entered the contest, the gloves came off. Calhounite John Clark's 1821 reelection as governor of Georgia over a Crawfordite opponent apparently convinced Calhoun that Crawford was weak enough to challenge for the presidency. Crawford and Adams had believed that Calhoun would ultimately endorse one of them for the office, so both were surprised when the secretary of war launched his own independent bid. Calhoun's campaign especially troubled Crawford because it meant two southerners would be competing for votes in their mutual home region. Suddenly, the cabinet split into two warring camps, with supporters of the administration (Adams and Calhoun) on one side, opposed by Crawford on the other. Adams famously asserted that "Crawford has been a worm preying upon the vitals of the Administration within its own body," while Calhoun instructed his followers "to point out *by arguments the objections to Mr. Cd . . . under which he must sink.*"[7]

No one declared the war openly, but Adams and Calhoun maneuvered against Crawford behind the scenes. Adams gossiped that the treasury secretary had been the secret prime mover animating every attack against Monroe during his first term. Congressional hostility toward the administration had been "stimulated by him and promoted by his partisans," Adams growled. "He has been felt when he could not be seen." Calhoun insisted that Crawford's "managing partisans" were using the same tricks they had employed against Monroe in the 1816 nomination tussle. When Crawford's presses began attacking both men, with Calhoun's War Department accused of wasteful spending and Adams faulted for his Federalist past, the two secretaries commiserated about their rival. Crawford's "watchwords," Adams blazed, were "Democracy, Economy, and Reform . . . Democracy to be used against me, Economy against Calhoun, and Reform against both." No other man in American history, Calhoun concurred fiercely, "with abilities so ordinary, with services so slender, and so thoroughly corrupt" had "contrived" to become a presidential candidate.[8]

The cabinet confrontations enraged Crawford. In proper republican fashion, he stoutly declared that he had not "sought, or claimed, or expected" any public office, including his entry in the 1816 nomination contest. "I was entreated to permit it to be done," Crawford insisted. He believed the 1816 nomination had been "clearly in my reach if I had been ambitious of it," so Monroe owed him politically for gracefully stepping aside. The treasury secretary deeply resented his cabinet adversaries' attacks on his character, and he insisted that he was not the mastermind behind the Radicals' harassment of the administration. Truthfully, Crawford was as much a tool as leader of the Radicals. *He* had not created the Radical faction as a means of winning the presidency; rather, *they* had selected him as their standard-bearer in the race. Though both sides cooperated closely to the clear benefit of Crawford's presidential bid, he never entirely controlled his spirited allies as much as Monroe, Adams, and Calhoun believed; in fact, some of them complained that Crawford should have done *more* to obstruct the president's agenda.[9]

Still, Crawford assiduously worked against his cabinet opponents to maintain his claim to the succession. He lamented that friends had warned him about Calhoun's treachery early on, but he had not resisted Calhoun's appointment as secretary of war when he could have prevented it. He declared that Adams engaged in political tricks aimed at winning the election. "I am afraid that his morality does not rise above considerations of this kind," the treasury secretary huffed. He claimed credit for "softening the asperities" in Adams's official correspondence, thus preventing embarrassment in America's diplomatic relations. Calling it justified financial prudence, but with its political motivation utterly transparent, Crawford and his subordinates began carefully scrutinizing his two rivals' account records kept on file in the Treasury Department.[10]

As the competition escalated in the background, cabinet meetings became tense affairs. "You well know what his conduct has been," Monroe groused to Attorney General William Wirt, "and how little it has been in harmony with theirs." The president considered sacking Crawford and even drafted letters demanding his resignation, but he never sent them. Instead, he decided "it comported better with the principles of our gov.^t & with my own character, to permit him to remain than to remove him." Principles and character aside, Monroe feared that firing the treasury secretary would only create a political martyr, intensify the Radical offensive, and, ironically, strengthen Crawford's presidential run. The treasury secretary was fully aware that "an intrigue for turning him out of office" existed, but he actually welcomed its political utility. "A state of irritation prevails," Crawford slyly informed one supporter, but "I believe it will not be injurious to me to remain in this state, or even to be removed from office." Since Monroe had correctly surmised the political value the treasury secretary might reap from his termination, Crawford remained in the cabinet, and the stressful relations between the secretaries persisted throughout the perpetual campaign.[11]

While Adams and Calhoun often tag teamed Crawford, they also waged their own lower-level scuffle. The two men had once been good friends, but their relationship cooled significantly once Calhoun failed to support Adams for president and joined the race himself. Their once sociable and supportive interactions became "delicate and difficult." To Adams's face, Calhoun claimed to be a "friend and admirer," but attacks against the secretary of state "multiplied tenfold"—easily rivaling those of Crawford's partisans—once the secretary of war declared his candidacy. Adams also remained bitter toward Calhoun for convincing him, before the secretary of war came out as a presidential candidate, to replace the Crawford-leaning *Democratic Gazette* with the *Franklin Gazette* as one of the official government printers for Pennsylvania. The new printer attacked the treasury secretary with vigor, but it also pushed Calhoun's candidacy and sharply critiqued the secretary of state.[12]

Calhoun greatly respected Adams, but he simply believed that the cultivated secretary lacked the killer instinct necessary for taking out a street brawler like Crawford. In a race pitting one non–slave owner against four slaveholders, "Mr. Adams [has] great advantages," Calhoun maintained, "if he knew how to improve them." A swing through the North inspecting the nation's defense installations had convinced Calhoun that the former Federalist Adams, despite being the only northerner in the race, lacked the united support of the region and even faced stiff opposition in New England. The secretary of war believed that once Crawford had been vanquished, Adams could be defeated by a South united behind Calhoun.[13]

For his part, Adams resented the youthful Calhoun for violating the "graduated subordination" that represented "the genius of our institutions." Presidential candidacies, Adams argued, should be based on age and experience. Calhoun's impudent attempt to jump ahead of older and wiser candidates disturbed proper republican order, suggesting that he lacked the gravitas to be president. "Precedent and popularity—this is the bent of his mind," the secretary of state sneered. "Primary principles involved in any public question are the last that occur to him." The two secretaries could concoct every conceivable political or principled justification for their battle, of course, but it simply represented their energetic pursuit of the same position.[14]

As the cabinet secretaries deployed "mines and counter-mines" against each other, the warfare grew so brutal that Adams even predicted the collapse of the administration before the end of Monroe's second term. With Jackson dismissed as a nonfactor and Clay regarded as a lightweight long shot, the cabinet war only damaged the secretaries, and as a group, they faced increasingly unfavorable scrutiny. "In their zeal for elevation they remind me of unt[r]ained Attendants at a Banquet jostling each other out of place," one Clayite noted, while a Jacksonian blared that "the Canker worms have been (already too long) gnawing at the very core & vitals of our Government & corruption stalks abroad." Naturally, Jackson offered a self-serving solution to the cabinet's shenanigans. "Was I President," the general bellowed, "I would Remove all who have come out as candidates for the Presidency—and fill my Cabinet with those whose whole time could be devoted to the duties of their office, and not to intrigue for the Presidency." To Jackson's great advantage, there would be even more fodder for the critics once the insiders' war escaped the confines of the cabinet.[15]

Congressional War: Clash of the Presidential Parties

Unsurprisingly, the candidates' congressional parties eagerly joined the battle their leaders were waging inside the cabinet. Real ideological differences underpinned the dispute. Crawfordite Radicals truly believed that federal spending and debt threatened the nation's postpanic economy, while Calhounites truly believed that any cuts to the War Department's budget threatened the nation's post–War of 1812 security. During the perpetual campaign to succeed Monroe, these legitimate policy differences became inextricably entangled with the competing presidential bids.[16]

Crawfordites fired the first shot. Since the War of 1812, the federal government's deficit spending had been largely financed by loans, which had increased the national debt from $45,000,000 to $99,000,000. The Panic of 1819 had significantly reduced the income necessary to pay down the debt. To remedy the situation, the Radicals had been calling for several years for "retrenchment": some combination of defense-related spending cuts and organizational efficiencies. Crawford's treasury report projecting the $5 million deficit further armed the Radicals in their proposed war on the War Department. In 1821, Georgia representative Thomas W. Cobb called for $3 million in government spending cuts, with two-thirds of the amount slashed from Calhoun's budget. When Kentucky's David Trimble declared, "To live upon loans is treason against posterity!," he clearly signaled that Clay's allies had joined with Crawford's. The tide had openly turned in favor of retrenchment.[17]

The House passed Cobb's radical bill 109–48. The Senate was more sympathetic to the War Department, so they countered with their own, less severe retrenchment legislation. Over the objections of the most rabid retrenchers, the Senate legislation was ultimately adopted by both houses of Congress. It significantly reduced the size of the army, trimmed the officer corps, and halved Indian Department appropriations. Perhaps most wounding to Calhoun, Monroe, and their vision of the nation's defense infrastructure, Congress also slashed fortification construction from an annual level of $800,000 down to $202,000, even specifying the forts to be axed. The battle lines could not have been more clearly drawn.[18]

Crawford and Calhoun, aided by their respective congressional parties, exploited the politics of retrenchment in an effort to damage each others' presidential campaigns. Congress ordered the 10,000-strong army be whittled down to 6,000 enlistees. Despite the dire complaints of Calhounite critics, the Radicals had simply taken the army off its war footing by more efficiently deploying smaller numbers of men. The plan to reduce the officer corps in proportion to cuts of the enlisted men provoked the far greater political firestorm. Instead of ordering particular cuts, Congress dropped responsibility for the politically sensitive specifics right into Calhoun's lap. Calhoun acted adroitly, however. In conjunction with a board of general officers, the secretary of war deftly brought the officer corps into line with the new retrenchment legislation through a clever series of discharges, demotions, and transfers.[19]

Naturally, some military egos were bruised in the process, and officers unfavorably affected by Calhoun's reduction plan complained to their congressional supporters, which ironically subjected Calhoun's congressionally mandated decisions to congressional criticism. The Crawford party in Congress immediately pounced on his allegedly questionable choices. The House Committee on Military Affairs launched an investigation into Calhoun's officer reduction methodology, while a secret executive session of the Senate scoured his proposed list of shuffled appointments. Monroe fumed privately as his favorite presidential contender faced withering criticism, insisting that the appointments were distributed with the "strictest impartiality." Despite all the bluster, Congress accepted almost all of Calhoun's decisions, blocking only two appointments. Spearheaded by ardent Crawfordites, the Senate rejected Colonel Nathan Towson as commanding officer of the Second Regiment of Artillery and Colonel James Gadsden as adjutant general of the army. Crawfordites insisted that improper personal preferences had governed the choices, since Gadsden was a "particular favorite" of Calhoun and Towson was "close personally" to the president. Suffering only two rejections from a list of about sixty appointments might make Calhoun's reduction plan appear highly successful, but during a perpetual campaign for the presidency, there was to be much ado about this nothing.[20]

A nasty, two-month-long contretemps ensued, as a livid Monroe, a recalcitrant Senate, and a bitterly divided cabinet bickered furiously—and quite publicly—over the two blocked appointments. The standoff remained unresolved, and the positions were left unfilled for the remainder of Monroe's term. Military efficiency, which both sides claimed to champion, seemed the primary casualty of the political scuffle, since the duties of the two posts had to be shouldered by other officers. Unsurprisingly, the candidates condemned each other for the imbroglio over the officers. Calhoun and Monroe dismissed the entire affair as a Crawford plot to embarrass Calhoun, while Crawford blamed Calhoun's "want of judgment" for embroiling the Senate and administration in a needless conflict. Army reduction only represented the opening skirmish as the war over retrenchment intensified.[21]

As much as Calhoun and Monroe abhorred the demands for army reduction, the Crawfordites' evisceration of the fortification program truly rankled them. Not only had Congress reduced the fortifications budget by three-fourths, it expressly halted construction of four of the six forts Calhoun was building. Proponents of the scaling back argued that the fortifications budget constituted 12 percent of the government's borrowing, totaling $8 million in fiscal year 1820–21 alone, a figure that they claimed simply could not be tolerated in the postpanic financial environment. The president did not agree. "Under the pretext of economy," Monroe seethed, Congress aimed "to cut up that system in many important parts, and in fact to reduce it to a nullity." By severing links in his unified chain of defenses, he insisted that the Radicals had forgotten the lessons of the War of 1812 and returned the United States to its prewar vulnerability.[22]

Monroe's own recalcitrance had been partially responsible for his defeat on the issue. Some of the less doctrinaire retrenchers had offered the administration a compromise, proposing that less money be allocated for smaller forts, but Monroe was unwilling to accept any limitations to his grandiose vision of defense. Calhoun blamed the situation on the "fallacious views" of the nation's finances that Crawford had peddled in his erroneous treasury reports. Both men pressured Crawford to coerce his allies into reversing the cuts, but the treasury secretary stoutly insisted that Congress had acted without his influence.[23]

Unfortunately for Calhoun, the increased congressional scrutiny of his beloved fort-building ventures only highlighted how woefully the construction projects had been mismanaged. Perhaps the most egregious failure of the program had been the fort at Rouse's Point on Lake Champlain. After construction commenced on this grand, thirty-foot, octagonal fort, surveyors realized the fort was being built one half-mile north of the border on Canadian soil. Derisively nicknamed "Fort Blunder," the entire site had to be abandoned at a loss of $275,000.

Fort Delaware, located on Pea Patch Island in the Delaware River, was nearly as troubled. Engineering issues bedeviled this star-shaped fort from the start. Its foundation pilings had been improperly situated in marshy soil, resulting in extensive cracking to the brickwork walls, and one section of 43,000 bricks had to be removed, repaired, and replaced. Ironically, construction of both forts had been initiated by Crawford, who had preceded Calhoun as secretary of war, but Crawford's party in Congress delightedly blamed Calhoun entirely. In the public's mind, Calhoun became associated with all defense-related problems.[24]

Calhoun probably deserved more of the blame for the setbacks the four other forts experienced, since he had supervised their construction from the start. Congress cut the funding for Forts Gaines and Morgan, two star-shaped masonry forts that were being built at the entrance to Mobile Bay in the Gulf of Mexico. Both projects had experienced construction delays. A War Department investigation revealed that Fort Morgan's contractor had received monetary advances far exceeding the building materials he had assembled on-site. When the contractor died, his estate was insolvent, which meant that his bondsmen were on the hook for the misspent government funds. One of those bondsmen, Nicholas Gouverneur, was a cousin of Samuel Gouverneur—Monroe's son-in-law, private secretary, and unofficial advisor to Calhoun's presidential campaign. If Monroe could induce Congress to resume funding the fort, a close relative of one of his most trusted confidantes might be financially salvaged. To maintain funding for the southern forts, he and Calhoun suggested transferring the "unexpended balance" of other War Department appropriations into the accounts covering the construction of the Mobile Bay forts. Adams had to remind the president and the secretary of war that funds appropriated for a specific purpose could not legally be spent on something else. Despite the administration's maneuvering, the two southern forts remained unfunded for three years.[25]

Monroe and Calhoun could at least be comforted that Congress had maintained funding for the centerpiece of the defense buildup, their two eponymous forts that safeguarded the entrance to the Chesapeake. The retrenchers had allocated $175,000 and $130,000, respectively, for the continued construction of Forts Monroe and Calhoun on the Rip Rap Shoals in Virginia. Unfortunately for Calhoun, congressional Crawfordites uncovered another contractor-related scandal. Elijah Mix had been hired in 1818 to deliver building stones for both forts. Calhoun had reviewed the contract, but it had been negotiated and signed by the War Department's chief engineer, Joseph Swift, and witnessed by Calhoun's chief clerk, Christopher Vandeventer. Apparently unknown to Calhoun, Vandeventer was Mix's brother-in-law, and he privately purchased one-half of the shares of Mix's contract. When the arrangement became public knowledge, Calhoun pressured Vandeventer into selling off his remaining shares, but the damage was done. In the minds of some ordinary citizens, the Mix/Vandeventer contract seemed to be another example of an odious sweetheart deal at the public's expense. Despite his real accomplishments—reducing costs and improving efficiencies in the War Department—the affair only further tarnished Calhoun's once-sterling reputation as an administrator.[26]

Calhoun was not powerless, however, and his own congressional allies counterattacked. His supporters successfully defended one of his politically valuable services, the Revolutionary War pension program. By law, anyone who had served at least nine months in the Continental Army merited monthly payments for life. Calhoun had expanded the program during his tenure, earning the gratitude—and, he hoped, future votes—of appreciative veterans. The most ardent Radicals called for cuts of one-fifth to all pensions, but the plan divided the proretrenchment forces. Northern and easterners, rather than southern and westerners, dominated the pension lists, so unsurprisingly, the Crawford and Clay men tended to favor the cuts while Adams's and Calhoun's supporters opposed them. Clay himself blasted the pension program, claiming that "never was there more public money spent with less practical benefit." His supporter Francis Brooke, from deep in the heart of pro-Crawford Virginia, even more scathingly denounced the pensions. Virginians, Brooke sputtered, objected to "support[ing] a large portion of the paupers of the north and the east under the imposing pretext that they are remunerating the old revolutionary Soldier for his blood & his Toils." In the end, Crawford's forces could never muster the votes necessary to deprive Calhoun of his beneficial political tool; the Senate supported the pension cuts, but the House overturned them by a large majority.[27]

Adams and his congressional minions had maintained a certain calculated distance as Crawford, Calhoun, and their parties clashed over retrenchment, but all three candidates became embroiled in the battle over rival speakerships. The House Speaker's considerable administrative powers helped him set the legislative agenda for Congress. He controlled committee assignments, including the chairmen; enforced House rules; and could convene a committee of the whole when he wished to discuss issues without voting. During a perpetual campaign, the Speaker could promote or impede legislation favorable—or unfavorable—to a presidential candidate. Accordingly, the three secretaries each backed Speaker candidates whom they believed would best support their White House bid. Unfortunately, Republican factionalism made this decision problematic because politicians routinely concealed or switched their allegiances. After Clay temporarily retired in 1820, New York's John W. Taylor served as Speaker for the remainder of the Sixteenth Congress. In the wake of the fractious debates over Missouri's admission, the antislavery and procompromise New Yorker had defeated the proslavery South Carolinian William Lowndes. Adams assiduously courted Taylor after his election, and both men ultimately agreed to a mutually beneficial relationship. Taylor supported legislative priorities agreeable to Adams, while Adams fed Taylor inside information about the administration's domestic policy agenda before it became public knowledge.[28]

The president and the secretary of war were not nearly as sanguine about the Speaker as Adams. After Taylor stacked the Military Affairs Committee with retrenchers, Calhoun and his mentor both worked behind the scenes to engineer Taylor's ouster. As a Clintonian, Taylor also faced opposition from many of his fellow New Yorkers, including Martin Van Buren. Calhoun, not yet realizing that Van Buren favored Crawford for the presidency, secretly conspired with New York's junior senator to elevate Virginia's Philip Barbour into the Speaker's chair over Taylor. Ironically, Calhoun's maneuver proved disastrous for his candidacy. Unbeknownst to the secretary of war, Barbour was a doctrinaire conservative and a closet Crawfordite. His ascendancy allowed the Radicals to dominate the House for the first time since 1807, which boosted the anti-Calhoun retrenchment agenda. Barbour's committee chairs proved equally adverse to Adams's interests, and the secretary of state severely chastised Calhoun for foolishly sponsoring a Speaker so inimical to the proadministration candidates. When Clay returned to the House in the Eighteenth Congress, Crawford backed Barbour's reelection as Speaker. Adams hoped Taylor might reclaim his old post, but Clay's influence over his fellow representatives simply proved too powerful. He returned to the speakership, defeating Barbour 139–42 after Taylor dropped out of the race. In the end, Clay, and not the secretaries, would direct House business during the critical presidential election year.[29]

As the retrenchment disagreements demonstrated, Crawford and Calhoun dominated the proxy war between the candidates' supporters in the legislature. Without any congressional party, Jackson played almost no role in the legislative tussles. Clay's absence from Congress relegated most of his allies to the sidelines, and Adams shrewdly stood back as his two administration rivals tried to destroy each other. Overmatched in sheer numbers of congressional supporters, Calhoun emerged as the clear loser and Crawford the winner as the perpetual campaign played out in Congress. Since retrenchment also enjoyed widespread popular support, in the minds of Republican voters, Crawford's commitment to economy appeared Jeffersonian, while Calhoun, despite his actual waste-cutting measures, became associated with bloated, overbudgeted bureaucracy. While Calhoun might have been down, however, he was not out; as the campaign spread from Congress into the newspapers, almost every candidate would endure "impressions unfriendly to their pretensions" courtesy of their rival aspirants.[30]

Newspaper War: Now for the Bad News

As the battle over retrenchment raged, the candidates extended their campaigns into the public sphere through the newspapers they controlled. They had been harassing each other in the press throughout Monroe's first term, but the attacks intensified as the critical election year approached. Just as Crawford and Calhoun had dominated the fight in Congress, at least initially, their papers took the lead in waging press-based attacks. Calhoun, hoping for a reversal of fortune in this phase of the campaign, welcomed the open warfare. "The more heat the better," the secretary of war insisted. "It will bring the fever to the surface, and fully develop what has been so long concealed from the knowledge of the publick." As a counter to the retrenchment narrative, Calhoun's *Republican* printed actual spending figures by department purporting to show that Crawford was the least economical secretary with the fewest spending reductions in the entire administration. Crawford dismissed Calhoun's suddenly showy offensive. He seemed to think that "success can be secured by importunity," Crawford drawled, "as heaven itself can be obtained by violence." While Adams's papers mostly avoided the newspaper fight over retrenchment, the bitter warfare reflected badly on all the secretaries. "The people will say 'if one tenth part of what these folks say is true it is time we make choice of a man unconnected with the administration,'" one of Clay's Ohio correspondents asserted.[31]

Like Adams, Clay tried to remain on the sidelines of the burgeoning press war. He and his supporters hoped that the lethargic pace of his campaign would immunize him from the cabinet's newspaper war, but he was soon drawn into a back-and-forth scuffle with Adams. As part of a routine 1822 investigation into settlement in the western territories, the House examined documents associated with the Treaty of Ghent negotiations. On the basis of a tip rumored to be based on an anonymous suggestion from Clay himself, the inquiry turned up an 1815 letter from Commissioner Jonathan Russell to then–Secretary of State Monroe. In the letter, marked "duplicate," Russell charged that his fellow commissioner Adams had been willing to grant Great Britain Indian trade rights in the West and navigation rights on the Mississippi in exchange for American fishing privileges off southeastern Canada, a swap that would have benefited New Englanders at the expense of other regions. Adams "would barter the patriotic blood of the West for blubber," Russell's letter thundered, "and exchange ultra-Allegheny scalps for codfish." If he had sought such a deal, it might seriously damage Adams's presidential campaign beyond his northeastern base.[32]

Russell, now a Massachusetts representative and Crawford supporter, validated the truthfulness of the letter, but unfortunately for him, Monroe had retained his copy. On a tip from Adams that the "duplicate" might be doctored, the president located the original letter in his personal files. Monroe's copy, marked "private," conclusively demonstrated that Russell had altered the duplicate letter with changes that exaggerated the charges against Adams. In Russell's "most diabolical" modification, his duplicate version claimed that Adams had violated explicit instructions from the Madison administration not to pursue the swap, while Monroe's copy asserted the exact opposite. The furious secretary of state confronted Russell, who admitted under Adams's withering examination that he had fabricated parts of the letter since he only retained an incomplete draft copy of the original, but that he had not altered any "facts." Adams produced a pile of State Department record books that proved otherwise and left Russell "alternatively flushing and turning pale." Eviscerating Russell privately hardly sufficed, however. "A vague and indefinite charge will be hanging over me," Adams declared, "to ruin my reputation as if it was distinctly proved." Working vigorously for nearly six months—it "totally absorbed all my morning hours . . . and all my faculties," he admitted almost sheepishly—Adams produced a series of newspaper articles that ruthlessly "annihilated" Russell. By printing both the duplicate and original letters side by side with adjoining commentary, Adams meticulously detailed Russell's duplicity.[33]

Russell feebly counterattacked. He submitted a third version of the letter to the *National Intelligencer*—"a triplicate!" Adams mockingly sneered—that matched neither the duplicate nor the original. "If he had done the same thing with a promissory note it would have introduced him to the penitentiary," an Adams ally bellowed. In the end, Adams's ferocious printed onslaught finally reduced Russell to sputtering that the secretary of state had somehow "tricked him" into releasing the duplicate letter. Ultimately, Adams published a hefty 256-page booklet, *The Duplicate*

Letters, the Fisheries, and the Mississippi, documenting the entire affair. His clever rebuttal successfully redirected the controversy from an analysis of the original charges, which contained grains of truth that might have damaged Adams's presidential campaign, into an investigation into the forged document, which only enhanced his standing. Perceived as the victim of a venomous smear campaign who valiantly fought back with vigor and intellect, Adams's presidential stock actually rose, even outside New England. "His Contest with Russell has elevated Adams immiensely [*sic*] both as an honest Man & as a Man of talents," Langdon Cheves observed.[34]

Clay watched bitterly as even Adams's critics lauded his response. The Speaker had probably inspired Russell to act against Adams, but without actually proposing a faked letter. Notwithstanding the clumsy document falsification and embroidered charges, Clay knew that Russell's accusations were fundamentally accurate. As Adams's fellow commissioner at Ghent, he had strenuously objected to Adams's support for the proposed swap. The Mississippi's navigation rights were "a privilege much too important to be conceded for the mere liberty of drying fish," Clay groused. Most of his friends advised him to stay out of the clash, dangling Russell's shredded reputation as a cautionary tale, but Clay seemed impervious to warnings. He claimed Adams had "labored to draw me into the controversy" by "misrepresenting" him in his enormous pamphlet.[35]

His public reasoning aside, Clay probably hoped somehow to validate the politically valuable charges against Adams and strengthen his own campaign in the West while avoiding association with an electioneering scheme. Accordingly, he published a letter in the *National Intelligencer* noting that Adams's account contained "no doubt unintentional" errors. "The hope may be confidently cherished," Clay added with an evident jab at his adversary, that navigation rights on the Mississippi "never will be hereafter deemed even a fit subject of negotiation with a foreign power." To avoid charges of electioneering, Clay promised to reveal his version of the Ghent negotiations "at some future period more propitious than the present . . . when there can be no misinterpretation of my motives."[36]

Adams quickly responded with his own sarcastic letter in the press. He would have derived "great pleasure" from correcting any errors had Clay found it "advisable now to specify any." Adams also promised to "vindicate contested truth" should Clay's account ever materialize. As a riposte to Adams, the Speaker finally published his own pamphlet, *Letters to John Quincy Adams, Relative to the Fisheries and the Mississippi*. Clay hoped this work would justify his role in the conflict and refute charges that *his* sectional stands at Ghent favored the West at the expense of other regions, but it never received the widespread distribution that Adams's booklet had commanded. Although the Speaker always strenuously denied any involvement in starting the controversy, Adams privately denounced Russell as Clay's "tool," insisting that Clay had been "circulating this poison" for years. Whatever the truth, if the strike had originated with any of his opponents, the plot badly backfired. The dispute enhanced Adams's standing at the expense of his presidential rivals. For his part, Russell never recovered from his bout with Adams. He left Congress after only a single term and the expression "to Jonathan Russell" an opponent, meaning to destroy his reputation overwhelmingly by refuting his lies, entered the political lexicon.[37]

While the press war over retrenchment and the Ghent negotiations were high-profile exchanges, almost every candidate received ongoing rough treatment in his rivals' newspapers. The nation's presses "pour forth continual streams of slander upon my character and reputation, public and private," Adams complained. Accusations ran from the frivolous to the formidable. Hostile editors labeled Crawford a "shameless parasite, a base dissembler," and dismissed him as a *"giant in intrigue* but a *dwarf in public service."* He had been an unfit minister, a tool of the British, and a proponent of prostitution. Critical papers denounced Adams as a quick-tempered, aristocratic monarchist with "lurking and distrustful suspicion in the eyes" who was unpopular even in New England. He did not pay his debts, had opposed the Louisiana Purchase, and was a "negligent" dresser who lacked a proper waistcoat and cravat and sometimes went to church barefoot. Opposition presses pilloried Calhoun as a lax administrator, a spendthrift bureaucrat, and a loose constitutional constructionist who was "seeking to foist a military despotism on the nation." Critics accused Clay of being too young, too inexperienced, and too devoted to western interests at the expense of nation to be president. He was a follower rather than a leader, and he had supported public legislation only because it benefited him personally.[38]

Clever editors modified their attacks to suit their target audience. Adams rivals' southern newspapers claimed that he favored tariffs and restrictions on slavery in Missouri for their largely antitariff and antirestrictionist readers; their northern editors reversed Adams's positions for their protariff, prorestrictionist readers. A Connecticut paper reminded voters that Crawford and Clay were slave owners "holding their fellow man in bondage, and not safe to be trusted with the liberties of the people," while one in Rhode Island countered that Clay favored emancipation, but Adams wished to extend slavery. "Mr. Adams has voluntarily resided for 7 years in a slave State and at this moment *is a slave-holder!*," the newspaper blatantly lied.[39]

Because Virginians had virtually monopolized the presidency at the expense of the rest of the union, newspapers in other states played on readers' fears of dynastic rule. Crawford and Clay might live in other states, one Illinois editorial carped, but "those gentlemen are *Virginians.*" Other papers openly denounced the *"Virginia dynasty,"* the *"Virginia succession,"* or the "Virginia influence." In Republican party strongholds, presses emphasized Crawford's partisan orthodoxy; the other candidates, a Richmond, Virginia, paper assured voters, "represent a new party broken off from the true Republican party." Adams correctly appraised the situation that almost every candidate faced from his opponents' newspaper attacks. "Against me I have in every section the passions and prejudices peculiar to its own situation and circumstances," he protested.[40]

Naturally, the detested opposition party proved an irresistible label to affix on one's opponents; Crawford, Adams, Calhoun, and Clay were each smeared as closet Federalists. Opposition newspapers insisted Clay violated Republican policy by supporting Federalist-inspired measures such as the national bank and federally funded internal improvements. Rival presses called Calhoun an "ultra-Federalist" who promoted "the idea of a grand and magnificent government" in Washington at the expense of the states.[41]

Crawford was pilloried for a twenty-five-year-old letter. During John Adams's quasi-war with France in 1798, Crawford, joined by several other young men in Augusta, Georgia, had dispatched a letter to Adams supporting his militaristic response to French naval aggression. Critics alleged that this "Augusta Address" demonstrated Crawford's support of the elder Adams's "reign of terror." They charged that Crawford also favored gag laws, antisedition legislation, and a standing army, none of which had actually been stated in the letter. Reprinted copies of the "Address" falsified some of the phrasing to make the letter appear to be more pro-Adams than the original. Crawford could only wearily respond that he had been a patriotic youth opposed to factionalism during wartime. He had been asked to support the "Address" precisely because he was a devout Jeffersonian Republican; Adams's most reviled legislation had passed only after Crawford had signed the letter.[42]

The younger Adams's Federalist problem exceeded that of every other because he had actually been a Federalist. Simpson's *Columbian Observer* maligned the secretary of state as "the Federalist of 1798, the libeller of Jefferson, the enemy of the rights of man, the contemner of Democracy ... and truly devoted to those destructive and ruinous measures of his Fathers' [sic] administration." Adams could only weakly answer that after he had been a Federalist, he had been "uniformly Republican," while his papers contended that he "had never been considered a sound federalist." Unfortunately for all the contenders, during a hostile, one-party election, newspaper accusations that a Republican candidate was actually a Federalist proved quite effective.[43]

While the charges and countercharges that spewed forth from the candidates' newspapers sullied their names to varying degrees, no attack proved more deadly than the allegations leveled by the mysterious "A. B." Beginning in January 1823 and continuing over the next several months, Calhoun's *Republican* printed a series of articles that accused Crawford of criminal corruption. Signed anonymously by "A. B.," these hit pieces blared that Crawford had knowingly deposited public money in unstable western banks and barred such funds from withdrawal. These deals amounted to compensation-free loans to nearly insolvent institutions, and the government lost money on the transactions when the banks failed. Crawford had also accepted depreciated currency from western banks, even when not backed by specie and barred by congressional resolution, and then lied about this "malfeasance" in his official reports to Congress. Over time, A. B.'s charges grew ever more lurid. He insisted that Crawford had speculated with Treasury funds in the western banks for his personal financial benefit and that Congress' official printer, the pro-Crawford *National Intelligencer,* had deliberately suppressed documents implicating Crawford.[44]

Unfortunately for Crawford, the charges resonated because they were based on real actions. During the Panic of 1819, despite his commitment to specie-backed paper money, Crawford had received unredeemable state bank notes into the US Treasury, redistributed this currency in states that accepted it at face value, and shifted federal deposits into some of the most troubled institutions. While his actions had saved some local banks from collapse, Crawford's real aim had been rescuing the national economy, not salvaging the state banks. Two special House committees convened hastily in 1823 and, dominated by his supporters, exonerated Crawford of any wrongdoing, but the treasury secretary's reputation suffered mightily. "Mr. Crawford is completely prostrate," one of Calhoun's partisans noted gleefully. "He has been . . . descending with an accelerated velocity every moment, since he received the propelling stroke from 'A. B.'"[45]

Though the accusations appeared in his flagship newspaper, Calhoun's direct level of responsibility for the A. B. attacks remains unknown. Like the other contenders, the secretary of war closely scrutinized the presses backing his candidacy, and his congressional party had also unsuccessfully supported resolutions calling for an investigation into Crawford's relationship with western banks over a year before A. B. sensationalized the scandal. A. B.'s charges destroyed Crawford's administrative reputation, just as the Crawfordites' hostile scrutiny of his forts and contracts had devastated Calhoun's. Fair or not, an odor of corruption would cling to Crawford into the final critical election year. The treasury secretary may have won the battle in Congress, but the secretary of war successfully counterattacked once the war reached the newspapers.[46]

The Costs of War: Perpetual Campaigning and the Politics of Corruption

Since republican belief forbade overt electioneering, the presidential candidates required other means of reaching voters. Their conflicts in the cabinet and Congress that ultimately reached the newspapers amply served this purpose. Battles over legitimate public issues in the course of press wars offered three methods of electioneering without electioneering: burnishing a candidate's political reputation, fostering a negative image of a rival, and defending one's own good name from an opponent's attack. Given that he was simply fending off a vile slanderer, no voter could accuse him of improperly campaigning for office. "Surely to parry the daggers of assassins is not to canvass votes for the Presidency," Adams cunningly observed in defense of the practice. The secretary of state proved especially adept at using defense as offense, overwhelmingly countering any criticism, no matter how slight, but every contender employed this strategy to electioneer covertly. A candidate's presses usually coupled defense with admiration. Laudatory newspaper coverage reinforced an upbeat image of his accomplishments while keeping his name before the public. There were pitfalls to positive image making, of course. Excessive praise from one's own newspapers could easily be dismissed as pandering puffery. Clay mocked the "ridiculous superlatives" that pro-Calhoun editors employed to promote his candidacy. "To compare him to Washington; to pronounce him a prodigy of genius! What nonsense," the Speaker sneered. Still, the benefits of positive self-promotion seemed to outweigh the risks.[47]

The perpetual campaign unsurprisingly favored the abuse of opponents over the cultivation of a positive public image. Adams acknowledged that the mudslinging was essential to the practice of presidential politics. "From the nature of our institutions," he opined, "the competitors for public favor, and their respective partisans, seek success by slander upon each other, as you add to the weight one scale by taking from that of the other." The candidates largely failed to realize that attacking each other amounted to a mutually destructive circular firing squad. In a one-party contest, with the allegiance of supporters subject to shifts, slandering rivals only discouraged potential future allies. "The effect of the stand taken here by Mr. Crawford's friends, partizans, and presses will be to alienate all the friends of the other Candidates," Clay observed, seemingly unaware that his own attacks produced a similar reaction in his opponents' allies.[48]

Beyond irritating elite politicians, political slurs repelled the very voters the candidates needed to win the election. The hyperpartisan presses cultivated a sense among readers that dissension dominated the ruling class. As Adams lamented, the negative campaigning that appeared necessary to win the election ironically suggested to voters that "caballing, bargaining, place-giving, or tampering with members of Congress" were also required. As the secretaries and the Speaker exaggerated each other's faults, public perceptions of government corruption intensified. "That scandalous defalcations in our public pecuniary agents, gross misapplications of public money, and an unprecedented laxity in official responsibilities occurred and been suffered under our government for the past six or eight years are faults not to be concealed," the *Statesman* luridly warned voters. Though the candidates tried to control the message that voters received through print medium, it was the readers and not the writers that determined the meaning behind the newspaper war. "Maladministration" emerged as a leading issue in the 1824 campaign.[49]

While a politician's reputation had always mattered in Early Republic presidential elections, the democratized contests from 1824 forward shifted the relevant audience. Instead of being judged mostly by one's fellow elite politicians, ordinary citizens now became important arbiters of a candidate's character. Attracting these ordinary people necessitated a perpetual campaign in which politicians transformed routine political debates over issues into a means of increasing one's own—or decreasing an opponent's—popularity with voters. Developments in 1824 proved enormously consequential, as echoes of the 1824 election reverberated in future contests. In a virtual repeat of the previous election, a nasty, mudslinging newspaper war dominated the 1828 contest. Voters in 1832, akin to those in 1824, assessed the candidates based on their position on economic issues, this time the rechartering of the Second BUS. Like the Republicans in 1824, the fractured Whig party fielded multiple candidacies in 1836 aimed at appealing to different constituencies. The Panic of 1837 proved just as central to the 1840 election as the Panic of 1819 had in 1824. A cabinet war over the annexation of Texas critically influenced the outcome of the 1844 contest. Perpetual campaigns were here to stay.[50]

While some of 1824's controversies may have been trumped up, what voters read in the newspapers defined the candidates' increasingly negative public images. Crawford developed a reputation as an overrated bureaucrat consumed by his ambitious schemes to win the presidency. "What talents has he ever displayed to Warrant it much less to merit [sic] it," one correspondent told Clay. Adams was denounced as an elitist intellectual unable to understand the concerns of ordinary Americans. Referencing the vision problems that plagued Adams after once looking at a total solar eclipse, one Clay correspondent jibed that "the Proffessor [sic] . . . has too much *water in his Eyes* to see common things." As always, his Federalist past fueled his critics. "*Adams can't be elected*," one insisted, "he is too Cold . . . he is *hated*—his Father's memory is enough." Another added that "with his 4th July garland flowers [and] . . . the glory of advocating the Surrender of the navigation of two thirds of the union to the British, he has secured himself early, if not dignified, *retirement.*"[51]

The two youngest candidates were not spared from attack. Calhoun's detractors pilloried his youthful inexperience and questioned his temperament for the job. As a representative, "he was then the most presuming man in Congress," one maintained. "He is now the most presuming man in the Nation—with fewer claims to the Chair of State than any other individual named, he is making bolder efforts to attain it." Another claimed that "his inexperience, Impetuosity of feeling &c. &c. prevented even a remote chance of his Election some twenty years hence." Critics caricatured Clay as a slick politico, with his obvious legislative skills overshadowed by his manipulative trickery. To his critics, he was impetuous, brash, power hungry, and immoral. Clay was like a "column that presents so beautiful a Corinthian capital [but] does not rest upon a broad basis of *Moral* confidence," Willie P. Mangum claimed, while John Randolph of Roanoke more wittily observed that "he stinks and he shines, like a dead mackerel in the moonlight." While dirtier than the Early Republic elections that preceded it, the sleaziness of the 1824 campaign easily rivaled that of its notorious successor election in 1828 and future elections during the Jacksonian era. It represented a clear transitional point toward more negative presidential campaigns. The *Southern Patriot* expressed the problem most succinctly, editorializing that "the candidates for the Presidency . . . are mutually and thoroughly reviled."[52]

The *Southern Patriot* should have omitted Jackson from its list of the loathed. Not seen as a serious candidate, without any party involved in congressional infighting, and almost completely ignored by his opponents' presses, the general marched blissfully above the fray as his rivals savaged each other. "The executive candidates are vying with each other—I stand alone," the general boasted. The presses Jackson controlled freely extolled his virtues and vilified his rivals, but faced little return fire during most of the long campaign. His followers denounced the *"trick upon trick, intrigue upon intrigue, and falsehood upon falsehood"* of the other presidential campaigns, allowing Jackson to run as a "virtuous outsider" set to take on the corrupt Washington establishment. While the other contenders trumpeted their illustrious records of political service, they dismissed Jackson precisely because he lacked one. The general turned this seeming disadvantage into an advantage. Jackson would enter the critical election year virtually unscathed politically, ready to lead the fight against corruption, with just the fresh face many voters sought.[53]

Unlike Jackson, his rivals would carry numerous political wounds into 1824, but none would be more battle-scarred than Crawford. As the frontrunner, he had faced the united opposition of the president and his fellow secretaries in the cabinet, endured pressure from both sides in the ongoing dispute between the administration and the Radicals in Congress, and suffered by far the most vilification in the combined presses of his adversaries. "He is under a distructive [sic] cross fire," Calhoun chortled. The strain of spending eight years in perpetual pursuit of the presidency may have proved too much for the ambitious treasury secretary. In September 1823, while visiting the Virginia home of his ally James Barbour over a hundred miles in the countryside southwest of Washington, Crawford was suddenly stricken with a debilitating illness that left him nearly blind, with slurred speech and paralyzed hands and feet. Contemporaries diagnosed Crawford's sickness as "inflammatory rheumatism," but he may have suffered a paralytic stroke. His illness may have been compounded by a severe allergic reaction to an overdose of lobelia, a popular nineteenth-century herbal purgative, that Crawford had taken to treat a skin infection. Confined to darkened rooms while he slowly recovered over the next four months, the usually energetic Crawford could not read, write, or attend to his cabinet duties. As the election year dawned, Crawford's ability to interact with his followers and directly control his campaign had been severely compromised. The war had been costly indeed.[54]

5

→ • ←

The Final Battles

A S HEATED AS THE perpetual campaign had been, nothing prepared the candidates for the furious conflict culminating in the election's final year. The political tools, new and old, that the candidates employed continued to drive presidential politics. Their triumphant social occasions received glowing coverage in their own biased newspapers, their organizations maintained the rancorous battling in Congress, and their letter writers continued spreading slanderous rumors about rival campaigns. As much as the candidates hoped to drive home their positive messaging to voters, the negative aspects of campaigning seemed to dominate. Factionalism further eroded Republican party unity, and slippery, side-switching politicians created ever more problems for the candidates.[1]

The voting public continued to scrutinize the contenders suspiciously for any violations of republican strictures against electioneering. "Every time [a candidate] acts personally in the Election it will hurt," one Clay supporter argued. "The public greatly approves a dignified & retired Course. It remains to be seen whether management, intrigue or Corruption Can eventually succeed." One of the candidates argued that such corruption was indeed already succeeding, or at least he made certain to air his contention for public consumption. "How can a republic last long under such scenes of corruption?" Jackson thundered. "Nothing but the redeeming spirit of a virtuous people . . . can redeem our nation from woe; and our republican Government from destruction." As the election played out, the political maneuvering necessary to win only strengthened the general's case to an increasingly anxious electorate. Jackson's conduct would ultimately help alter the rules of the presidential game, shifting the focus from elite insider maneuvering to popular out-of-doors appeals. Presidential elections were in transition.[2]

Fortunes and strategies varied for each candidate in the momentous final year of the election. The outsider Jackson accepted an insider position in the Senate to bolster his political resume, while launching a "charm offensive" to improve his image. Crawford captured the coveted congressional caucus nomination, but many in the electorate objected to the corruption intrinsic to this insider tactic. Calhoun faced unexpected campaign setbacks in North Carolina and Pennsylvania, which provoked the unexpected collapse of his presidential effort. Clay ramped up his campaign's focus on policy issues, with dramatic fights in Congress over internal improvements and tariffs, but his efforts displeased as many voters as they pleased. Adams concentrated on buttressing his reputation as a diplomat, but his treaties proved ironically problematic for his presidential campaign. Most important, the "A. B." affair reached its dramatic denouement. Though centered on Crawford, the most shocking political scandal of the entire election tainted every candidate's reputation, except that of outsider Jackson.

Barbarian inside the Gates: General Jackson Storms Washington

While Jackson had spent most of Monroe's second term as the outsider candidate running against the "corrupt" capital insiders, he would venture deep into the heart of enemy territory as the campaign entered its final climactic year. When Crawfordite senator John Williams, an open critic of Jackson's adventurism in Florida, sought reelection from Tennessee's state legislature in 1823, Jackson backers John Eaton and William Lewis hoped to replace him with a supporter of the general's candidacy. They tried assembling a coalition behind other candidates while pressuring Williams to drop Crawford in favor of the general. When neither tactic worked, rumors circulated that Jackson lacked the unanimous support of his home state. If Tennessee elected a pro-Crawford senator, Jackson's presidential campaign would appear every bit as weak as his rivals had always claimed. Without Jackson's knowledge, Eaton and Lewis gambled by placing Jackson himself in nomination for the Senate seat as the only Jacksonian capable of beating Williams. A Jackson victory would be an uphill climb, since the incumbent enjoyed broad popularity in the state legislature and many members had already committed to his candidacy.[3]

Though Jackson coyly insisted that he had played no role whatsoever in snaring his Senate nomination, he immediately decamped to the Capitol in Murfreesboro. While virtuously reiterating his stance against election-eering, the general unstintingly reminded the legislators of Crawford's unpopularity in Tennessee. His strong-arm campaign worked. Jackson overcame Williams 35–25, a close margin, but an amazing accomplishment considering Williams's high profile. In one deft maneuver, Jackson and his organization had solidified his presidential campaign both statewide and nationally. His hold on Tennessee was virtually beyond challenge now. A Senate term would also add legislative experience to his paltry political resume—barely more than a year combined as a congressional represen-tative and senator over a quarter-century earlier. With proper republican sentiment, Jackson publicly claimed that he had hoped to remain retired, but would reluctantly serve to deprive Crawford of Williams's caucus vote. Even when moving to the inside, Jackson would try to maintain his out-sider status.[4]

Jackson regarded Washington, DC, as a modern Babylon, a city with magnificent buildings that concealed every sort of political wickedness. Though the grand public edifices damaged during the British attack in the War of 1812 had been repaired, the capital city retained touches of its rus-tic origins. Ornate carriages frequently overturned in the muddy streets during the swelteringly humid spring and summer, while two-foot-long snakes occasionally invaded posh drawing rooms. Real reptiles aside, Jackson remained more wary of the politicians who slithered along the grimy streets of Washington—many had censured him as an impulsive troublemaker. "My enemies . . . denounced me as a man of revengefull [sic] Temper and of great rashness," he admitted ruefully.[5]

Determined to refashion his reputation, Jackson deliberately listened more than participated in congressional debates. While carefully concealing his "honest indignation" with routine political practice in Washington, he bragged that "I have become a perfect Philosopher. . . . My enemies have become confounded, & dismayed, in not being able to irritate me." Jackson made only one speech in his first Senate term, in favor of increased defense spending, and that stance only reinforced his warrior-hero image. His tactics demonstrated that the general was as politically savvy as the capital politicos he condemned. Remaining mostly silent allowed Jackson to avoid taking any controversial stands on issues, minimized his proclivity for making enemies, and countered his reputation for recklessness. "The opinion of those whose minds were prepared to see me with a Tomahawk in one hand, & a scalping knife in the other has greatly changed," Jackson crowed gleefully.[6]

Being close to his fellow senator from Tennessee, Eaton, undoubtedly eased Jackson's entry into capital politics. Eaton had played an outsize role in the general's campaign already, serving as Jackson's cheerleader, confidante, fundraiser, publicist, and chief strategist. The two men frequently gossiped about the state of the race and bounced ideas off each other, and Eaton even supplied Jackson with suggested phrasing for his political correspondence. Jackson's Senate service also provided him firsthand access to the all-important political rumor mill. He passed a variety of the latest gossipy tidbits into his correspondence network while simultaneously reaffirming his outsider status with the caveat, "However, I know but little upon the subject, as I neither met with the politicians, or conversed on the Presidential question."[7]

Proximity to the powerful also allowed Jackson to reconcile with some long-standing enemies. Since his decision to run for president, the general had quietly tried to resolve many of his outstanding disputes. Jackson mended fences with Thomas Watkins, a critic of his killing of Charles Dickinson in an 1806 duel. He suddenly settled in his opponent's favor a long-standing lawsuit with Andrew Erwin. Once he reached Washington, Jackson restored civil relations with Clay; ended a seven-year feud with fellow general Winfield Scott; exchanged dinners with his bitter foe John Cocke; and, in a move that "you never would have expected," as a stunned Eaton put it, he even patched up his vicious quarrel with Thomas Hart Benton, who had wounded Jackson in an 1813 barroom brawl. "It is a pleasing subject to me that I am now at peace with all the world," he proudly informed his wife Rachel. Crawford's name remained on Jackson's enemies list, of course; Jackson continued to regard the treasury secretary as "that arch-fiend." Settling with his old adversaries served as yet another method for Jackson to undercut the criticism that he lacked the proper temperament necessary for the presidency.[8]

Just as Jackson's Senate service signaled a more aggressive phase of his presidential bid, his campaign in the states began gathering steam. Pennsylvania especially showcased the general's emerging prominence. Thanks to his robust statewide newspaper network, led by the indefatigable Stephen Simpson and his *Columbian Observer*, Pennsylvania Democrats (the name Republicans in the state had adopted) were turning increasingly Jacksonian. At a March 1823 nominating convention for state races, the Family Party—supporters of Calhoun, as we saw in chapter 2—planned to anoint the secretary of war as the Democrats' preferred presidential candidate. Instead, Jackson fanatics staged a "wild demonstration" in favor of the general. A Philadelphia meeting in January 1824 proved even more favorable to Jackson. Each presidential candidate was represented by a standard bearing their name. Attendees could signal their preference by gathering under the insignia representing their favorite, but in "a trial at the place where the other candidates expected to make an impression," only Jackson's standard attracted any followers. Ultimately, eleven counties and the city of Philadelphia committed to attending a convention in Huntingdon to name a slate of Jackson electors. In Pennsylvania, at least, Jackson seemed unexpectedly poised to upset the Republican elites.[9]

While gaining politically in a key mid-Atlantic battleground, Jackson also showed surprising strength in North Carolina. In presidential politics, the state had almost always followed Virginia, so North Carolina was expected to favor the treasury secretary. Substantiating this conventional wisdom, one-half of North Carolina's state legislators endorsed Crawford in late 1823. Calhoun's in-state allies secretly organized district meetings to form a unified "People's Ticket" of electors opposed to Crawford. They planned to claim the majority of spots on the ticket, relegating minority positions to the Jackson and Adams men. Working with the general's minions proved exasperating, however. "They are an obstinate sett [sic]," one Calhounite claimed, with one Jacksonian insisting that "if elected to support Jackson, he would vote for no other man." In the end, the general's men abandoned any pretense of cooperation with his rivals. Emboldened by Jackson's muscular movement in Pennsylvania, they forced the Calhounites off the People's Ticket and claimed the majority of electors. "The people are beginning to stir, and when they do they will be heard," Jackson asserted as he followed these developments.[10]

The general had assessed the situation correctly. The burgeoning Jackson movements in two states well outside his home region finally caught the attention of his presidential rivals. "The unfortunate nomination of Gen. Jackson," one frustrated Pennsylvania supporter informed Clay, "has so possessed the public mind & the disorder has broken out in so many fresh places that your friends have been unable to make headway." Eaton chuckled at the "fear and trembling" Jackson's emergence had abruptly produced among the secretaries and their supporters. "When the people are . . . openly proclaiming the man who rests strong in their affections," he noted with amusement, "alarm is produced, from an apprehension that such a spark, may presently be fanned into a flame." Their sustained dismissal of Jackson's candidacy left his opponents suddenly scrambling for a strategy to blunt his mounting popularity.[11]

Adams adopted the softest approach, trying to co-opt Jackson into his own campaign. He had long harbored hopes of hitching the general's bandwagon of followers to his own presidential star. Adams had always admired Jackson, often defending the general's controversial activities during the Seminole War. He plotted to draft him as his vice presidential running mate, openly asserting that Jackson would add "the peculiar advantage of the geographical association" to his ticket. As the expressly northern candidate in the race, Adams certainly realized that running with a slaveholding westerner—to say nothing of a national celebrity hero—would enormously increase his appeal to voters outside New England. The secretary's organization began spreading rumors that Jackson preferred playing junior partner to Adams. Adams airily dismissed concerns about Jackson's reputed intemperate impulsiveness. The vice presidency is "a station in which the

General could hang no one," Adams explained to his nervous followers. "It would afford an easy and dignified retirement in his old age." The secretary of state seemingly forgot that he was only four months younger than the "elderly" Jackson. When rumormongering proved insufficient to corral the general, Adams personally planned a showy social campaign to win him over.[12]

To commemorate Jackson's victory in the Battle of New Orleans, Adams decided to host a colossal party on the battle's anniversary, January 8, 1824, with the heroic general himself feted as the guest of honor. Adams timed his event perfectly. It occurred shortly after Jackson arrived in Washington to assume his Senate seat, but before the congressional caucus due in February. Accordingly, Jackson would be available to attend and Adams might convince the general to serve as his running mate just prior to the Republican caucus.[13]

The Adamses spared little expense or effort for their spectacular affair. Louisa Adams hand-delivered almost 500 invitations while laboring for weeks over the food, music, and decor. Her husband fretted meticulously over the details, personally supervising the placement of party decorations on the big night. The result was a feast for the senses. From two blocks away, bonfires guided the guests to the Adams residence. The home itself was festooned with garlands, lanterns, and flowers. The dance floor inside was decorated with a chalked design that proclaimed "Welcome to the Hero of New Orleans" embellished by eagles and flags. Over a thousand guests watched Louisa gracefully escort a gracious Jackson through the festivities. The party served as another newspaper victory for Adams, too. It was relentlessly hyped by his presses beforehand and celebrated just as flamboyantly afterward.[14]

Adams's festivities impressed most of official Washington and even awed Jackson. "The party at [M]rs. Adams was the largest I ever witnessed at a private house," the general enthused. The affair failed to achieve its main objective, however, as Jackson moved no closer to serving as Adams's vice president. With his campaign's positive developments, Jackson had begun to taste victory, and he was not about to accept a seat anywhere but at the head of the table. As rumors persisted that Jackson would subordinate his own ambitions to Adams's, he blamed his rival's organization for the whisper campaign that aimed at diminishing his candidacy. "The friends of Mr. Adams . . . not only are guilty of the grossest misrepresentation," Jackson noted testily, "but practice an unpardonable outrage upon . . . the freedom, & sovereignity [sic] of the people." His own supporters grew so annoyed that they floated their own counterrumor that Adams had agreed to serve as secretary of state under Jackson. No matter how much it irritated the general, Adams continued his attempted downgrade well into the fall of 1824 and long after its evident futility. Unfortunately for both men, Adams's efforts invited their mutual opponents to start another rumor that the two were cooperating in a secret coalition. Crawfordites labeled the pair the "Holy Alliance," which unfavorably associated Adams and Jackson with the detested absolutist monarchs of Europe.[15]

Where Adams had unsuccessfully dangled carrots to entice Jackson, the remaining power elite in Washington took a stick to the general instead. After almost a month of Jackson's charm offensive, coupled with his dramatic rise out in the states, in mid-January, the Crawfordite Philadelphia *Democratic Press* broke a shocking scandal. The newspaper claimed that in 1817, Jackson had advised then president-elect Monroe to balance his administration between the two parties by appointing at least two Federalists to his cabinet. If true, the allegations might seriously damage Jackson's campaign both in Pennsylvania, where the Federalists remained a sizable minority loathed by many in the Democratic majority, and with hyperpartisan Republicans nationwide. Jackson only vaguely recalled the correspondence, and he desperately sought a copy of it. Monroe claimed to be unable to locate the damaging letter, yet he could somehow "very well recollect" that the seven-year-old missive "did you honor. It expressed . . . a generous exercise of power, by the Republican party, in a way to . . . draw the Union together." "Intrigue is the order of the day here," Jackson snarled. "The object is, by the publication at this moment to produce an effect upon Pensylvania [sic] who is about to form an electoral Tickett [sic] to support me." The suspicious timing of the release certainly justified Jackson's surmise.[16]

While Jackson initially denied the story, once he received his copy of the letter from his son, he realized there was truth behind the slander.

The general had indeed recommended Federalist William Drayton, a colonel who had served under Jackson in the War of 1812, as Monroe's secretary of war. The other "Federalist" that he had advocated, however, had been then a Republican, Adams as secretary of state, so the claim that he favored two Federalists was clearly exaggerated. The episode took an unexpected twist when Monroe himself was accused of sharing Jackson's letter with various politicians, with a version anonymously mailed to Pennsylvania senator Walter Lowrie. The principals involved engaged in a four-month fight in the newspapers, bickering over the propriety of "publishing private and confidential correspondence." In the end, after a conference between their advisers, Jackson and Monroe released to the *Columbian Observer* and the *National Intelligencer* the letters both men had exchanged in 1816 and 1817, as well as their 1824 correspondence on the subject. Newspapers across the nation reprinted the eagerly awaited letters.[17]

Once it entered the public record that Jackson had indeed pressed Monroe to appoint a Federalist cabinet secretary, many believed the general's campaign had been irreparably damaged. Jackson's recommendations were "tantamount to a declaration that political principles and opinions [were] of no importance in the administration of government," Albert Gallatin noted disparagingly. In response, Jackson justified his support of a Federalist on patriotic rather than partisan grounds. Lauding Drayton's personal character, Jackson added that "men, call them what you will, who risk life, health and their all in defense of their country are entitled to share the offices of the Government." In an even more clever maneuver, he invoked two of the nation's beloved founding icons to validate his actions. "I can truly say of [Drayton], that we are all Federalists, we are all Republicans," Jackson insisted, quoting Jefferson's inaugural address. He later added that "the voice of Washington, in his farewell address . . . was that party animosity was not to be encouraged." Jackson managed to turn a negative, support for an enemy partisan, into a positive, association with figures from the nation's hallowed republican past.[18]

Privately, Jackson blamed the treasury secretary for the entire ruckus. "Mr. Crawford's friends have become desperate and will do anything," he growled. The general largely exonerated Monroe for his role in the

controversy, merely charging him with naivety. The president clearly deserved far less of Jackson's trust. After the scandal broke, Monroe insisted that Jackson's correspondence was only located "after a long search,
and in an old forgotten trunk." His claim failed to explain how a long-stored
letter that only he knew about could be "well recollected" both by himself
and other politicians. Following his extended public campaign denying any
involvement whatsoever in the affair, Monroe finally admitted privately to
Adams that though he had not *read* Jackson's letter to anyone, he had "al-
luded" to its contents. Indeed, at least four politicians would ultimately
concede that Monroe had shown them the letter. The president probably
realized that sharing Jackson's damaging correspondence with Pennsylvania's politicos might have blunted the general's unexpected advance in the
Keystone state, with Calhoun as the principal beneficiary. Printing Jackson's letter in a Crawford newspaper would give the attack the appearance
of a Crawford-orchestrated plot and scrub Monroe's fingerprints from the
intrigue. While only circumstantial evidence implicated Monroe in such
a scheme, it certainly fits with his secret backing of Calhoun's presidential bid.[19]

Ironically, whether or not Crawford or Monroe had directly plotted to
undermine Jackson with his pro-Federalist letter, the affair ultimately
strengthened the general's campaign. While his rivals' presses labeled Jackson "the Federal candidate for the Presidency" and suggested that "the man
who disclaims Party should by Party be disclaimed," Jackson's own papers
countered that the general simply championed nonpartisan appointments
of well-qualified individuals for the national good, just as Washington and
Jefferson had done. Most Jackson-leaning Republicans accepted this justification, and they defended the pro-Federalist letter—either half- or wholeheartedly, depending on their feeling toward Federalists. Unexpectedly, the
opposition party provided Jackson with his greatest gains. Jackson was
now the only Republican candidate who had rejected his party's Federalist
proscription policy in writing. Since he had done so seven years earlier and
long before the current campaign, his sentiments seemed truthful rather
than an electioneering ploy. Once again, Jackson's presidential foes had
misjudged his unorthodox campaign, to their own detriment.[20]

While Jackson may have been strengthened, the publication of his damaging correspondence signaled a new front in the electoral war. The candidate who had once been ignored by his rivals' newspapers suddenly endured the same withering attacks his opponents had faced for three years. While some opposition presses focused on his lack of civil administrative experience, most exclaimed that his "martial" temperament rendered him unfit for high office. The hard-nosed general who had summarily executed undisciplined militiamen, incarcerated martial law violators, and mercilessly hanged alleged British spies might endanger American liberty. As the general watched the escalating denigration, he began sounding like the other contenders. Opposition newspapers "heap upon me every scurrilous slanderous abuse that falsehood can suggest," Jackson complained, caricaturing him as "a sort of saw head & bloody bones, fit only to scar[e] children."[21]

Since the general's military record served as the raison d'être of his presidential run, these attacks aimed to undermine the foundation of his candidacy. Jackson privately conceded that as a military commander he had occasionally acted unconstitutionally, but he blamed such breaches on the "critical situations" he faced in wartime. In public, Jackson ignored the ill-treatment. Just as he had remained calm during Senate debates meant to provoke his temper, the general surmised that such press strikes aimed at provoking his violent response, thereby validating the criticism against him. Instead, Jackson predicted that the newspaper assaults would backfire. "The subjects the[y] embrace . . . will increase my standing with the nation," the general shrewdly observed. "They will elect me, contrary to their wishes, by their *abuse*." Indeed, press attacks that warned voters about Jackson's "dangerous" military record also reminded them of Jackson's "glorious" military record. Ultimately, the voters would decide which version of Jackson was running for president.[22]

Out with a Whimper: Crawford and the Death of "King Caucus"

While Jackson marched purposefully into 1824, Crawford limped—physically, mentally, and politically—into the last year of the election. Though slowly recovering from his incapacitating September affliction, the treasury sec-retary's job, campaign, and political standing had each suffered in the interim. "If I was to judge from the appearance today of the treasurers friends," Jackson chuckled, "I would suppose he is politically (as he notably is) sick." His rivals gleefully circulated rumors that Crawford would surely die, initiating a wild frenzy to capture his supporters and voters. Despite his opponents' hopes, Crawford's condition steadily improved through the winter, and by April 1824, he rejoined cabinet meetings for the first time since the previous summer.[23]

Though numerous historians have blamed Crawford's debilitating ill-ness for his poor showing in the election, the treasury secretary's health garnered surprisingly little attention from rival presses. "You see nothing now in the papers respecting the health of Mr. Crawford," a chagrined Clay acknowledged. While elite politicians freely gossiped about the subject, the secretary's potential physical unfitness for high office never became a press-ing campaign issue for ordinary voters. Though his condition was serious, Crawford always seemed to be steadily improving, so his sizable organiza-tion and newspaper network held firm during his ongoing travails. Craw-ford was hardly the "virtual corpse" depicted in many historical accounts.[24]

Perhaps his rivals avoided publicly disqualifying Crawford for his sick-ness because several of them had suffered crippling health setbacks as well. In the fall of 1822, Clay contracted a severe "bilious fever" while attending to business in Ohio. With the Speaker bedridden for several months, ru-mors circulated that he had actually died. Clay's persistent illness forced him to decline a proposed electioneering swing through western New York in 1823. Although not as severely, the Speaker's health problems slowed his campaign just as Crawford's had affected his.[25]

However significant Clay's troubles, Jackson's medical issues easily trumped the Speaker's. Courtesy of his past duels and bar fights, the gen-eral carried two bullets in his body, one in the chest and the other in the upper left arm. The lodged bullets, combined with the lingering effects of his bouts with malaria and dysentery, seriously compromised Jackson's health. His brief stint as military governor of Florida almost killed Jack-son, and from 1821 onward, he was in pain every day. The general endured acute chest congestion, chronic cough, periodic pulmonary hemorrhages, sporadic fever, debilitating stomachaches, severe osteomyelitis, and the occasional abscess that he lanced himself. He self-medicated with huge doses of mercury and lead-based drugs that were actually slowly poisoning him.[26]

Throughout the long campaign, Jackson deluged his correspondents with a litany of his ailments. His health problems rendered him at times unable to read, write, travel, or concentrate on his campaign. "I apprehend, that I will never regain my health," the general sighed. "My constitution has recd so many severe trials—that it is too much weakened." Considering the state of nineteenth-century healthcare, a serious illness could sideline any candidate at any time, so overtly criticizing Crawford for his physical issues would have been problematic.[27]

Crawfordites put their chief's ill health to good use. They tried to induce his rivals to abandon their own runs and join his ticket as vice president, dangling Crawford's allegedly imminent death as a surefire route to the presidency. Some flattered Adams, claiming that Crawford's "highly probable" death required them to select a "quality" vice president like the secretary of state. Adams, who was carefully following Crawford's recovery, rejected all such overtures by claiming that his supporters would refuse to, yet again, subordinate a northerner under another southern president.[28]

Crawford's allies made an even stronger push to recruit Clay. Van Buren himself grew convinced that a Crawford/Clay ticket uniting the South and West would best defeat Adams and Calhoun and preserve Republican party unity. He assured Clay that accepting the vice presidency now ensured "his eventual elevation to the Presidency." Convinced he could win the highest office himself, Clay rebuffed the offer in proper republican fashion, proclaiming that "it is my fixed determination to enter into no arrangements, to make no bargains." To the detriment of both sides, the negotiations between the Crawford and Clay organizations only fueled rumors that both men were cooperating in a secret coalition aimed at benefiting Crawford. Jackson's newspapers argued that a vote for Clay was really a vote for Crawford. Clay's alliance with the nefarious treasury secretary only proved, the *Nashville Gazette* insisted, "that the prospects of subordinate office under a superior, whose schemes he aids . . . is with him a more governing principle than . . . obedience to the will of the people." Crawfordite efforts to shunt two rivals into a lesser office ultimately ended in failure.[29]

While illness and running mate machinations may have distracted Crawford and his minions, the treasury secretary and his organization remained focused, as they had from the outset of the campaign, on winning the congressional caucus nomination. In pursuing his party's official endorsement, Crawford was merely following the path blazed by his three predecessors. The first Republican congressional caucus had selected Jefferson and Burr as the party's nominees in 1800. The initial conclave had been envisioned as a means to grant official party approval to nominees already backed by popular public opinion. Because its earliest iteration lacked set rules and formal organizational structure, ensuing caucuses were plagued by poor attendance, intraparty bickering, and popular criticism that the caucus seemed to be directing rather than following public opinion. Congressional caucuses often became forums for politicians opposing the official nominee. Monroe, who had himself challenged Madison in the 1808 caucus, only narrowly edged Crawford 65–54 in the one held in 1816. Despite its checkered history, Crawford avidly sought the official Republican endorsement. The treasury secretary had labored for eight grueling years building an organization, distributing patronage, and assembling the congressional party necessary to win a caucus vote. His formal Republican nomination would be the crowning achievement of his traditional campaign for the presidency.[30]

Caucusing had long been a staple of American politics, predating even the Constitution. State politicians often used such gatherings to help pass legislation, dole out patronage, make nominations for elected office, and plot party strategy. Regardless of its time-honored status, congressional caucuses for presidential nominees had been criticized in every electoral cycle since their initial use. The shopworn arguments for and against the caucus were rehashed for the 1824 contest. The Cincinnati *National Republican* reprinted an 1808 anticaucus manifesto verbatim. Opponents argued that caucuses were unconstitutional, undemocratic, unnecessary, and unethical. Since US congressional politicians were constitutionally barred from serving as presidential electors, granting these same men the right to pick nominees violated the Constitution. Because ordinary voters in popular elections increasingly chose the electors, granting elite politicians in Washington control over the nominee was seen as undemocratic. Without a Federalist opponent, Republicans could dispense with this unnecessary partisan relic. Because congressmen were notorious for trading favors, pedaling influence, and self-interested voting, giving Washington politicians a voice in picking the nominees invited corruption. Contemptuous critics labeled it "king caucus," emphasizing its lack of republican virtue.[31]

Proponents countered that caucuses simply represented the constitutionally protected free expression of individuals. Since the national legislature convened the caucuses, the official nominee best represented the national will of ordinary voters, would help to balance competing state claims, and was certain to support the party's doctrines. No more democratic method of designating the party candidate existed, and past nominees Jefferson, Madison, and Monroe had proven to be principled statesmen, not crooked politicians. Caucuses prevented electoral college intrigue, so they certainly had not promoted corruption. Exaggerating its historical importance, Crawfordites championed the caucus as the ultimate Republican institution, with the probable favorite positioned as the true Republican heir to Jefferson. Caucus supporters appealed to tradition, defending the conclave as "the good old way," "an old landmark," and a "keepsake from the purest days of democracy."[32]

Despite the principled stances on both sides of the debate, caucus supporters were usually members of the majority faction expected to win a caucus vote while opponents were usually members of a minority faction with little hope of dominating the gathering. Many politicians in the majority who vigorously favored caucuses were known to oppose such conclaves once their faction slipped into the minority, with caucus losers labeling the winners corrupt intriguers. The congressional caucus had now "met with the displeasure of several gentlemen with whom I have served in caucus more than once," Crawfordite Samuel Smith observed disgustedly. "Men are governed by the consideration of whether the caucus will or will not support their favorite candidate." Politicians from states supporting Crawford tended to champion the congressional caucus, while those from states supporting other candidates generally denounced it.[33]

The presidential candidates followed similar self-interested logic. Expecting to be competitive, Crawford, Adams, and Clay supported the caucus, while the less viable contenders, Calhoun and Jackson, opposed it. With verbal commitments from Republicans representing Georgia, New York, Virginia, North Carolina, and even twenty New Englanders, Crawfordites judged that they commanded the solid majority of congressman necessary to win the caucus vote. There would be little trouble from Adams or Clay. The secretary of state had publicly defended the caucus as fully constitutional. "It is in its essence caballing," he admitted privately, but "I consider it one of the least obnoxious modes of intrigue." Clay agreed to attend a caucus himself, "provided the members who compose it speak the sentiments of those whom they represent." Unsurprisingly, the trio of procaucus candidates each commanded a significant number of allies in Congress, so each harbored hopes of engineering a victory, especially if the caucus divided among the large number of candidates.[34]

Unlike their fellow contenders, Calhoun and Jackson opposed congressional caucus nominations. Initially Calhoun had been noncommittal about attending one, but his poor showing in the congressional war with Crawford probably convinced him to come out against a caucus that he seemed unlikely to win. The secretary of war informed Van Buren that he would decline a congressional caucus nomination even if offered one. His newspapers began running editorials criticizing the caucus as an unprincipled and undemocratic tool of managing politicians, and Calhoun's followers joined the mounting outcry against it. Intentionally invoking the name of Crawford's faction, one Calhounite savaged the caucus as "*radically* vicious." It "throw[s] all power into the hands of a few managers, who will eventually prostitute their power to corrupt & selfish ends," he grumbled.[35]

With few congressional supporters and virtually no chance of winning the traditional nomination, Jackson rejected the caucus from the outset of his campaign with even greater vigor than Calhoun. "I touch not, handle not this unclean thing," the general bellowed. "I hope the people . . . will not be intrigued out of their direct right of electing the President." His supporters echoed their hero and assailed the caucus just as forcefully. Considering the general's burgeoning support in the state, Pennsylvania unsurprisingly emerged as a prominent battleground against the caucus. At a late 1823 political meeting in Philadelphia, Jacksonians hissed a procaucus Crawfordite off the stage. "There arose a universal cry of no caucus!—down with him!—Out with him!" one stunned Calhounite related. "The poor fellow was glad to get off with his whole bones." Early the following year, boisterous Jacksonians disrupted a procaucus meeting. Editor Stephen Simpson leapt on a table, waved his hat, and shouted, "Three cheers for General Jackson!" In the ensuing melee between pro- and anticaucusers, the fighting knocked down a stove pipe, the room filled with smoke, and the attendants dispersed without passing any resolutions. Many Jacksonians believed that defeating the caucus even trumped electing the general.[36]

Disregarding the objections, Crawford and his followers had little choice but to press onward, as the treasury secretary had predicated his entire campaign on winning the official Republican nomination. As with much of the anti-Crawford effort throughout the perpetual campaign, Calhounites led the attack against Crawford's caucus. Early in 1824, fourteen Calhoun-supporting congressmen from Pennsylvania issued a "Circular" proclaiming their intention to boycott a caucus. Clay and Adams initially held back from joining an outright rejection, maintaining their own chance of winning and hoping that Crawford's health might decline even further, forcing him to drop out. The two contenders waited until the very end of January before finally joining the anticaucus movement.[37]

Adams, who had already been carefully gauging how various members might vote in a caucus, visited his ally John W. Taylor in the Capitol, and the two men spent three hours assessing the situation. Shortly afterward, the secretary of state, who had never once voiced any objections to the caucus, suddenly declared himself "utterly averse" to the undemocratic, unconstitutional, and corrupt party nomination. "I wished my friends to take any measures in concert with others opposed to it," he proclaimed. Meanwhile, Clay initially believed he was many members' second choice for president, and he might win the nomination as a compromise choice if the caucus deadlocked. Once he arrived in the capital and began counting congressional noses, Clay realized that Crawford would certainly be the official nominee. Unless the treasury secretary's adversaries cooperated, Clay argued, Crawford would "infallibly succeed against them all."[38]

Accordingly, Calhoun's ally Samuel Ingham, Clay supporter Richard Mentor Johnson, and Adams's Taylor coordinated their activities. The trio ironically convened a caucus of like-minded followers, who eventually agreed to boycott the caucus en masse. The "friends of Calhoun, Clay, Jackson, & Adams . . . are united in the determination to give the caucus a death blow," one Calhounite chortled. "The explosion will blow up Mr. Crawford's machinery & put an end to his hopes forever." In one final, frantic gambit to stave off defeat, New York Crawfordite C. C. Cambreleng dangled a future nomination to both Clay and Adams in exchange for supporting Crawford in this year's caucus. Cambreleng "promise[d] that by acceding to this arrangement now, the service to the party would lay up a fund of merit for promotion at a future election." The deal mimicked Crawford's tactic in gracefully accepting Monroe's 1816 nomination, but Adams and Clay both rejected the offer this time around. As hopes for a robust caucus faded, opposition presses mocked the Crawfordites' pretensions. "The poor little political bird of ominous note and plumage . . . was hatched at Washington on Saturday last," the *Baltimore Morning Chronicle* taunted. "The sickly thing is to be fed, cherished, pampered for a week, when it is fondly hoped it will be enabled to cry the name of Crawford, Crawford, Crawford."[39]

As various members publicly declined to attend, the disconsolate Crawfordites soldiered on, with Virginia's James Barbour stoutly insisting that "I by myself, I" would caucus even if no other members joined him. The caucusers convened on February 14 at 7 p.m. in the House chamber. The night was cold and dreary, apt weather for Crawford's increasingly bleak campaign. Van Buren had tried to coerce two legendary Republicans into attending, but Nathaniel Macon and John Taylor of Caroline both opted out, citing the unconstitutional nature of the proceedings. The highest-profile participant that the Wizard of the Albany Regency could conjure up was Maryland's venerable Samuel Smith, a congressman since 1793 who had joined in the first caucus. Precaucus predictions had ranged as high as 115 members attending; in the end, only 66 of the 240 Republicans in Congress actually appeared. Van Buren had opened the affair to the public, hoping to refute charges that the caucus was a "secret cabal," but the decision backfired when the spectators outnumbered the caucusers. Four states accounted for two-thirds of those gathered—sixteen from New York, fifteen

Virginians, nine from North Carolina, and eight Georgians. Five states sent one participant only, while ten went completely unrepresented.[40]

The Crawfordites were genuinely stunned by the meager turnout, and even the anticaucus coalition expressed surprise at the effectiveness of their boycott when several Crawfordites failed to show up. One member, disheartened by the low attendance, motioned to postpone, but Van Buren himself sternly led the effort to defeat any delay. Ignoring the hostile cries from the gallery of "Adjourn! Adjourn!" accompanied by the thumping of walking sticks, Crawford was overwhelmingly nominated on the first ballot by sixty-four votes, opposed by two for Adams, one for Jackson, and one for Macon. Depending upon the presidential proclivities of the reporter, the galleries either erupted in applause for Crawford countered by "a small coterie" of hissers, or in "much hissing" with only "scattered applause" for the nominee. Regardless of audience reaction, the results laid bare the ugly truth behind Crawford's fading candidacy. In the last congressional caucus ever held, the treasury secretary had been nominated by a minority of Republicans in Congress, less than one-fifth of that body, and by the smallest percentage of members compared to prior caucuses for first-time nominees. Crawford's supposedly massive, unstoppable organization compelled only scanty attendance for the signature event of his entire campaign.[41]

The caucus also nominated Albert Gallatin as Crawford's running mate. Gallatin received fifty-seven votes with nine others scattered among an array of candidates including, in an obvious dig, one for Adams. A former congressman, diplomat, and long-serving secretary of the treasury in the Jefferson and Madison administrations, Gallatin's nomination served as repayment after he favored Crawford over Monroe in 1816. As a Pennsylvanian, Crawfordites expected Gallatin to nudge that all-important mid-Atlantic state into the treasury secretary's column. As a protégé of Jefferson, he would reinforce Crawford's links to the party's glorious Republican past. Gallatin's nomination also effectively balanced the ticket geographically and ideologically. Not only would a northerner now be paired with a southerner, but, as treasury secretary, Gallatin had staunchly supported federally funded internal improvements, while Crawford did not.[42]

Unfortunately for Crawford, as the consummate Washington insider, Gallatin also reminded voters of treasury secretary's immersion in the capital's unsavory political establishment. Objections to Gallatin's nomination surfaced almost immediately. Critics argued correctly that Gallatin, who had been born in Geneva, Switzerland, was ineligible to serve as vice president, or president should the need arise (the Constitution mandates that only natural-born citizens could hold those offices). Over his long years of service, Gallatin had also amassed numerous political enemies. They readily disparaged his competence, claiming that Gallatin had left the treasury in significant disarray when he resigned his post. Crawford's organization renewed begging Clay to step in and replace their embattled vice presidential nominee, but the Speaker continued rejecting every effort to demote his candidacy. Van Buren finally prevailed upon Gallatin to step aside, and he withdrew in humiliation on September 18. Crawfordites resignedly suggested that each state select a local favorite for vice president on their Crawford tickets.[43]

Ultimately, all of Crawford's rivals cooperated to derail the caucus. Once he accepted the official nomination, opposition presses intensified their attacks, depicting him as a corrupt, elite insider. Crawfordites dismissed the objections as politically motivated, self-interested propaganda spread by his unsuccessful competitors. The other candidates opposed the caucus "not from any repugnance to the practice, as their previous conduct had shown," Benton insisted, "but because it was known that Mr. Crawford . . . would assuredly receive the nomination." Indeed, candidates Adams, Calhoun, and Clay had all caucused in the past. Most hypocritically of all, Richard Mentor Johnson, one of the most vocal opposing voices, had served as secretary of three previous caucuses. In a political culture increasingly reliant on popular participation, the anticaucus forces emerged victorious, however. As with much of the coordinated attack against the treasury secretary throughout the long campaign, Crawford's rivals managed to turn his strength into a weakness, transforming his support within the party into a corrupt intrigue by politicos. Instead of positively influencing public opinion as it had in the past, Crawford's caucus nomination became a burdensome liability.[44]

Of all of Crawford's rivals, Jackson probably benefited the most from the treasury secretary's caucus nomination. Although part of the long, ongoing, mainstream criticism of caucusing within Republican party ranks,

Jacksonians had been the earliest and noisiest opponents of a potential Crawford nomination and of caucusing in general. Jackson linked caucus opposition to the central theme of his campaign. "Should the people suffer themselves to be dictated to by designing demagogues," he noted fiercely, "their present happy Government . . . must sink under the seeds of corruption." He made two correct predictions. Jackson asserted that Crawford's caucus nomination would damage his presidential campaign and that "this will be the last of King caucus—its Funeral Knell well will be sounded throughout the union."[45]

Just as Crawford's campaign had focused on winning one, Jackson's centered on denouncing the caucus nomination. The general's correspondence teemed with condemnations of the practice. Eaton's *Letters of Wyoming* included a sternly worded rejection of the caucus. Editorials in the *Columbian Observer* derisively nicknamed it the "Second Hartford Convention," evoking memories of that notorious 1814 conclave at which Federalists from New England, disgusted by the ongoing War of 1812, contemplated secession from the union. Resolutions passed at a Jackson meeting in Pennsylvania reviled it for "promoting intrigue and corruption, and . . . usurption [sic] of the rights of citizens." Jackson's entire campaign—correspondence, newspapers, state nomination speeches, meeting resolutions, and pamphlets—expertly reinforced his messaging against Crawford, the caucus, and corruption. Jacksonians used the caucus to skewer all of Jackson's presidential rivals. Congressional caucusers "are near to the executive, as well as to the great offices of State, of the Treasury, and of War, to all of which there is great influence, and patronage attached," one Jackson backer insisted. In contrast, they praised their hero for his opposition to the odious practice. "*My* candidate requires no caucus," another Jacksonian proclaimed, "*His* caucus was in the hearts of the people." For Jackson, Crawford's nomination simply proved that "Babylon" did indeed have a "great whore."[46]

Casualty of War: The Surprising
Collapse of the Calhoun Campaign

While Calhoun and his minions had successfully orchestrated the anticaucus effort that undermined the focal point of Crawford's candidacy, they continued concentrating on the states central to the secretary of war's own campaign. Every contender had harbored designs on capturing North Carolina and Pennsylvania, but Calhoun, positioning himself as the southerner with northern appeal, staked his entire candidacy on winning the pair. Accordingly, Jackson's emerging prominence in both states represented an existential threat to Calhoun's candidacy.

In North Carolina, the Jacksonians' forced expulsion of Calhounites from the People's Ticket exposed the secretary of war's campaign as a project hatched by elite politicians opposed to Crawford, rather than a unprompted popular movement. In perhaps the greatest achievement of Jackson's 1824 campaign, his tireless forces worked meticulously over several months, populating the People's Ticket with pro-Jackson electors. Without any central party machinery, the general's North Carolina campaign coordinated local public meetings via newspapers and correspondence committees that nominated electors or replaced those unwilling to serve. Federalists helped turn the tide against the secretary of war. With the general's pro-Federalist letter assuring many that a President Jackson would not "proscribe and persecute the Federalists," several became Jackson electors on the People's Ticket. Facing these Jacksonian efforts, Calhoun's operation in North Carolina suffered a complete breakdown.[47]

Beyond his push in North Carolina, Calhoun had expended even greater effort to win Pennsylvania. He had successfully courted Philadelphia's Family Party. Representing wealthy manufacturers and bankers, the Family Party favored economic nationalism. By joining with Calhoun, they envisioned a new, progressive alliance between Pennsylvania and South Carolina, supplanting the more conservative Virginia/New York axis. Family Party politicians had orchestrated nearly every key advance of Calhoun's campaign. They made up the state's US congressional delegation that asked an allegedly "surprised" Calhoun to run for president in December 1821.

They distributed pro-Calhoun literature in Pennsylvania and organized the ill-fated attempt to secure Pennsylvania's nomination for Calhoun at the state convention in 1823. When John Shulze, the pro-Calhoun candidate for governor in 1823, won office by the largest majority in Pennsylvania history, the secretary of war appeared primed to capture the northern part of his two-state nationalist strategy.[48]

Calhoun had not factored in Jackson's emergence, however, and the general's forces had a few surprises in store for the secretary of war. Once Pennsylvania's Jacksonians announced in January that they planned to attend a convention in Huntingdon to select a ticket of electors, Democratic state legislators, most of them supporters of Calhoun or Crawford, issued a countercall for a convention in Harrisburg. Calhounites secretly plotted to use the convention to draft a Calhoun presidential ticket, with Jackson relegated to the vice presidential slot. Jackson's backers correctly suspected that the Harrisburg convention was a Calhounite stratagem, and, once again, Stephen Simpson rallied the troops. He recommended that the Huntingdon delegates vie for slots at the Harrisburg gathering instead "and thus beat the enemy in their *strong hold,* and on *their own ground!*" Simpson organized "Hickory Clubs" for Jackson supporters; these attracted numerous young, politically unaffiliated, and previously inactive voters. The Jackson clubs, combined with an extensive newspaper network, formed the popular movement necessary to combat the regular Democratic Party machine.[49]

With the general always more popular with western rank-and-file Democrats than eastern political elites, Jacksonians easily swept delegate elections in Pennsylvania's western counties. More shockingly, with the enthusiastic support of urban artisans, they carried 10 of 14 wards in Philadelphia. Jackson's support, in a city supposedly solid for Calhoun, stunned the Family Party in the very epicenter of their power base. "Heaven knows what will be the upshot," one bewildered Calhounite exclaimed, "but it seems to me that Jackson is carrying it away from all the rest." Faced with losing control over Pennsylvania's patronage to the state's other factions as the popular general swamped the hapless secretary of war, George Dallas, the leader of the Family Party, wisely conceded defeat. He personally sponsored a resolution endorsing Jackson's presidential candidacy at a citywide meeting in late February. Without even consulting Calhoun, Dallas had effectively withdrawn him from contention in Pennsylvania. The March 4 convention in Harrisburg turned into a virtual rally for the general, with a pro-Jackson electoral ticket approved almost unanimously 123–2.[50]

While Pennsylvania had a history of holding state delegate conventions to pick gubernatorial nominees, the Harrisburg assembly was the first-ever delegate convention held for a presidential nominee. After Jackson's victory there, Pennsylvania's Democrats of all types consolidated behind his presidential bid. The general attracted his share of wealthy businessmen, merchants, and lawyers, but the bulk of his followers were "small farmers, miners, rivermen, and mechanics." Pennsylvania's Jacksonians, whom one Calhounite had once disparagingly dismissed as "the grog shop politicians of villages & the rabble of Philadelphia & Pittsburgh," rocked the political establishment across the nation. "I confess that nothing in the course of this canvass has surprised me more than that Pennsylvania should have selected Jackson," a dazed Clayite admitted. With his stunning Pennsylvania upset, in the eyes of his presidential rivals, Jackson went from farce to factor almost literally overnight.[51]

No politician proved more shocked than Calhoun himself. Only three weeks prior to his astonishing reversal of fortune, the secretary of war, declaring that "Penn^a. is firm as a rock," insisted that he would capture the Harrisburg nomination. Reeling over Dallas's switch to Jackson, he counseled his supporters "to hold our position, and wait events," but the convention's results sealed Calhoun's fate. His dual failures in Pennsylvania and North Carolina meant that the two pillars supposedly buttressing his candidacy had collapsed, effectively taking his entire campaign with them. With his electoral fortunes rendered untenable, Calhoun suspended his campaign for the presidency. The man who had once hoped to be everyone's runner-up ended up run over by the Jackson juggernaut. As a consolation prize, Calhoun's supporters in Pennsylvania pushed for his vice presidential nomination on both the Adams and Jackson tickets. As the election played out, Calhoun, though personally favoring Jackson, pursued a neutral course carefully designed not to alienate followers of either of his rivals.

Perhaps Calhoun had indeed been everyone's second choice for president, because he ultimately proved agreeable as a vice presidential nominee to both the Jackson and Adams organizations. Matching the tactical mastery with which he had weakened Crawford throughout the perpetual campaign, Calhoun had engineered a win-win vice presidential bid. He would triumph regardless of which man captured the presidency. In Calhoun's mind, at least, he was well positioned for a future presidential run.[52]

Jackson's ouster of Calhoun immediately strengthened his campaign. Much of Calhoun's organizational support in North Carolina and Pennsylvania transferred to the general. "The mist into which Calhoun's bubble broke settles upon Jackson," Adams cogently noted. Calhoun's once-mighty newspaper network also disbanded, with Jackson frequently the beneficiary. Most prominently, Calhoun's *Patriot* and *Raleigh Star* began editorializing for the general. Electorally, Jackson's triumph over Calhoun transformed him into a credible alternative to Clay in the Northwest, nudged mid-Atlantic states Maryland and New Jersey in his direction, and even strengthened his support in his home region in the Southwest.[53]

While Calhoun may have been disappointed in his personal finish, he and Monroe surely celebrated his campaign as a whole. Defeating Crawford, Calhoun had once hyperbolically observed, "is of the highest importance to the lasting interest of this Republik. Almost as much depends on it as on the late war." Accordingly, both men had dedicated significant effort throughout the president's second term to frustrating the treasury secretary's succession. By crossing swords with Crawford in cabinet debates, contesting his party in Congress, publishing damaging newspaper attacks against him, and assembling the coalition that torpedoed the caucus, Calhoun had done far more than any other candidate to deny Crawford a victory. With far fewer elite and popular supporters at his disposal than his rivals, the secretary of war inflicted maximum damage with minimal resources. Indeed, Calhoun's strategic focus on undermining Crawford's candidacy with destructive attacks proved a key development in the outcome of the election of 1824.[54]

Raising the Issues: Clay's Quixotic Quest in Congress

As the election year unfolded, Jackson, Crawford, and Calhoun had each exploited the Eighteenth Congress to further their campaigns. Jackson used
the session to enhance his resume, Crawford to capture the caucus nomination, and Calhoun to tarnish Crawford's prize. No candidate had made congressional legislating the central feature of their campaign, however, until
Clay reappeared in Congress in late 1823. Not only could he count on the
esprit de corps of his fellow members should the multiple candidacies result
in a House election for the presidency, the speakership would allow Clay
to conduct an unusual presidential campaign, using congressional legislation to attract voters. All the candidates had taken positions on important
issues, but none would center his presidential bid as directly on policy as
Clay. He had learned the power of the speakership throughout his service in
Congress. During Monroe's first term, by opposing the president's foreign
policy and spearheading the compromise over Missouri's admission, Clay
had vaunted into the rarified ranks of credible presidential contenders. In
1824, the Speaker became the first American presidential candidate to run
an overtly issues-based campaign.[55]

Using legislation to attract voters was essential for Clay, who lacked access to the patronage or funding necessary to sustain a newspaper network
as the secretaries did. All of Clay's congressional speeches were printed by
the *National Intelligencer,* and copied in other newspapers across the country, at no cost to Clay. Since verbatim transcripts were employed, his campaign messaging would be directly conveyed to voters unfiltered by the
media or his adversaries and in exactly the form he wished. Indeed, Clay
spent countless hours correcting the notes the *Intelligencer* editors would
use to typeset his speeches. As an added bonus, drafting and passing legislation comprised the routine duties of a congressman, so Clay could hardly
be accused of electioneering.[56]

Clay called his platform the "American System," a patriotic moniker he
had coined in the Sixteenth Congress, but based on policies he had been
pursuing throughout his career. The American System included high protective tariffs and a network of federally funded internal improvements,

including roads and canals. The Speaker believed that these progressive policies would strengthen the nation's domestic market and shower prosperity on all citizens. Clay argued that America needed his system now more than ever. By bolstering domestic manufacturing, it would help fortify an economy devastated by the Panic of 1819. By building roads and canals, it would improve the weaknesses in the nation's defense infrastructure that the War of 1812 had exposed. By creating interconnections between regions, it would help heal the bonds that had been frayed by the divisive sectional battle over slavery in Missouri and the partisan bickering over the war. In theory, the American System offered tangible progress to every voter. In practice, the devil would be in the details.[57]

Clay focused on internal improvements first, a seemingly prudent course, given that they were wildly popular with the public and many politicians. Despite the broad backing for the general concept of internal improvements, judgment on individual projects was usually based on self-interest. Rather than supporting Clay's theoretical, overarching, planned, and organized system, many politicians and citizens alike assessed public works projects based on their value to personal or local interests. Legislators and the ordinary voters supporting them routinely opposed funding projects in other states that they had supported in their own. In general, westerners coveted increased market access, so they almost always supported federal funding to improve their less developed infrastructure. The mid-Atlantic states usually favored extending their existing system of improvements, but discouraged any that created competitive economic rivals outside the region. New Englanders had already built an excellent system, so they resisted financing any extensions to other regions that might facilitate a drain of their own population. The South, with low population growth, usually rejected nationally subsidizing any projects. Support for federally funded internal improvements managed to be both broad and narrow at the same time.[58]

Apparently unconcerned about the potential political pitfalls surrounding the issue, Clay delivered four dramatic, well-publicized speeches outlining his plans for federally funded internal improvements in the first three months of 1824. "Is not that Union best invigorated by an intimate, social, and commercial connexion between all parts of the confederacy?" Clay argued with his usual rhetorical panache. Prompted by the House Speaker, a committee of the whole drafted a "Bill to procure the necessary Surveys, Plans, and Estimates, upon the subject of Roads and Canals." This legislation allocated $160,000 to map out routes deemed nationally important for commercial, military, or public mail purposes, but largely confined the actual surveying to the western and mid-Atlantic states. After vigorous debate, the House passed the bill 113–86, the Senate concurred by a vote of 25–21, and Monroe signed the legislation on April 30, 1824. Reaction proved predictable, with voices from the South criticizing Clay's bill and those from the West or the mid-Atlantic supporting it. South Carolina governor John Wilson griped that his state "will be grievously assessed, to pay for the cutting of a canal across Cape Cod." Contrarily, Erastus Root, the lieutenant governor of New York, gushed, "Your zeal upon that subject fastens your friends in the western part of this state."[59]

Despite Clay's close association with the issue, one of his presidential rivals also supported federally funded internal improvements. Though Jackson had once insisted unequivocally that only the states possessed the power to fund internal improvements, he now evasively repositioned himself. "Congress can constitutionaly [sic] apply their funds to such objects . . . where they are of a character national, not local," he proclaimed prolixly, "but the general government . . . cannot exercise an exclusive jurisdiction and invade the Soverignty [sic] of the States." He voted for the survey bill and proved quite receptive to funding all defense-related infrastructure during his Senate term. In private discussions, Adams and Crawford paid largely formulaic lip service to the benefits of internal improvements, but offered little concrete action to support the policy. While his rivals may have agreed with him to varying degrees, the public identified Clay as the prime political mover behind federally funded internal improvements. "The industry and talents of the illustrious statesman, CLAY," one Rhode Island newspaper editor waxed lyrically, defeated "a hydra . . . determin[ed] to suppress those marches of national improvement."[60]

Clay followed up his internal improvements victory with a push for new protective tariffs, an issue that usually sparked contentious debate. Tariffs were taxes on imported goods; they had been promoted in the United States as far back as the Washington administration as a means of promoting domestic industry. In the post–Panic of 1819 economy, devastated manufacturers in the mid-Atlantic and northwestern states began demanding new tariffs to help shelter their already-stressed businesses. The southern and southwestern states, with economies more reliant on exporting agricultural produce, and New England, with its numerous connections to international trade, generally objected to any new tariffs that would hike prices for products they purchased or imported. Much like federally funded internal improvements, broad majorities supported tariffs in principle, but in practice only if they protected the narrow special interests in their home regions, states, or localities.[61]

After Clay stocked the House Committee on Manufacturing with pro-tariff representatives, it introduced a "Bill to amend the several acts for imposing Duties on Imports" in January 1824. Congress laboriously bickered over the legislation for two months, with Clay addressing his colleagues on nine occasions. "Are we doomed to behold our industry languish and decay yet more and more?" Clay pleaded. The final tariff bill mandated an ad valorem tax (meaning that the rate was a fixed percentage placed upon the value of the commodity, generally 35 percent) on a host of imports, including burlap, bleached cotton yarn, straw bonnets, marble, lace, carpeting, tarred cordage, tacks, steel wire, anvils, anchors, rifles, cutting knives, iron screws, quills, tiles, black lead pencils, candles, castor oil, wheat flour, potatoes, corks, beer, beef, butter, cayenne pepper, plums, raisins, books, foolscap (a type of paper), window glass, and apothecaries' vials. The broadest and most controversial increased duties were placed on imported iron, woolens, cotton, hemp, and cloth bags.[62]

The bill protected such a diverse array of domestic industries that it corralled support from various localities for different reasons. Hemp growers in Kentucky, cast-iron manufacturers in Pennsylvania, Nantucket's whalers, lead miners in Missouri, sugarcane growers in Louisiana, and textile producers in New York and Ohio all heartily supported it. Conversely, the wide range of taxed imports allowed critics to attack the tariff on specific items. New England's shipbuilders objected to the duties on iron, hemp, and sail duck (a canvas-like fabric), all raw materials essential to their industry. Duties on cotton bags and cheap woolens used for enslaved workers' clothing incensed southern and southwestern cotton planters. Weavers in Massachusetts blasted the increased cost for imported wool. Even temperance advocates complained that taxes on imported spirits would only encourage "a loathsome *still* on every side of the picture." Clay cavalierly dismissed the bill's critics. "Do you ever expect to see a tariff adopted which will satisfy every body?" he demanded hotly. "Perfection in matters of detail, if ever attainable, must be left to the future." The Speaker had apparently concocted the legislation just perfectly enough. In April, it narrowly passed the House 107–102 and the Senate 25–21. Monroe signed the tariff into law in May.[63]

Clay had some prominent company in support of his legislative triumph. Jackson and his fellow Tennessee senator Eaton were the lone "ayes" for the tariff bill from the Southwest. The votes of both men proved crucial to passing the legislation, but supporting the bill was the first potential misstep of the Jackson campaign. The southern slave states were the largest consumers of imported cotton bags. In the Senate committee that worked on the bill, Jackson successfully fought to have the duty on cotton bags lowered. When the bill reached the floor, however, he flip-flopped and supported a compromise—"two immaterial amendments," he claimed dismissively—that reinstated a higher duty on cotton bagging.[64]

Jackson had obviously betrayed the will of his southwestern constituents—and for suggestively political reasons. His change of heart on the cotton bag tariff occurred simultaneously with his battle with Calhoun for Pennsylvania's nomination. Jackson already feared that his pro-Federalist letter had damaged his standing with the notoriously anti-Federalist Pennsylvania Democrats. Passing a tariff that would be popular in the state probably seemed essential to his presidential campaign. Jackson stoutly justified his maneuver, insisting that he had only supported "a careful and judicious Tariff." He insisted that the bill was necessary to protect raw materials essential to the nation's defense infrastructure, to lower the national debt, to avoid tax increases, and to help redistribute labor to an understaffed manufacturing sector. Practically channeling Clay, Jackson proclaimed that "it is time we should become a little more *americanized.*"[65]

While he may have improved his standing in Pennsylvania, Jackson endured a furious negative reaction in his home region. Adamsites in Tennessee staged meetings to denounce Jackson, and even some of his closest friends and family members broke with the general over the issue. Jackson endured an unprecedented torrent of critical press. One Alabama broadsheet heatedly blared that his tariff vote "gave decisive proof that Gen. J. is entirely devoted to this new and oppressive system of taxation." Even Jackson's hometown *Nashville Whig* condemned the general's vote. The furor surrounding his tariff vote rankled Jackson more than any other occurrence in the long election, probably because the general realized his political pandering to Pennsylvanians undercut the very basis of his campaign message against corruption. In the end, Jackson weathered the storm, and most of his regional supporters forgave his tariff apostasy, while his mid-Atlantic backers applauded his vote.[66]

Considering the heat Jackson had taken over his tariff vote, Adams and Crawford wisely remained circumspect about the bill. Employing some politically prudent equivocation, Adams claimed to have little "knowledge of its details" or any "decisive opinion upon them," but he "hoped its operation would be satisfactory to those whose interests it was particularly adopted to promote, without being oppressive upon the agricultural and commercial interests." Daniel Webster, his fellow New Englander and one of the tariff bill's more vocal opponents, carped that "our friend J.Q. is as bad upon it as any of the rest" of the presidential candidates. Yet, one of Adams's supportive newspapers positioned the secretary of state as an opponent of Clay's "extremes of a prohibitory policy." In terms of the tariff, Adams could be depicted as standing on almost any side of the debate.[67]

Crawford also hedged. While insisting that he broadly rejected protectionism, he conceded that tariffs crafted to raise revenue or promote key domestic industries were occasionally necessary. His organization split on the issue. Crawfordite southerners opposed the tariff. Many were openly delighted that the vote on cotton bagging had dented Jackson's seemingly impervious regional popularity. Meanwhile, Crawford's normally tariff-averse northern supporters favored the bill, rationalizing this self-interested stance as a Republican party-building measure.[68]

Whatever his rivals' opinions on the issue, Clay became the public face of the protective tariff movement, just as he had with internal improvements. Unsurprisingly, he received plaudits from the special interests that had supported the bill and criticism from those that had opposed it. "Of all of our public men, I think you best understand the great interests of this great Country," a Rhode Island lawyer raved. Meanwhile, Francis Brooke, Clay's chief supporter in Virginia, lamented that "your Speeches on the Tariff had made a Strong impression against you." Indeed, Clay's tariff bill battered as much as bolstered his presidential campaign. While he had touted the nationwide good that increased taxation would create, Clay devoted three of his nine speeches on the tariff to lauding the hemp industry. When southerners complained about the increased taxes on imported cotton bags, Clay insisted that domestic hemp bags would serve as the ideal replacement.[69]

The optics of his stance proved problematic. Hemp growers were concentrated in his northwestern home region. Clay himself grew the crop, and he was heavily invested in hemp rope manufacturing. Southerners argued that cotton bags far surpassed the hemp version in quality, so Clay was demanding that they spend more money on an inferior product that would enrich him personally and support the already-profitable hemp bag industry in his home state. To some, Clay's legislative work on tariffs and internal improvements seemed to be just more insider maneuvers by a corrupt politician. Detractors denounced both programs as "electioneering schemes" aimed at making Clay president.[70]

In their attempt to appeal to voters at the local level, Jackson, Adams, and Crawford had each abandoned any pretense to a uniform national position on the tariff and internal improvements issues, the former overtly and the later pair more circumspectly. Contrarily, Clay adopted a consistent, national position on both. Since he had hoped to become synonymous with both tariffs and internal improvements in the public's mind, Clay's strategy to run as the issues candidate proved quite successful in that sense. Unfortunately for the Speaker, his problem was not the messaging but the message. Clay had sold protective tariffs for their broad economic value, but critics countered that they simply benefited narrow special interests, including Clay personally, at the expense of national concerns. The Speaker had pushed federally funded internal improvements for their national usefulness, but critics argued that he was simply surveying roads for his constituents in Kentucky at the expense of other states' taxpayers. While he claimed to be the champion of America, his opponents accused Clay of simply dressing his naked self-interest in a handsome nationalist suit. Ultimately, the voters would decide if the clothes fit the man.[71]

International Front: Adams and the Bitter Fruits of Diplomacy

Clay and Jackson may have been held accountable for their votes in Congress, but Adams frequently interacted with the legislature himself, so voters could also judge him for his departmental work. During the perpetual campaign, he averaged nearly 250 official visits with congressmen per month, which did not include his impromptu "chats" at the theater, church, or his residence. Adams usually spent at least a half-hour with each man, with three hours reserved for the truly important discussions. Every presidential campaign required networking with congressmen, but Adams especially relied upon the legislature. Since successful international negotiations served as his principal qualification to succeed Monroe, Adams needed the Senate to sanction the various pacts he submitted for approval.[72]

By 1824, he had already successfully produced an impressive string of diplomatic triumphs, with five treaties accepted by Congress and two more pending. Once the divisive tariff bill finally passed, Adams submitted for Senate approval a slave trade convention that he had negotiated with the British. The agreement had a tortured history. Despite prohibition of the transatlantic slave trade since 1808, illegal privateers had continued to smuggle slaves into America. In 1818, British foreign secretary Lord Castlereagh proposed a slave trade convention with the United States that sanctioned a reciprocal right to search suspicious vessels flying the flag of either nation. Though the ends may have been morally laudable, the entire cabinet rejected Castlereagh's means. Granting the British a right to "visit and search" any American vessel anywhere sounded too much like their practice of impressing US sailors, a still-unresolved issue that had helped trigger the War of 1812. As a former Federalist always suspected of pro-British proclivities, Adams unsurprisingly denounced Castlereagh's proposal more harshly than any other administration figure. Granting the British the right to search American ships "would be making slaves of ourselves," Adams snarled.[73]

The convention proposal gathered dust until 1823, when the US House of Representatives voted 131–9 to define the slave trade as piracy, instructing the Monroe administration to negotiate its abolishment with any European maritime power. The "piracy" designation served as an attractive fig leaf, concealing the fine line between searching for slave traders and impressing American sailors. Adams drafted a new proposed convention with Britain. It sanctioned a reciprocal right of search once both nations had officially declared the slave trade to be piracy, ensured captured traders would be tried in their home countries, demanded indemnities for abuses of the right to search, and forbade removal of any person from any vessel, the so-called anti-impressment clause.[74]

After both nations signed the new convention, Adams submitted the treaty to the Senate for approval on a stormy morning in May 1824. In an election year, the ensuing political storm was utterly predictable. While there had been broad agreement in Congress only one year prior for permitting reciprocal searches for slave traders, the Senate summarily rejected Adams's latest handiwork. Crawfordites organized a showy public campaign, sensationally accusing Adams of abandoning the United States' traditional opposition to impressment. Ironically, in the cabinet debates surrounding the convention, Adams had been the loudest voice opposing British searches of American ships. Crawford, who had been the principal proponent of moderating Adams's tough initial stand against the British, now claimed he had never approved of the secretary of state's concessions; his supporters portrayed him as chief critic of impressment. The Senate amended the convention to restrict searches to the African coastline only and ratified the treaty 29–13. The British rejected the American alterations, and the convention was never enacted.[75]

Adams tried to defend himself with an unsigned, lawyerly editorial in the *National Intelligencer*, carefully distinguishing between the right of searching pirate vessels against the right of search in general, but he became enmeshed in yet another dustup with the Crawford-leaning newspaper. When the *Intelligencer* published documents related to the treaty, they curiously omitted the 1823 House reports that had reopened negotiations and sanctioned a British right to search in the first place. The documents were "suppressed on the pretext of a want of room for them," Adams fumed, yet they had enough space for "nearly a whole column of counter-argument." Crawfordites gleefully spread a rumor that Adams himself had deliberately withheld the documents. Though the *Intelligencer*'s editors apologized for the oversight, they were furious when Adams reprinted the House reports in his own *National Journal*.[76]

As the imbroglio played out, Crawfordites surreptitiously circulated a handbill alleging that Adams opposed any suppression of the slave trade, while Crawford, vice president of the American Colonization Society since its 1817 inception, staunchly favored curtailing the odious practice. Criticizing Adams's slave trade convention proved doubly advantageous as an electioneering tool to his presidential rivals. The former Federalist Adams could be painted as soft on impressment, and derailing the treaty sullied his glorious record of diplomatic achievement, the very foundation of his presidential campaign.[77]

Like many northern politicians, the secretary of state had a complicated relationship with slavery. As a senator in the early 1800s, Adams voted against prohibiting the importation of slaves into the Louisiana Territory. As an American diplomat and secretary, he championed southern claims for compensation for slaves removed by British forces during the War of 1812, helped US citizens attempting to extradite escaped slaves from Canada, and opposed the American Colonization Society's attempt to repatriate free blacks to Africa. Despite his severe private reservations, Adams publicly supported the Missouri Compromise, which admitted a slave state into the union.[78]

While he may have publicly compromised with slavery, in private, and almost exclusively with his antislavery supporters from New England, Adams often sounded much more like an abolitionist. He insisted that "slavery is the great and foul stain upon the North American Union," and prayed for its total "extirpation." Because he needed support from all sections to win the presidency, Adams's public/private dichotomy allowed him to talk tough with northerners opposed to slavery without seeming tough on slavery to southerners. As a vote-seeking politico, he prudently never answered any letters that requested his opinions on any slavery-related issue. Trying to straddle both sides cautiously left Adams open to a multipronged attack. Crawford's northern supporters claimed Adams favored extending slavery, while southern Crawfordites alleged he favored restricting it. Adams hoped that voters would remember his numerous successful diplomatic forays rather than the election-year failure of the slave trade convention.[79]

A. B. Unmasked! The Many Faces of Ninian Edwards

Like Adams, Crawford conducted his own election year business with Congress, but his work proved even more combative. While the 1823 congressional investigation into A. B.'s shocking charges over criminal corruption had exonerated him of any wrongdoing, as we saw in chapter 4, the House still had an outstanding resolution from May 1822 requesting the Treasury Department's correspondence with western banks regarding government deposits. The voluminous documents and Crawford's intervening illness delayed the project, but the secretary finally complied with the resolution in March 1824.

In his cover letter with the submitted correspondence, Crawford disputed the testimony that Illinois senator Ninian Edwards had made during the House's 1823 A. B. investigation. Edwards had claimed that as a director of the Bank of Edwardsville in 1819, he had instructed the bank's receiver, Benjamin Stephenson, to withhold acceptance of public funds because the bank was in danger of failing. In Edwards's presence, Stephenson had written to Crawford communicating these dangers, but he subsequently received written orders from the treasury secretary to deposit public funds anyway. When the Bank of Edwardsville eventually failed, the government lost the deposits it had placed there. If Edwards had testified truthfully, then Crawford may have indeed been guilty of malfeasance, as A. B. had been mercilessly insisting throughout the previous year. Crawford's cover letter challenged Edwards directly. He informed the House definitively "that no such letter from the Receiver is to be found in the files of the Department; that the officers employed in it have no recollection of the receipt of such a letter; and that . . . no answer to any such letter, directing the Receiver to continue the deposits, was ever written to him by the Secretary of the Treasury." Either Edwards or Crawford was lying, and because Stephenson had died in 1822, there appeared to be no way to resolve the dispute.[80]

Following Edwards's testimony during the A. B. investigation, Monroe had appointed him minister to Mexico. On the verge of departing for his new assignment when Crawford submitted his accusatory letter to the House, Edwards prepared a reply while en route, dispatching it to Speaker Clay from Wheeling, Virginia. While he ludicrously "disclaimed any other construction" of his accusations "than the most innocent of which they are susceptible," Edwards's latest missive insisted unequivocally that Crawford had mismanaged his departmental funds. He maintained that the treasury secretary had accepted unredeemable paper notes from western banks in contravention of an 1816 congressional resolution, underreported the amount of those notes in his reports to Congress, illegally deposited public money in failing banks, deliberately suppressed documents proving these charges, and committed perjury during the House's 1823 investigation. Perhaps most explosively of all, Edwards admitted that he himself was the mysterious A. B.[81]

The minister's letter dropped like a bomb right into the middle of the presidential race. As the charges and countercharges flew, the salacious scandal embroiled the principals, Congress, and the administration in an entrancing public scandal. "One or the other must fall never to rise again," Jackson proclaimed excitedly. "It was politically a question of life and death to them both," Calhoun agreed.[82]

Hardly a stranger to political controversy, Edwards had been long involved in Washington's insider political machinations. He was born into a well-connected Maryland family; he entered politics in Kentucky and aligned with the Pope family, Clay's principal rivals in the state. After creation of the Illinois Territory in 1809, Edwards's powerful friends in Washington secured his appointment as the second governor. Once Illinois became a state, the legislature picked Edwards as its first senator in 1818. Serving in the national capital during the perpetual 1824 campaign, Edwards naturally became enmeshed in the presidential race. Edwards initially backed Adams, but he switched to Calhoun after the secretary of war promised to help secure his diplomatic appointment. As a member of the secretary of war's organization, Edwards unsuccessfully conspired to replace the *National Intelligencer* with Calhoun's own *Republican* as the official printer of Congress and eagerly became the prime purveyor of rumors that Clay had been behind Russell's attack against Adams using the Ghent letters. When Calhoun dropped out of the race, Edwards admitted to Adams that he had switched to the secretary of war only because Calhoun seemed better positioned to defeat Crawford, Edwards's "paramount" objective. Adams gratefully welcomed the return of his capricious crony.[83]

Both sides tried to control the narrative surrounding the blossoming A. B. scandal. Edwards's supporters claimed that Crawford had deliberately procrastinated in submitting the documents until Edwards had left town and would be unable to defend himself. Crawfordites responded that, in fact, Edwards had been in Washington when Crawford's cover letter reached Congress, and he had purposely departed, leaving his false accusations to influence voters in the fall. The treasury secretary himself had always suspected that Edwards was part of a coterie of Calhounites behind the "insidious conspiracy."[84]

Pressured by Crawfordites, Clay had little choice but to convene a select House committee to investigate the entire affair. The Speaker carefully balanced the committee's politics. It included three Crawfordites, Chairman John Floyd, his fellow Virginian John Randolph, and George Owen of Alabama; Adams's House leader John W. Taylor; Clay's own ally from Ohio, Duncan McArthur; Louisiana Jacksonian Edward Livingston; and Webster, who had favored the now-withdrawn Calhoun. The select committee immediately demanded that Edwards return and testify, dispatching the House's assistant doorkeeper to locate and escort Edwards back to the capital.[85]

Since Monroe had just selected him as minister to Mexico, Edwards's stunning revelation also directly entangled the administration in the scandal. Crawfordites insisted that a nefarious quid pro quo had occurred. Edwards had supplied the anonymous A. B. slanders against Crawford, and the president had rewarded him with a plum diplomatic assignment. "Having sown his seed," Van Buren hissed, "he obtained from Mr. Monroe the appointment." Exasperated, Monroe blamed Edwards for dragging him into a controversy related to the presidential election. He convened three emergency cabinet meetings—excluding Crawford, of course—to plot the administration's response to the crisis. The cabinet debated immediately recalling Edwards. Adams and Calhoun objected. "A prodigious stir has been made about catching him . . . to excite odium against him," Adams sputtered. "[It] had been used to divert public attention from the merits of his allegations . . . and to prepare for a whitewashing of Crawford." The secretary of state certainly understood that tactic; he had employed the same strategy in destroying both Jonathan Russell and his Ghent accusations. In the end, Monroe only ordered Edwards to stop and await any congressional command to return.[86]

In one unprecedented fourteen-hour marathon session, the cabinet also debated Edwards's potential "resignation" as minister. Monroe favored forcing him out immediately. "He would thereby disengage himself and the Executive from the imputation of a concert together," he reasoned desperately. Adams hoped to let Edwards resign of his own accord, while Calhoun "warmly" objected to any removal of Edwards, arguing that even his resignation would be tantamount to an admission of guilt. The trio based their divergent opinions on personal political calculations—Monroe was protecting his personal reputation, Adams his ally, and Calhoun his longstanding campaign against Crawford. Ultimately, Monroe acceded to his subordinates' wishes and decided to retain Edwards while the congressional investigation played out.[87]

While the capital breathlessly awaited Edwards's return, the select committee proceeded with its investigation. With Edwards unavailable, the group produced an initial report on Crawford's activities to be supplemented by Edwards's testimony when he eventually returned. The committee's preliminary findings covered six accusations. They agreed on six points. First, Crawford could not be charged with "having mismanaged public funds." Second, Crawford had indeed accepted notes not backed by specie from some banks in repayment for their treasury debts, which had been forbidden by the 1816 congressional resolution, but he had correctly done so to prevent more bank failures. Third, with only one minor omission, Crawford had not misreported the amount of those "uncurrent notes" that the treasury had received from the banks. Fourth, while he may have "misconstrued the effects" of the contracts between some banks and the treasury, he had not deliberately misled Congress because he had submitted the actual contracts with his reports to the legislature. Fifth, Crawford had failed to inform Congress about the public deposits in three local banks, but it had been an accidental oversight. Sixth, Crawford had excluded some of his personal correspondence with bank directors from his congressional reports, but the "papers so omitted were immaterial" and not "withheld from some improper motives."[88]

Edwards's supporters reacted furiously when Crawford's numerous "excuses" were conveniently accepted. "Was it lawful to allow a bank, or any body, to use public money for one or two years, or a single day, and return it in depreciated notes?" Samuel Ingham protested hotly. Edwards's defenders complained that the intimidating power of a potential Crawford presidency had unduly biased the committee against him. Even some Crawfordites expressed surprise that a House committee comprised of conflicting candidate supporters would issue a report so favorable to Crawford, especially during a superheated election year. Edwards had not fared so well, however. In perhaps the greatest blow to his credibility, the investigation discovered that many western bank directors, including Edwards, had pressured Crawford to invest public money in their failing institutions during the panic. The exact crime that he had charged Crawford with committing had been "very much desired and promoted by Edwards himself," one Adamsite noted resignedly.[89]

The new report that Crawford submitted to the committee had been presented and partially written by his chief clerk. Unfortunately for the treasury secretary, just two days before his testimony was scheduled to begin, Crawford suffered a relapse of his illness. In this latest bout, he suffered partial paralysis, his tongue swelled, which slurred his speech, his eyesight became blurry, and, most troubling of all, he experienced hallucinations, raving that Ninian Edwards was stealing his horses and planning to shoot him. "He appeared to be much more infirm than Mr. Jefferson at the age of 82," one visitor reported of the 52-year-old Crawford. The Washington rumor mill was again abuzz with speculation that Crawford's relapse would force him out of the race, but much to the chagrin of his political foes, Crawford once again escaped death. Although plagued by ongoing speech and vision difficulties, Crawford had largely recovered by September. He could walk firmly, read newspapers, and write in a scrawl; in November he resumed attending cabinet meetings.[90]

As Crawford recuperated, his accuser finally returned to Washington. Edwards reappeared in late May and faced the select committee in June. Erstwhile Calhounite Samuel Ingham coached Edwards on his written submission to the investigators, suggesting the weaknesses in Crawford's testimony that Edwards could exploit. "Do not forget that you are writing for the popular eye and ear, which requires things be made plain," Ingham counseled. "Let your reply be mild, and forbear to draw any conclusions as to motives." Unfortunately for Edwards, his testimony and the witnesses he called largely rehashed the information the committee had already reviewed and dismissed in the month prior. Even more damaging, the House members deeply probed his own role as A. B. When seeking confirmation as minister to Mexico in March, he had strongly implied under oath that he was not the mysterious anti-Crawford author. Several witnesses testified that Edwards had "positively and solemnly denied" being A. B., dismissed A. B.'s anti-Crawford accusations, and even praised the secretary's "integrity and propriety" in managing the treasury. The committee's final report, issued on June 21, echoed their preliminary investigation and totally exonerated Crawford. Edwards's lies had severely damaged his own standing, so he received most of the public condemnation. Still, the final report hardly represented a total victory for Crawford, given that it documented a number of his mistakes, misstatements, and dubious decisions. Crawford's reputation as a competent financier, tarnished by hints of corruption, certainly suffered.[91]

While the Senate had long adjourned, Van Buren remained in Washington to watch over the House proceedings and surreptitiously review the committee's final report. It "did not contain a single harsh comment" about Edwards, Van Buren related, "a feature which I was very desirous it should possess and to which I took some pains to reconcile our friends who were naturally excited and justly indignant." Indeed, the committee had predictably fractured along partisan lines, pitting supporters of the opposing presidential contenders against each other. Crawfordites sought to laud Crawford's administrative skills and censure Edwards's "frivolous and malicious" accusations. Supporters of the other candidates tried to expunge all criticism of Edwards and moderate the "proposed panegyric" of Crawford. Sparing Edwards in the report was another of Van Buren's political masterstrokes, however, because it gave the document the appearance of impartiality rather than of being a partisan Crawfordite whitewash of their candidate's transgressions. The report ensured public awareness of Edwards's lies, but seemed reasonable because it avoided personal attacks or even censure of the embattled Minister. Because he appeared to have lied about Crawford's activities with western banks, deliberately misled the Senate to receive his ministerial appointment, and then fled after making his false accusations, Edwards's public reputation had been utterly ruined.[92]

Edwards's troubling testimony sparked yet another crisis for the administration. Not only had the president's hand-picked minister clearly lied under oath during his confirmation hearings, but Calhoun had been implicated in furthering the plot against Crawford. The committee discovered that Edwards's original charges against the treasury secretary had not been mailed directly to Clay, to whom they were addressed, but in fact had come to the House through the War Department. Edwards refused to answer direct questions about Calhoun's involvement in the affair, and when he was about to admit that the secretary of war had recommended him as minister to Mexico, Livingston cut him off. "This stopping of the testimony would operate worse on the public mind than if everything had come out," Adams noted despairingly. Openly blaming Monroe for the A. B. attacks, Crawfordites publicly pressured the administration to sack their devious minister. Meanwhile, Edwards's supporters claimed that a good man would be sacrificed to further Crawford's presidential bid. "The President was so harassed that he scarcely knew where to set his foot," Navy Secretary Samuel Southard acknowledged.[93]

Monroe convened three more emergency cabinet meetings to address the fiasco. The sessions included two exhausting daylong discussions, with the men eating their meals together and working late into the evening. Calhoun admitted that he had indeed received Edwards's packet of charges before it reached the select committee. Adams argued for full disclosure given that the unpleasant truth had already become public knowledge, but Wirt and Southard convinced Monroe to avoid admitting anything that "might connect unnecessarily the Administration with the odium." Monroe and almost the entire cabinet agreed that Edwards should be terminated to prevent "the Government itself catching the infection with which his name is tainted." Only Adams defended him, insisting that the committee had not censured Edwards, but in fact proved that Crawford had made "glaring misstatements," just as Edwards had charged.[94]

The meetings devolved into gripe sessions condemning the treasury secretary and reviewing in minute detail his every offense since 1819. The entire cabinet agreed that "Crawford's career had been an uninterrupted series of attacks upon the Administration, always disavowed or disguised by himself." Adams insisted that Crawford never renounced or restrained the perfidious conduct of his Radical friends. Calhoun complained about Crawford's dereliction of duty during his illness, including illegally authorizing his daughter to sign his name on official documents. Monroe produced an 1822 letter—the president seemed to always have old, politically valuable correspondence at the ready—in which Crawford blamed Adams and Calhoun for the "prejudices against him."[95]

Amid all the Crawford-bashing, the cabinet received word that Edwards had resigned, solving that problem for them. The embattled minister insisted that Crawford was guilty, but he quit to spare Monroe any further embarrassment. Unfortunately for Edwards, by resigning, he only seemed to confirm that he had lied under oath to obtain the appointment, and his reputation had been completely destroyed. Although later elected governor of Illinois, he never again played any role in Washington politics.[96]

The entire A. B. episode was probably a combination of traps that Calhoun and Crawford had tried to spring on each other. Calhoun's organization, including Monroe, seemed to know A. B.'s secret identity from the outset. "I look with some curiosity for 'A. B.,'" Calhounite Southard, with tongue firmly in cheek, wrote teasingly to Edwards during A. B.'s initial revelations in 1823. "He is a troublesome fellow. I wish I could find him out." Crawford's informants reported that Calhoun had been secretly closeted with Edwards for hours on end, presumably working on Edwards's report to the select committee. "I never doubted that the plot against my reputation was your handi-work and originated in a brain so fertile in mischief," Crawford contemptuously informed Calhoun after the election was over.[97]

Monroe and Calhoun countered that Crawford had deliberately reignited the controversy in 1824 to embarrass the administration and tarnish Calhoun's candidacy. The A. B. issue had "in great measure been forgotten" since 1823, Monroe insisted. Crawford calculatingly waited until Monroe appointed Edwards as his minister to send his cover letter to Congress. He planned to catch Edwards in a lie, simultaneously implicating the president and the secretary of war in an insidious intrigue to scuttle his candidacy. The entire affair "has been one of the most painful of my public life," Monroe lamented.[98]

If Crawford and Calhoun had indeed engineered two countervailing traps, nearly every power player in the election tumbled into them. The president's minister, a close political ally of the secretary of state, had charged the secretary of the treasury with committing crimes and published his accusations in the secretary of war's newspaper, with the entire affair papered over by the Speaker's committee. It had been a sorry spectacle indeed and probably reinforced the public's perception that Washington was a cesspool of corruption. As usual, though, one candidate adroitly sidestepped the mess entirely. Jackson had recused himself from the case. "I would not sit upon his trial," the general insisted. "It is a subject I intend to take no part in." Wisely, and perhaps purposely, Jackson avoided the issue that ordinary citizens most closely associated with corruption in the capital.[99]

For political junkies, the A. B. incident served as a microcosm of the election itself. It pitted multiple candidate organizations against each other, with the fight conducted dramatically within Congress. It featured dueling rumors, correspondence that both hurt and helped, and social politics deployed as a weapon. It had been fueled by a scuffle over patronage and

energized by side-switching politicians routinely transferring their allegiance among the presidential candidates. It boasted the most spectacular
cabinet war of the entire election, with breathless coverage in the newspapers eagerly devoured by the electorate. As with every other episode in the
long campaign, those voters would have the final say over the meaning of
the A. B. affair.

Conflicting Strategies: Varied
Approaches to a Politics of Corruption

With the fiery resolution of the A. B. episode, the campaign entered its
waning months. Each candidate adopted a different strategy for his final
appeal to voters. Crawford's effort had always relied primarily on elite politicians. Since he had been sidelined by illness, he turned to Van Buren to
take charge of his faltering campaign. Fortunately for Crawford, Van Buren
was the ultimate Washington insider and wily political fixer, a man his enemies insisted was "as slippery as an Eel." The New York senator had arrived
in Washington in 1821 without a preferred presidential candidate, but soon
gravitated to Crawford. A firm believer in the positive societal worth of political parties and earnest champion of partisan unity, Van Buren blamed
Monroe for the Republican Party's disintegration and believed the treasury
secretary was best suited to reunite their warring factions. Crawford also
represented a continuation of the Virginia/New York axis's control over
presidential politics, which conveniently increased Van Buren's personal
political power. He tried to apply at a national level the same tactics of party
management and discipline that he had used so effectively in state politics.
"I made my *debut* in the art and business of President-making," Van Buren
recalled proudly.[100]

Van Buren certainly needed all of his numerous political skills, because
the Crawford campaign had reached a critical stage. It had been an underwhelming year for the treasury secretary. Crawford had been attacked as a
scheming intriguer, his caucus nomination had been only weakly supported,
his reputation for competency had been undermined in a sensational

congressional hearing, and now he was too sick to manage his own presidential run. Not ones to spare the wounded front-runner, his rivals piled on with a fresh attack. As secretary of war in 1816, Crawford had submitted a report on Indian affairs that claimed Native Americans faced extinction unless they became more Americanized. "Let intermarriages between them and whites be encouraged by the government," he argued, because Indians were superior to "the fugitives of the old world." His 1824 opponents dusted off the old report, charging in a new pamphlet that Crawford was an aristocrat, bigoted against European immigrants with an indecent bias in favor of Native Americans. The new attack only further diminished his fading popularity.[101]

Van Buren decided it was high time to bring out the big gun: none other than the revered father of the Republican Party, Thomas Jefferson. He knew that Jefferson preferred Crawford as Monroe's successor, and he hoped the iconic founder would publicly endorse the treasury secretary. Gaining open support from the elder statesman would surely boost Crawford's crippled candidacy. It helped that Jefferson had little affection for Crawford's principal antagonist. As Virginia gentlemen, Monroe and Jefferson maintained superficially cordial relations, but the pair secretly disliked each other intensely. "His enmity to Mr. Monroe was inveterate, though disguised, and he was at the bottom of all the opposition to Mr. Monroe in Virginia," Monroe's son-in-law George Hay insisted.[102]

On a visit to Monticello, Van Buren listened courteously as the nattering old politico rambled on about his turn-of-the-century conflicts with those reprehensible Federalists. "He seemed never to tire in his review of the past," Van Buren observed politely, but his mission ended in failure. While Jefferson admitted to favoring Crawford, no formal endorsement would be forthcoming. The former president claimed his age "forever excluded [him] from any interest in the management of public concerns." Jefferson's disappointing decision practically typified Crawford's entire campaign—enthusiastic support from the political elite that never translated into broad public appeal.[103]

While Crawford's late electoral efforts were relatively staid, Clay commenced one of the most aggressive stretches of his entire campaign. He dispatched his close ally, Louisiana senator Josiah Johnston, to New York and Philadelphia in June in a last-ditch attempt to capture the mid-Atlantic states. Johnston complained that Clay had neglected to organize his many supporters there, so "the other parties have gain'd ground by our supineness." To remedy the situation, he created committees of correspondence centered in New York City and Philadelphia, and they initiated a furious flurry of letter writing. He arranged meetings between the Speaker's allies and then widely disseminated the resultant addresses and resolutions. Clay's mid-Atlantic effort had been so unassuming that the regional newspaper war had ignored him almost as much as Jackson. "There is one advantage at least you enjoy by having no press," Johnston admitted ruefully. "You certainly provoke no hostility."[104]

To rectify the situation, Johnston finally established a newspaper network dedicated to Clay's candidacy. He secured the Philadelphia *Aurora* and the *Patriot* in New York City for Clay, penned laudatory articles about the Speaker for inclusion, and sent copies of the final printed broadsheets to Clay's friends in eight states. He was so desperate for press coverage that Johnston even accepted editorial support from two Federalist papers in New York. For his own part, and still cognizant of the issue-oriented nature of his campaign, Clay encouraged Ralph Ingersoll Lockwood, a young New York lawyer, to compose a pamphlet extolling the Speaker's stance on federally funded internal improvements and protective tariffs. Clay himself tweaked a circular praising his nationalist views that had been published by his Kentucky committee of correspondence. Johnston scattered thousands of copies of both hagiographic pamphlets across the union.[105]

The newfound urgency suddenly animating Clay's forces seemed barely to change the trajectory of his campaign, however. The exchange of correspondence amounted to little more than the same men who had been supporting Clay from the outset circulating feel-good letters among themselves. The meetings Johnston organized were sparsely attended, and though Clay's diminutive press network began churning out newspapers, they were fewer in numbers and years behind those of his rivals. Even stressing the issues behind his candidacy seemingly failed to deliver the votes. Clay petulantly grumbled that southern opposition to his tariff policy had not been "counterbalanced by any espousal of my cause in Pennsa. and other quarters, where the Tariff was so much desired." Johnston correctly blamed Clay's dearth of mid-Atlantic state support on his lackluster, unorthodox campaign strategy. "Your Cause . . . sank everywhere under the want of direction & management," he admitted with chagrin. "With a little activity & money a sufficient number of presses would have been engaged." Unfortunately for Clay, his vigorous push in the waning months seemed far too little and much too late to affect the outcome of the race.[106]

Because he had already conducted a more energetic campaign than Clay, Adams remained much less active than the Speaker as the election approached. The secretary of state went home in September to visit his father. The pair were quite close, so Adams hoped to quash a false rumor that the elder Adams had declined to bequeath his estate to his son that had produced "unfavorable political impressions concerning my personal character." Adams spent a month in New England, carefully tending to his core constituency. He flatly declined to appear at a grand public dinner in his honor held at Faneuil Hall in Boston, claiming that it might be labeled a political stunt. Instead, he hosted a series of intimate private dinners for his closest allies, which could hardly be labeled as electioneering by his rivals. Adams diligently reminded his guests that he alone could best represent their interests and secure their patronage positions. Long the master of social campaigning, Adams's final exertions once again demonstrated his supremacy in this aspect of the war for votes.[107]

Jackson avoided obvious electioneering as much as Adams did. Instead of scrambling like Crawford and Clay, he rested quietly at home, expecting to reap the electoral rewards of his well-conducted campaign. Like much of the general's good fortune through the long election, another lucky coincidence dropped directly into his lap. In August 1824, one of the few living Revolutionary War figures made a triumphant return to the scene of his heroic youthful exploits. Invited in celebration of the fiftieth anniversary of the nation's independence, Marie-Joseph Paul Yves Roch Gilbert du Motier, known popularly as the Marquis de Lafayette, spent the next thirteen months traveling by stagecoach and steamboat to all twenty-four states. He visited battlefields, attended veterans' reunions, and witnessed spectacular entertainments staged in his honor. Poets wrote odes feting him, artists painted noble portraits of his likeness, young women strewed flowers in his path, and tens of thousands of Americans personally witnessed the living legend as he progressed on his epic journey. As we shall see, the warm glow enveloping Lafayette reflected favorably on Jackson, reminding ordinary citizens that another popular military hero was seeking their votes in the upcoming election.[108]

Most commentators remarked on the European political implications of Lafayette's tour, noting the unflattering contrast between democracy in the United States and the despotism of Bourbon France. Lafayette's impact on American politics may have been greater still. His iconic image served as a stark counterpoint to the lingering problems that had plagued the United States for over a decade. His battlefield success in the revolution contrasted unfavorably with the military failures of the War of 1812. His antislavery views rebuked the concessions to slaveholders in the Missouri Compromise. His unselfish service to the young American republic reproached the greedy commercialism that many believed had prompted the Panic of 1819. For Americans worried that their nation was in decline, Lafayette's visit only reminded them just how far from their founding ideals they had tumbled. With a strong sense of nostalgia as their founders were dying one by one, tinged with fears that the next generation of leaders would not live up to their valiant forebears, Lafayette's visit chafed a raw nerve in the American psyche.[109]

Because he was acclaimed throughout the union, Lafayette's appeal cut across all partisan, political, and factional lines. Every presidential candidate naturally tried to bask in the reflected glory from the famous Frenchman. In early October, Clay personally wrote and widely publicized the patriotic resolution inviting Lafayette to Kentucky. Adams made an even splashier connection. In October, he spent five ballyhooed days with Lafayette. In Philadelphia, the pair met a dying woman in the Pennsylvania Hospital for Sick and Insane Persons, passed through a line of surly convicts at the penitentiary, reviewed a parade of over 4,000 schoolchildren, and listened to orphans singing hymns. They also visited Independence Hall and examined a Spanish chestnut tree that George Washington had planted before his retirement. For his part, Crawford eagerly led the cabinet delegation that welcomed Lafayette to Washington in mid-October. In return, Lafayette publicly expressed his personal friendship with the treasury secretary—the pair had met when Crawford served as minister to France in 1813. Almost every contender attempted to drape Lafayette's heroic mantle at least partially around their own candidacy.[110]

Jackson alone never interacted with Lafayette before the election. Although he had been in the crowd that witnessed the Marquis's landing in Charleston in 1777, he only officially met Lafayette in December 1824, when they accidentally ran into each other in the Washington hotel where both were staying. Despite lacking a preelection connection, Jackson benefited enormously from Lafayette's visit nonetheless. As a tribute to his victory in the Battle of New Orleans, Jackson had been presented with Washington's spyglass and pistols, the latter originally a gift from Lafayette. Cleverly, he connected these artifacts with his own presidential bid. "To be thought worthy of this deposit," he informed Rachel, "[is] a triump [sic] over my enemies, of honest worth, over corruption." His supporters also grasped the connection. "In one word," a Jacksonian from Pennsylvania gushed, "*he has acted like a Washington.*"[111]

During the revolution, the thirteen-year-old Jackson had served as a courier for the local militia in South Carolina. Once captured by the British, as a prisoner-of-war Jackson was treated inhumanely, confined in an underground cell, and almost starved to death. Should any voter forget Jackson's connection to the nation's storied past, the *Letters of Wyoming* earnestly reminded them to "Remember, he was of the Revolution!" In the ongoing political struggle between liberty and power, Wyoming insisted that Jackson was the champion of the republicanism handed down from the founders. Fortunately for Jackson, nostalgic voters celebrating Lafayette's visit and concerned about the declension of the nation's corrupt politics probably could not help but remember Jackson's own connection to the revolution as they cast their ballots in the fall.[112]

As the perpetual campaign finally neared its compelling conclusion, the insiders were clearly running differently than Jackson the outsider. Crawford pinned his hopes on high-profile establishment figures, Clay on belatedly matching the efforts of other campaigns, and Adams on his skill at social politicking with other insiders. Only Jackson seemed truly connected to Lafayette's unprecedented, triumphal tour. In the end, the voters would decide whether the insiders or the outsider deserved to succeed Monroe. As we will see in chapter 6, Jackson's populism proved well suited, and Crawford's elitism ill suited, to increasingly democratized presidential elections. Meanwhile, Clay's issue-oriented campaign and Adams's socializing were important aspects of the emerging Jacksonian presidential politics. As the candidates prepared to face their judgment, none knew what to expect from the unconventional one-party election, however. Adams, expressing what all of them probably felt, fretted, "Prospects everywhere, nothing to be relied upon anywhere."[113]

6

→ • ←

The War within the States

"A MAN DRAWN BY FOUR horses or a carriage by eight to the four cardinal points of the compass are an admirable hieroglyphic of our approaching presidential election," Adams suggested cogently. Indeed, with the exception of the mid-Atlantic states, each region had fielded a champion expected to succeed with the voters in their area—Adams in New England, Crawford in the South, Jackson in the Southwest, and Clay in the Northwest. Candidates were generally sympathetic and knowledgeable about the needs and concerns of voters from their home base, but to win the presidency they required at least an aura of nationalism to attract voters from other regions. As a result of the complexity of running twenty-four state campaigns, however, no candidate competed in every state or even every region. Unsurprisingly, candidates focused on competitive areas where they believed they possessed at least a chance to win, so the race winnowed down to five somewhat individual races—Adams versus Crawford in New England, Crawford versus Jackson in the South, Jackson versus Adams and Clay in the Southwest, Clay versus Jackson and Adams in the Northwest, and a four-candidate free-for-all in the mid-Atlantic states.[1]

To achieve victory, each candidate had to navigate through opposing currents. Voters from different states or regions would judge by distinct sets of standards. For instance, the Panic of 1819 had not affected all Americans equally. It had amplified the divide between debtors and creditors, artisans and farmers, and exporters and importers while pitting towns against cities, the coast against the interior, and state against state. Most debtors lived in the South and the West, but owed money to creditors from the North and the East. Similarly, tariffs were generally more popular in the North than the South, while the East resisted federally funded internal improvements that westerners coveted. The Missouri Compromise had created two schisms; it had not only divided an antislavery North from a proslavery South, it also split East from West. Many westerners strongly objected to eastern politicians controlling a western state in ways that no eastern state would permit. Regardless of a citizen's pro- or antislavery sentiments, reaction to the compromise also intensified in proportion to a state's proximity to Missouri. Meanwhile, the threat of Federalism and the opposition to amalgamation mattered far more in the older states, where the Federalists persisted as a minority political force, than in newer states that never experienced the "taint" of Federalism. These conflicting circumstances complicated campaigning; positions popular in Georgia might repel voters in Illinois and vice versa.[2]

One issue transcended and encompassed all these concerns. Many voters worried that corruption had overtaken the political system. One of Jackson's correspondents enumerated "the aberration[s] (from the old republican principles)" which has infected the political process: "The excessive accumulation of offices, . . . the affectation of European & princely etiquette . . . the lust of office and pride of power about the seat of the General government." Only hypervigilant voters could ensure that their political leaders would honor the nation's traditional republican values.[3]

By an act of Congress, voting occurred between October 27 and December 1. Most states featured statewide winner-take-all popular elections for electors, while some chose electors by district; only six states retained the legislature's control over elector selection. Franchise laws and turnout varied greatly by state (see table 1). In rural areas especially, any convenient location could serve as a polling place for popular elections, including post offices, stores, or even private homes. Election officials usually remained inside with the ballot box and voter records while voters stayed outside and handed their ballot to the officials through a window. Eligibility generally went unchallenged unless the voter was not recognized by the officials. There were no "official" ballots. Tickets, with the candidate's name followed

TABLE 1. Election data by state in the presidential election of 1824

STATE	ELECTION TYPE	ENFRANCHISEMENT	TURNOUT (% OF ELIGIBLE VOTERS)	CANDIDATES
NEW ENGLAND				
Connecticut	Statewide popular	Property requirement (most white males could vote)	15	Adams; Crawford
Maine	Popular by district plus 2 statewide	All white males could vote	Unknown	Adams; Crawford
Massachusetts	Statewide popular	Taxpaying qualification (most white males could vote)	30	Adams; Crawford
New Hampshire	Statewide popular	All white males could vote	Unknown	Adams
Rhode Island	Statewide popular	Property requirement (only 1/2 white males could vote)	12	Adams; unpledged
Vermont	Legislative	—	—	—
SOUTH				
Georgia	Legislative	—	—	—
North Carolina	Statewide popular	Taxpaying qualification (most white males could vote)	42	Crawford; Jackson
South Carolina	Legislative	—	—	—
Virginia	Statewide popular	Property requirement (only 1/2 white males could vote)	12	Adams; Clay; Crawford; Jackson

(continued)

TABLE 1. Election data by state in the presidential election of 1824 (*continued*)

STATE	ELECTION TYPE	ENFRANCHISEMENT	TURNOUT (% OF ELIGIBLE VOTERS)	CANDIDATES
SOUTHWEST				
Alabama	Statewide popular	All white males could vote	50	Adams; Clay; Crawford; Jackson
Louisiana	Legislative	—	—	—
Mississippi	Statewide popular	Taxpayers; property-owning militiamen	46	Adams; Jackson
Tennessee	Popular by district	Freeholders with at least 6 months' residence	27	Adams; Clay; Crawford; Jackson
NORTHWEST				
Illinois	Popular by district	All white males could vote	25	Adams; Clay; Crawford; Jackson
Indiana	Statewide popular	All white males could vote	37	Adams; Clay; Jackson
Kentucky	Popular by district	White males with 2 years' rural or 1 years' urban residence	25	Adams; Clay; Crawford; Jackson
Missouri	Popular by district	All white males could vote	20	Adams; Clay; Jackson
Ohio	Statewide popular	Taxpaying qualification (most white males could vote)	37	Adams; Clay; Jackson

STATE	ELECTION TYPE	ENFRANCHISEMENT	TURNOUT (% OF ELIGIBLE VOTERS)	CANDIDATES
MID-ATLANTIC				
Delaware	Legislative	—	—	—
Maryland	Popular by district	All white males with 1 year's residence	54	Adams; Clay; Crawford; Jackson
New Jersey	Statewide popular	Taxpaying qualification (most white males could vote)	33	Adams; Crawford; Jackson
New York	Legislative	—	—	—
Pennsylvania	Statewide popular	Taxpaying qualification (most white males could vote)	22	Adams; Clay; Crawford; Jackson

Source: Derived in part from McCormick, *Second American Party System,* 33–20.

by his list of electors, were printed by the candidate or his organization and then distributed by hand. Alternatively, newspapers published the ballot, which could be cut out and carried to the polling place. In high-turnout elections that generated significant voter interest, the grounds around the voting window could become quite hectic and congested, full of voters, the electors, their representatives, ticket agents, onlookers, and even the occasional "tough" employed by one faction to prevent voting by another.[4]

With an increasingly democratized electorate, the candidates needed their own representatives in each state to reach the voters, but since all were Republicans, none could rely on the existing party apparatus. Contenders with demonstrated popularity in a state counted on their friends there to select, organize, and then print the ticket of electors, but occasionally candidates had to solicit the electors personally. The candidates sometimes exploited public meetings and legislative caucuses, staples of traditional politics, to produce electoral tickets. Tickets produced by public meetings often created confusion. Too many or too few electors might be chosen, tickets might improperly overlap districts, or a selected elector might refuse to stand. In the newer states with less experience in presidential campaigning, electors might even self-nominate, so voters had to trust that a self-styled "Adams elector" would, in fact, vote for Adams when the electoral college convened.[5]

None of the presidential hopefuls ran in all of the eighteen states with popular elections. Because the candidates were running their own campaigns, fielding a ticket in a particular state was often determined by their organizational strength and regional strategy. While a candidate's popularity in a state certainly factored into their decision to run there, limited resources also circumscribed efforts to achieve nationwide ballot access. Accordingly, historians have sometimes mischaracterized the voting results, suggesting, for example, that Jackson and Clay "were completely shut out" in New England, or that the general "ran poorly" in the region. Clearly, all the candidates would have received votes in states where they were "shut out" if their campaigns had not been personally burdened with assembling tickets in the eighteen popular elections.[6]

The four presidential campaigns yielded quite different results. Adams assembled the most national effort, fielding tickets in seventeen of eighteen states with popular elections. Jackson followed with thirteen state tickets; Crawford with twelve; and Clay, in his customary last-place position, with ten. Failure to assemble a ticket of electors in a particular state had grave electoral consequences. Regardless of the number of voters who might have preferred a candidate, without a ticket of electors in a state, he received no popular votes there. While campaigning state by state had been chaotic, the results (see table 2) offered some clarity. Jackson led the field with robust pluralities in both popular and electoral votes, while Adams finished a strong second. Crawford and Clay badly trailed the leaders. Though Clay barely edged Crawford in the popular vote, the treasury secretary enjoyed a slight lead in the electoral college. No candidate received a majority of electoral votes; the election would have to be resolved by a second contest in the House of Representatives. The routes each man had taken to achieve his final tally clearly demonstrated how presidents would be made in the forthcoming Jacksonian era.[7]

Hail the Conquering Hero: The General Wins the Battle

Jackson's winning electoral vote margin rested on his strong performance in his home region. Clay had once considered the Southwest a part of *his* western home base, but Jackson's entry had scrambled the Speaker's careful political calculations. Not only was the general from the Southwest, his military exploits appealed to numerous citizens living there. As the scourge of the Creeks and the Seminoles, Jackson's formidable reputation as an Indian fighter comforted people who feared Native American attacks. As a wily negotiator with Indians—Jackson was notorious for his one-sided, deceptive treaties favoring European Americans over Native Americans—the general gained a following in states where Indians still controlled large swaths of territory that European Americans coveted. Contrarily, Clay, a fierce critic of Jackson's military activities and with more sympathetic views of Native Americans, rapidly lost ground to the general in the entire region. The issues he stressed also worked against his campaign in the Southwest. While internal improvements were regionally popular, southwesterners reviled his tariff legislation (with the exception of Louisianans). Jackson

TABLE 2. Vote totals for the presidential election of 1824

STATE	JACKSON			ADAMS			CRAWFORD			CLAY		
	POPULAR VOTE	% OF POPULAR VOTE	ELECTORAL VOTE	POPULAR VOTE	% OF POPULAR VOTE	ELECTORAL VOTE	POPULAR VOTE	% OF POPULAR VOTE	ELECTORAL VOTE	POPULAR VOTE	% OF POPULAR VOTE	ELECTORAL VOTE
NEW ENGLAND												
Connecticut	0			7,556	79.25	8	1,978	20.75		0		
Maine	0			10,289	77.32	9	3,018	22.68		0		
Massachusetts	0			31,851	82.28	15	6,860	17.74		0		
New Hampshire	0			9,454	100	8	0			0		
Rhode Island	0			2,142	91.46	4	0	8.54		0		
Vermont						7						
Regional subtotal	0			6,1292	83.79	51	11,856	16.44		0		
SOUTH												
Georgia									9			
North Carolina	20,417	56.65	15	0			15,622	43.35		0		
South Carolina			11						24			
Virginia	2,890	18.11		4,071	25.51		8,565	53.68	24	430	2.69	
Regional subtotal	23,307	44.82	26	4,071	7.83		24,187	46.52	33	430	0.83	

STATE	JACKSON			ADAMS			CRAWFORD			CLAY		
	POPULAR VOTE	% OF POPULAR VOTE	ELECTORAL VOTE	POPULAR VOTE	% OF POPULAR VOTE	ELECTORAL VOTE	POPULAR VOTE	% OF POPULAR VOTE	ELECTORAL VOTE	POPULAR VOTE	% OF POPULAR VOTE	ELECTORAL VOTE
SOUTHWEST												
Alabama	9,461	69.35	5	2422	17.75		1,663	12.19		96	0.70	
Louisiana			3			2						
Mississippi	3,307	65.56	3	1,738	34.44		0			0		
Tennessee	19,947	96.19	11	224	1.08		316	1.52		250	1.21	
Regional subtotal	32,715	82.98	22	4,384	11.12	2	1,979	5.02		346	0.88	
NORTHWEST												
Illinois	1,143	24.28	2	1,540	32.72	1	847	17.99		1,012	21.50	
Indiana	7,444	46.94	5	3,093	19.50		0			5,321	33.55	
Kentucky	6,433	27.50		120	0.51		3	0.01		16,837	71.97	14
Missouri	1,167	34.32		191	5.62		0			2,042	60.06	3
Ohio	18,373	36.74		12,315	24.63		0			19,318	38.63	16
Regional subtotal	34,560	35.56	7	17,259	17.76	1	850	0.87		44,530	45.81	33

(continued)

TABLE 2. Vote totals for the presidential election of 1824 (*continued*)

STATE	JACKSON			ADAMS			CRAWFORD			CLAY		
	POPULAR VOTE	% OF POPULAR VOTE	ELECTORAL VOTE	POPULAR VOTE	% OF POPULAR VOTE	ELECTORAL VOTE	POPULAR VOTE	% OF POPULAR VOTE	ELECTORAL VOTE	POPULAR VOTE	% OF POPULAR VOTE	ELECTORAL VOTE
MID-ATLANTIC												
Delaware						1			2			
Maryland	14,470	44.22	7	14,189	43.36	3	3,371	10.30	1	695	2.12	
New Jersey	10,342	51.76	8	8,406	42.07		1,233	6.17		0		
New York			1			26			5			4
Pennsylvania	35,893	76.07	28	5,403	11.45		4,184	8.87		1,706	3.62	
Regional subtotal	60,705	60.77	44	27,998	28.03	30	8,788	8.80	8	2,401	2.40	4
National total	151,287	41.83	99	115,004	31.80	84	47,660	13.18	41	47,707	13.19	37

Source: Adapted from Dubin, *United States Presidential Elections: 1788–1860*, 31–42.

Note: Totals do not include 365 popular votes for unaffiliated electors, 200 in Rhode Island and 165 in Illinois. The results for popular votes reported here vary somewhat from other sources, such as Parsons, *Birth of Modern Politic*, 98–99, and Ratcliffe, *One-Party Presidential Contest*, 279–80. There was no "official" tally of popular votes. Historians have pieced together the totals from newspapers accounts and state archives, so tallies are frequently inconsistent.

also blasted Clay as a corrupt insider, linking him to Crawford, the ultimate Washington villain. As the election season unfolded, taking the Southwest from Jackson proved a bridge too far for Clay and the other candidates.[8]

Despite Tennessee's acrimonious internal political divisions and Jackson's numerous enemies there, the state unsurprisingly voted almost unanimously for the general. Jackson also triumphed in Alabama and Mississippi. Both states were highly dependent on cotton and slavery, while they maintained strong connections to the federal government to facilitate Indian removal, land sales, and internal improvement projects. Though Jackson's tariff position had angered the cotton planters in both states, his support for internal improvements and his military reputation overcame any opposition. The general also gained three more electoral votes from winning Louisiana's legislative election. Adams captured two votes from the same election, proving the only candidate able to poach from Jackson in his home region. The secretary of state, with his control over government printing, had secured favorable press coverage, and his defense of Jackson's military exploits endeared him to many voters. Numerous Yankee merchants resided in southwestern urban centers, and Adams's deliberately ambiguous tariff position had snared him a portion of the planter vote. Still, Adams only managed a far distant second place finish across the region. Crawford, with his partiality toward Georgia in local land sales—at the expense of Alabama—still fresh in the minds of angry voters, fared even worse than Adams. Clay's supporters amounted to less than 1 percent of popular vote totals; southwesterners almost unanimously endorsed local favorite Jackson over the other westerner, Clay.[9]

As well as he had performed in the Southwest, Jackson demonstrated his real strength outside the region. While the other candidates had amassed more than half their electoral votes from their home bases, Jackson's Southwestern votes amounted to only about one-quarter of his final tallies. He gained seven electoral votes from popular elections in the northwestern states Indiana and Illinois while proving even more dynamic in the South and the Mid-Atlantic. As we have seen in chapter 5, North Carolina's political elite, as usual meekly following Virginia's lead, supported Crawford. Insurgent Jacksonians hijacked the Calhounite People's Ticket for the general. Clay, prime advocate of the unpopular tariff, did not run in North Carolina, and Adams, although he attracted a minority following, never fielded a ticket there either. Jackson's convincing victory, with almost 57 percent of the vote, stunned most political observers. Despite facing the near-unanimous opposition of North Carolina's Republican movers and shakers, astonishingly, the general's ticket polled majorities in two-thirds of the state's counties.[10]

Crawford carried North Carolina's geographic and political power center, Raleigh and its environs in the middle of the state, along with the Piedmont region bordering Virginia. Jackson triumphed in the west bordering Tennessee, with eastern tobacco and rice planters on the Atlantic, and in nineteen of twenty-three traditionally Federalist counties. The general assembled his winning coalition by diverse appeals to varying constituencies. Based on his pro-Federalist letter to Monroe, Federalists hoped President Jackson might abolish the Republicans' hated proscription policy. The general's successful military exploits attracted militiamen. "In almost every Captain's company the drums were beating and fifes whistling for the hero of New Orleans," one Crawfordite disgustedly claimed. Eastern and western North Carolinians had long sought funding for internal improvements, but had been denied by a handful of stingy political leaders from the middle who controlled the state's politics and purse strings, so Jackson's vote in favor the Clay's bill appealed to them. Many Jackson voters, tired of North Carolina playing second fiddle to Virginia, simply rejected the candidate so closely associated with their powerful neighbor. "It is time for North Carolina to stand alone," one former state legislator maintained, "time to break the chain of Virginia influence." Distrust of Washington's establishment politicians transcended and encompassed all these concerns for Jackson's voters. "The very existence of our republican government," the *Salisbury Western Carolinian* shrieked, "depends upon the success or the failure of the present struggle of the people against the schemes and machinations of a caucusing aristocratic combination of politicians." Jackson's image as an anticorruption political outsider simply resonated with more North Carolinians than that of a career politico like Crawford.[11]

Calhoun had once predicated his national victory on carrying the Carolinas. He successfully transferred the allegiance of South Carolina's legislators from their favorite son to a Jackson/Calhoun ticket. Jackson won the state's legislative election, further frustrating Crawford's dreams of solid southern support. Meanwhile, Pennsylvania had been the other planned keystone of Calhoun's campaign. As we have seen in chapter 5, his elite political supporters there had backed the secretary of war as a means of shattering the Virginia/New York axis and elevating Pennsylvania's stature, but Jackson's grassroots forces overwhelmed Calhoun at the state Republican convention in March. Western Pennsylvania had been the first hotbed of Jacksonian support outside his native Tennessee, but in the fall election, the Jackson ticket attracted voters from across the state, easily swamping the Adams, Crawford, and Clay offerings by a three-to-one margin. The National Road, connecting the Potomac and Ohio Rivers, had been the first highway built by the federal government. Clay's support for terminating it in his birth state, Virginia, rather than in Pittsburgh helped torpedo his efforts. Meanwhile, Crawford's opposition to protective tariffs and Adams's lukewarm support from Pennsylvania's still-powerful Federalists fatally undermined each of their campaigns.[12]

Jackson captured ballots from almost every voting bloc. Skilled artisans and poor immigrants believed that Jackson's tirades against corruption promised real improvements in the battered economy. Scotch-Irish, Irish, and German Pennsylvanians found Jackson, the vanquisher of the British at New Orleans, culturally appealing. The general had cleverly publicized his church-building efforts at the Hermitage, which helped him secure Methodist, Baptist, and Presbyterian ballots. Jackson's heroic military exploits attracted young, first-time voters. Courtesy of Jackson's pro-Federalist letter, many in the opposition party eagerly anticipated his lifting of the Republicans' proscription policy; the Federalist stronghold in Lancaster County voted overwhelmingly for the general. Jackson's outsider campaign aimed at toppling a corrupt political establishment encompassed these concerns. Built on arguments that had been circulating in Pennsylvania for years, Jackson's in-state literature warned that "intrigues . . . among the official Gentry at Wash. [were] poisoning & strangling our Infant republic." Where Calhoun had faltered, Jackson flourished, taking both North Carolina and Pennsylvania, the original raisons d'être of the secretary of war's campaign.[13]

Jackson fared reasonably well in other mid-Atlantic states. Though he only received one elector in New York's legislative election, Jackson performed much better in the region's popular elections. New Jersey's elite Republican politicians were busy supporting the cabinet candidates, but Jacksonians in south Jersey, after two unsuccessful attempts to nominate a Jackson-only ballot, finally crafted a People's Ticket a mere eight days before election day. Despite the late entry, the Jackson-only ticket carried 52 percent of the electorate, a less commanding margin than in Pennsylvania, but a victory nonetheless. New Jerseyan voters apparently heeded Jackson's in-state literature to "take for your President a man from your own body, untainted by the corruption of a court, and uninitiated in cabinet secrets."[14]

The race in nearby Maryland proved closer still. Electoral participation there usually ranked highest in the nation. With presidential electors selected in a popular vote by district, each candidate possessed eleven chances to walk away with electoral votes. All four candidates competed, but there were no statewide tickets. Electors were either self-nominated or picked by meeting in each district. Unsurprisingly, in a competitive four-man contest in which each district election mattered, Maryland validated its national reputation. The state enjoyed the highest turnout in the union at 54 percent of the eligible electorate, one of only two states to surpass the halfway mark in voter participation. In the popular vote, Jackson barely edged Adams; both men received about 15,000 ballots, with their totals separated by less than three hundred votes. Jackson swept more districts, however, earning seven electoral votes to Adams's three. Crawford dropped well into third place with more than four times fewer votes than the leaders, but he captured one district, taking one electoral vote. In yet another humiliating finish, Clay, who had expected to carry at least two districts, fell just short of an insubstantial seven hundred votes total and earned no electoral votes whatsoever.[15]

Crawford's Radical retrenchment policies remained quite unpopular in Maryland. Adams easily defeated the treasury secretary in the rural areas around Baltimore, in the ethnically English slaveholding strongholds in southern Maryland, among coastal tobacco growers, and with state employees. The general's supporters were located primarily in the city of Baltimore and in western Maryland. Baltimore's economy had substantially suffered in the panic, so Jackson's anticorruption message helped him carry the city's working class. The general's advertised piety swayed voters here as well, with Jackson leading among Methodists, Baptists, and Presbyterians. The factionalized Federalists, still quite active in Maryland, unsurprisingly split in their presidential choice, and Federalist electors appeared on the Adams, Jackson, and Crawford tickets. Calhoun had relentlessly courted Maryland's Federalists, and most of his high-profile supporters there flipped to Jackson, but ordinary Federalist voters broke almost evenly between the general and the secretary of state.[16]

Without competition from a mid-Atlantic state candidate, the region's elections were the most broadly and bitterly fought contests in the cycle. Every candidate offered something to the mid-Atlantic electorate. Clay's tariff and internal improvements legislation had been crafted as a panacea for the postpanic high unemployment and depressed commerce that continued to burden the region. Crawford had excelled at coalition building as he assembled his mighty organization, which appealed to partisan Republicans facing their own fractured state parties. Adams claimed that his skills in diplomacy and administration promised protection for the diverse special interests in the Mid-Atlantic. Jackson separated himself from the other three. As the anticorruption outsider, he would save the mid-Atlantic states from further depredations by intriguing federal politicians. In the end, the general's message most resonated in the Mid-Atlantic. Coupled with his western and southern wins, Jackson commanded over 40 percent of the national popular vote and the field-leading ninety-nine electoral votes. Ironically, the outsider given little chance to win became the front-runner to triumph in a House election.[17]

Still the Stepping-Stone: The Secretary
of State's Solid Second-Place Finish

While Adams may have distanced himself from his family's Federalist legacy, he hoped to equal his father's electoral dominance in New England,
a region the elder John Adams had carried unanimously in two consecu-
tive elections in 1796 and 1800. The son's aspirations proved well founded.
Winning both popular and legislative elections, Adams swept all six New
England states, capturing fifty-one electors in the process. This haul comprised more than one-half his final tally and made him the only candidate
in the race able to completely sweep his home region. Still, despite the
prospect of breaking the South's quarter-century, six-term hammerlock on
the presidency, only one in five eligible voters bothered to turn out, the
lowest percentage for any region. Perhaps New England's voters simply decided their ballots were superfluous, since none of Adams's rivals offered
much of a challenge to his regional ascendancy. Clay had enjoyed a boomlet
of support—two Federalist newspapers had endorsed him, and the region's
wool producers avidly advocated his tariff policies—but his lackluster campaign failed to field any electoral tickets. Jackson had likewise opted out
of New England, so both westerners received no popular or electoral votes
there. Independent Republicans and Federalists repulsed by the "turncoat"
Adams formed tickets for Crawford, but the treasury secretary's scandal-
plagued reputation, southern identity, and opposition to protective tariffs
yielded an uninspiring, lopsided showdown tilted dramatically in favor of
the native-born Adams. Whatever the level of their national appeal, the
Adams family's dynastic dominance in New England continued unabated.[18]

The secretary of state proved much less of a vote magnet elsewhere.
He was completely shut out of electoral votes in the South while receiving only a scattering of electors from other states—three from legislative
elections in Louisiana and Delaware and four from popular elections in
Illinois and Maryland. Ultimately, the fabled New York legislative election boosted Adams into his strong second-place showing. With thirty-six
electoral votes, a whopping 15 percent of the national total, New York offered
the biggest reward in the entire election, and every candidate conspired
to carry off the trophy. A plethora of competing interests comprised the

electorate in New York. Manufacturers, merchants, industrialists, shippers, and farmers all vied for political attention, while the state's domestic and international economic ties drew the focus of New Yorkers both east and west. Representing this complex mixture, Republicans in New York had splintered into a bewildering array of shifting factions, endlessly complicating every political calculation. "After living a dozen years in New York, I don't pretend to comprehend their politics," one New England émigré observed bemusedly, "It is a labyrinth of wheels within wheels, and it is understood only by the managers." The two principal groups were allied to Martin Van Buren and DeWitt Clinton respectively. Conventional wisdom suggested that since Van Buren supported Crawford, and Van Buren's Albany Regency controlled the legislature, and the legislature picked the electors, Crawford would carry New York.[19]

Van Buren faced a challenging task, though. Having barely beaten back an attempt to replace the legislative election with a popular one in 1823, he now confronted a group of notoriously fickle politicos. By a simple majority vote, each branch of the legislature voted for a slate of electors. If the slates matched, then electors were considered selected, but if they differed, both chambers met in joint session to negotiate a unified slate. The Regency controlled the Senate, but not the Assembly. With thirty-two senators and 125 assemblymen, the winning slate needed seventy-nine votes. Clay's American System policies had attracted numerous devotees, especially legislators from western New York. New England émigrés, traditional Dutch New Yorkers, and Federalists leaned Adams. Even more troubling for Van Buren, some Regency Republicans never truly embraced Crawford. Many disliked his opposition to protective tariffs and internal improvements, and the hoary Virginia/New York axis itself had become increasingly unpopular. For voters in the nation's largest state, a Crawford presidency meant four more years of undeservedly playing second fiddle to the much-smaller Virginia. When Van Buren counted heads, he realized that Crawford and Adams each commanded about sixty votes, while forty members favored Clay; only by expert strategic management would Crawford triumph in New York.[20]

The state's politicians had developed a national reputation for their slick maneuvering, and they successfully maintained that standing. Van Buren had struck up a secret alliance with the Clayite minority, brokering a mixed slate of electors containing twenty-nine Crawford and seven Clay men. Van Buren's list cleared the Senate, but faltered in the Assembly. After a three-day deadlock, Van Buren convinced cautious Crawfordites in the Assembly to vote for an Adams ticket. Since each chamber now had a designated slate, a joint session would decide between the two. Van Buren had contrived the entire plot based on the smug assurance that the Crawford/Clay ticket would easily defeat the Adams slate in the joint session. Foolishly, he had not informed his Clay allies about his plan, so when the Regency Assemblymen voted for the Adams ticket, Clay's followers naturally assumed Van Buren had deserted them. Adams's manager Thurlow Weed smartly countered with his own clandestine Clayite alliance. He negotiated a new combined slate of twenty-nine Adams and seven Clay electors, but secretly printed the ballots himself to keep the maneuver entirely concealed.[21]

The ballot counting in the joint session quickly revealed Weed's stealthy maneuver, stunning the overconfident Crawfordites. When the joint session chairman Erastus Root plucked the first Adams/Clay ballot from the box, he was so flustered he could only sputter, "A printed split ticket!" Bedlam erupted, with desperate cries of "Treason!" from the Crawfordites. In the final tally, the Crawford/Clay ticket received 76 votes, the Adams ticket 59, and the Adams/Clay ticket 19; three ballots were left blank. Since the seven Clay electors received ninety-five votes total from two tickets, they were selected. Twenty-five Adams electors had garnered seventy-eight votes, one short of an absolute majority. The Adamsites claimed that the three blank ballots meant that only seventy-eight votes were actually needed. After two hours of angry debate, the Adams men were approved, along with some token Crawford electors on a second ballot. Ultimately, Adams left New York with twenty-five electoral votes; Clay seven; and Crawford, the erstwhile front-runner, with a meager four. Once again, the treasury secretary's vaunted organization had fumbled at the finish. Van Buren "looks like a wilted cabbage," one Adamsite chortled.[22]

Though he had been bested by Adams, the cunning Van Buren still possessed one last card to play. When the electoral college convened in December, Van Buren, ably assisted by Adams men and Clintonians working for Jackson, applied ample political pressure on New York's electors. Accordingly, one Clayite voted for Jackson, one Adams elector voted for Crawford, and two other Clay electors failed to appear and were replaced by Adams men. Van Buren's latest machinations netted one additional electoral vote each for Adams, Crawford, and Jackson, all at the expense of Clay. "I know not the secret springs which have produced such a strange result," the deflated Clay admitted. Had he uncovered the true source of these "secret springs," Clay would have realized that Adams was the fountainhead. While the secretary of state had proved admired enough in his home base to sweep the popular elections in New England, the political schemers he had recruited in other regions were crucial to his legislative election victories.[23]

Don't Follow the Leader: The Unhappy Conclusion of the Hapless Crawford Campaign

Despite the front-runner's lofty prospects, as we have seen, Adams outmaneuvered Crawford in New York and Jackson out-polled him in North Carolina; ultimately Crawford staggered into a weak third place finish behind the leading pair. Unsurprisingly for a candidate popular with elected politicians, the treasury secretary garnered almost half of his final tally in legislative elections. Supplementing the five votes in New York, as expected, he gained nine more from his home state's legislative election. Unfortunately for Crawford, though he added two more from Delaware's legislative election, the process only reinforced his reputation as a scheming politico. When a joint session of the legislature convened to pick the electors, fourteen favored Adams, eleven Crawford, and five opted for Jackson, but almost all members were open to bargaining. Needing an absolute majority of sixteen votes to win, only one Adams elector cleared that bar on the first ballot. Two Crawford electors obtained fifteen votes, however—just one short of victory. The Senate Speaker, who was chairing the joint session and had already voted for Crawford as a member, voted again as chairman, giving Crawford two electors. Adams had clearly been cheated, but the results stood.[24]

Virginia's popular election proved one of the few bright spots for Crawford's beleaguered campaign. In presidential politics, the Old Dominion had dominated both the South and the nation. A Virginian had run for president in each of the nine elections held since the United States adopted the Constitution. Although justifiably proud of its historic importance, the state gained a reputation for doctrinaire, impractical conservatism. After a visit to Richmond, Monroe's son-in-law George Hay bemusedly told Adams that the politicians there were *still* discussing the now twenty-five-year-old Virginia Resolutions, authored by James Madison in 1798 to denounce John Adams's "unconstitutional" Alien and Sedition Acts. The Virginians act "as if they belonged to another planet, and have not the remotest conception of the present state and condition of Virginia's influence as a member of the Union," Hay chuckled. The landed gentry controlled political life in the Old Dominion, with east Virginians disproportionally represented in the legislature. Western Virginians enjoyed a more diverse economy than those in the east, so they were more receptive to internal improvement funding and less rigidly opposed to protective tariffs.[25]

Initially, the east backed Crawford and the west favored Adams, but as Jackson's campaign gained steam, he started poaching supporters from the secretary of state. Thomas Ritchie's influential Richmond *Inquirer* tried to tip the scales toward Crawford, proclaiming him the true Jeffersonian in the race. The newspaper dismissed Adams as an ultra-Federalist committed to high tariffs and Jackson as a ruthless warrior ill-suited for the executive chair. A rump caucus of state legislators formed a pro-Crawford electoral slate. Jacksonian and Adamsite supporters tried and failed to unite behind one anti-Crawford ticket. Ultimately, all the candidates fielded an individual ticket in Virginia, one of only five states with a contested four-man race. Despite the plethora of options, voters seemed unexcited by their choices.[26]

Election day results reflected their apathy. Only 12 percent of the eligible electorate turned out, one of the lowest percentages in the union, but Crawford easily garnered over 50 percent of those who voted. The treasury secretary amassed his totals mostly in the east, sweeping the Tidewater and Piedmont, with Adams and Jackson splitting the west for about 26 percent and 18 percent of the final tally, respectively. Despite the concerted effort Clay had expended to win Virginia, he limped away in humiliation with a measly 430 votes, under 3 percent of the ballots. The Speaker had

long understood the utter disdain Virginians harbored for his positions on
tariffs and internal improvements, yet he somehow continued to believe
his birth in the state would sway the voters there. "I should indeed have
been highly gratified if my native state had thought me worthy of even a
second place in her confidence and affection," Clay remarked peevishly after
his fourth-place finish. Crawford's appeal in Virginia ironically rested on
factors that diminished his electability in other states. His reputed Jeffersonian principles, his opposition to protective tariffs, his position as the
official Republican nominee, and his influence with elite politicians—
the exact sort of men who controlled Virginia—all buttressed his convincing win. In his only state popular vote victory in the entire election,
Crawford snared all twenty-four of Virginia's electoral votes. The treasury
secretary also eked out one additional electoral vote from his third-place
finish in Maryland's popular election.[27]

Crawford's failure to sweep the South typified the problems besetting his
campaign. Though he technically defeated Jackson in the region, winning
thirty-three electoral votes there to twenty-six for the general, his victory
was hollow at best. Superficially, the four Southern states had seemed as
secure for Crawford as New England had been for Adams. Rural, agricultural, and hostile to protective tariffs, they appeared to be easy wins for a
candidate who had been born in Virginia, lived in Georgia, and espoused
the Jeffersonian line against tariffs. As with so many aspects of Crawford's
misbegotten campaign, theoretical advantages only fitfully translated
into actual election-season success. Carrying a solid South should have
served as a springboard to his national victory, but his nasty fight with Calhoun and his reputation for political chicanery had cost him the Carolinas.
Running as the "anti-Adams" in New England, Crawford had polled only
16 percent of the vote while performing even more poorly in the Southwest
and Mid-Atlantic. In the Northwest, his opposition to federally funded internal improvements, cheerleading for the BUS, and scandal-mired management of public deposits had forced him to sit out almost every state
contest there. With his defeats and disappointments across most of the
nation, the one-time front-runner could now only follow the leaders into
a House election.[28]

Setting Star in the West: Clay's Issues Become the Issue

Thanks to Jackson's popularity, Adams's political skills, Crawford's support from Republican elites, and his own deficiencies as a campaigner, Clay's bid for the presidency flopped almost everywhere. Despite grassroots support in New England, he never fielded any electoral tickets there. The same story played out in New Jersey. Unconnected to the Speaker's national organization, over a thousand enthusiastic Clayites had spontaneously rallied in support of his candidacy at public meetings in Bergen, Morris, and Essex Counties in north Jersey, but on election day they had no Clay ticket to cast. While Jackson, his fellow westerner, racked up big victories in Pennsylvania and Maryland, Clay finished dead last in both popular elections. The result was no different, even when he tried; despite the effort he had poured into winning Virginia and New York, he still trailed the field in both states.[29]

Even bad luck seemed to cling to Clay's campaign. He was quite popular in Louisiana. Clay's tariff bill taxed imported brown sugar expressly to protect sugarcane, the state's cash crop, while his stance on internal improvements promised relief from flood loss and bad roads. Jackson's legendary triumph over the British in the Battle of New Orleans earned him quite a following, of course; the city had designated its central plaza "Jackson Square" six months after the general's titanic victory. However, Jackson's controversial arrests after he declared martial law in New Orleans had soured many on his presidential bid. In Louisiana's legislative election, Clay's son-in-law, Martin Duralde, personally managed the Speaker's campaign. About thirty-one of fifty-eight members supported Clay. The Speaker only needed thirty votes to win, yet somehow his feckless campaign snatched defeat from the jaws of victory. Two of his supporters suffered a carriage accident and missed the vote, another lost a challenge to his seat by an Adams man, and two more arrived late. No candidate achieved a majority, but the tiny Adams faction cleverly cut a deal with the Jacksonians to split the electors 3–2 in favor of the general. Despite his ample support in Louisiana, the Speaker was completely shut out of electoral votes there.[30]

Naturally, Clay hoped for redemption in his home base. Since the War of 1812 ended, the Northwest had suffered from a trade imbalance, numerous bank failures, a shortage of cash, and a poor transportation system that limited market access. Many northwesterners seethed that profits from sales of their public lands somehow ended up in the pockets of easterners. Clay expected his issues-based campaign would appeal to voters across the region, arguing that his American System would vastly improve the Northwest's fragile economy; indeed, northwestern congressmen had voted overwhelmingly for Clay's tariff and internal improvements bills. Not every issue worked in his favor, however. His association with the detested BUS, the very reason Crawford had opted out of most northwestern elections, worried even his friends and neighbors. Antislavery sentiment also permeated Ohio, Indiana, and Illinois, and some of his allies feared that Clay's much-heralded compromise with slavery in Missouri might cut into his vote totals. Despite the Speaker's breezy optimism about his chances in the Northwest, pitfalls clearly remained in his path to victory.[31]

Unsurprisingly, Kentuckians expressed a "universal passion" for their favorite son. Clay smashed a Jackson ticket, winning over 70 percent of the ballots cast. He also coasted to victory in Missouri, the state he had personally ushered into the union in 1820, with 60 percent of the popular vote. His plan to add the other northwestern states to his victory column ended much less favorably. In Indiana, two caucuses of state legislators nominated electoral slates for Adams and Clay, while Jackson relied on a grassroots movement. Echoing Pennsylvania, but on a smaller scale, eighteen of the general's supporters from only a handful of counties attended a delegate convention, the first ever such assembly organized for a presidential candidate in Indiana. Surprisingly, the general's ad hoc ticket carried the balloting, with almost one-half of popular votes cast. While Indianans applauded Clay's stance on internal improvements, his support for the BUS cost him the election there.[32]

The Speaker fared no better in Illinois. With electors selected in a popular vote by district, Jackson, Adams, and Clay each offered a ticket in all three areas. Because the governor had announced the configuration of the districts only a few weeks before the election, disorder was the order of the day, as a bewildering array of self-nominated electors offered themselves to voters. Only one Adams elector ran in each district, which helped consolidate his vote total, while the general's voters could choose from at least two—and up to five—Jackson electors. Adams actually captured a plurality of Illinois's ballots, but his voters were concentrated in one district, so he received only one electoral vote. Jackson carried the other two districts, earning two electoral votes. Sweeping the panic-ravaged districts, Jackson benefited enormously from opposition to the BUS, while Clay's support for it hobbled his campaign. Crawford, the other candidate closely linked to the bank, tried running in Illinois, but one of his electors campaigned without ever uttering the name Crawford. Antislavery sentiment also weakened support for Clay. In August, voters had resoundingly rejected a new state constitution that might have permitted the introduction of slave labor, and Adams's electors had been publicly identified with the antislavery cause. While Clay hoped that issues such as tariffs and internal improvements would deliver Illinois to his column, the voters chose to focus on the bank and slavery instead.[33]

Ohio offered the most contested and exciting contest in the Northwest, as Clay, Jackson, and Adams all competed vigorously in a statewide popular election for sixteen electoral votes, the most valuable prize in the region. Parties supporting the three contenders were assembled almost from scratch, with little connection to any other political factions, including the governor's race, which had been held only two weeks prior. Clay's party in the legislature constructed his ticket of electors, which was ratified at a meeting in Columbus of about three hundred "friends of 'An American System.'" Aided by favorable press coverage, Jacksonians convened a state delegate convention in May. Much like the tiny affair in Indiana—only seventeen delegates attended—the Jackson convention still represented the first ever state delegate convention in Ohio. The Adams organization lagged behind his opponents', but still managed a few meetings that nominated a slate of electors. The three clashing campaigns raucously roused their supporters on election day. "The cannon are now roaring and the drums beating before my door, and I hear the loud huzzas," one excited observer reported. Ohio had been viewed as a slam dunk for the state's close neighbor, but Clay only barely edged out Jackson 39 percent to 37 percent, with Adams falling to third at about 25 percent of the vote.[34]

Economic concerns dominated the election. Clay's hope that the issues he championed would underwrite his success proved warranted. His literature stressed the Speaker's contributions to furthering federally funded internal improvements, and his voters, seeking increased economic development, favored such projects. Clay racked up healthy majorities in counties along the proposed state canal and National Road routes. The Speaker fared far more poorly in areas devastated in the panic. Since the economic downturn, anti-BUS sentiment had soared in Ohio. Cincinnati's economy had been especially ruined and residents were still reeling from another minipanic in May 1824. The BUS, with its involvement in the devastating collapse of local banks, seemed like an eastern "swindle" perpetrated on innocent westerners, and many Ohioans blamed the politicians who promoted the scam. Meanwhile, Jackson's literature in Ohio trumpeted him as "the CANDIDATE OF THE PEOPLE," in opposition to "an organized corps of *Leading men* and intriguing politicians"; the majority of his voters lived in economically distressed regions. Adamsites tore a page out of Jackson's playbook and ran the secretary of state as the outsider, antiaristocracy candidate running against Clay, the candidate endorsed by most of the state's political heavyweights.[35]

Slavery and cultural politics also factored into the race. Many Ohioans opposed slavery; the state legislature even vowed in January 1824 to work against this "national evil." In response, Clayites claimed that the Speaker had channeled "the spirit of George Washington" in settling the Missouri question; he also stood for gradual emancipation, while Adams's views on the future of slavery were unknown. Despite these counterarguments, the nonslaveholding Adams outperformed his opponents among antislavery religious groups, including Quakers, Presbyterians, Seceders, and Baptists. New England émigrés also trended toward the secretary of state, while Jackson was more popular with the Scotch-Irish and Pennsylvania Dutch, groups traditionally hostile to the English. Still Clay peeled off a number of votes from the cultural favorites in these communities, demonstrating the widespread appeal of his policies. In Ohio, at least, the Speaker finally gained voters with the issues-based candidacy that had been so costly elsewhere.[36]

Clay performed well in his home region, capturing thirty-three electoral votes from the Northwest, but his opponents denied him the clean sweep he desired, expected, and needed, with Jackson winning seven and Adams one electoral vote. Attributing his defeats in Illinois and Indiana, along with Jackson's near upset in Ohio, to forces outside his campaign, a chagrined Clay pointed the finger of blame at everyone but himself. "The discouragement of my friends—the power of the Atlantic press—the influence of Governmental patronage—the fabrication of tales of my being withdrawn" had all contributed to his northwestern setbacks, he insisted. Indeed, Clay's tiny organization, nonexistent newspaper network, lack of patronage, and rumors of an alliance with Crawford had hampered his campaign across the nation. Despite Clay's analysis, however, the very issues he had supported contributed to his fate in the Northwest. While he focused solely on tariffs and internal improvements, which certainly earned him significant votes, his support for the BUS, his compromise with slavery, and his association with unsavory Washington politics repelled other voters. The Speaker learned a hard lesson about running for president in an increasingly democratized electorate. While politicians might try to target specific constituencies with carefully crafted policy positions, it was the voters who would decide which issues mattered the most. Hampered by bad decisions, flawed premises, and false hopes, Clay's campaign for the presidency never really got off the ground.[37]

Analyzing the Returns: The Fate of Four Different Candidacies

As heated as the contest had been, turnout proved quite subdued. Over 360,000 citizens voted, representing only 27 percent of eligible voters, with the strongest participation in the mid-Atlantic states and the weakest in New England. Given that many contests were lopsided formalities for the expected winner, many voters, convinced that their ballot was unnecessary, simply stayed home. Voters also generally participated in greater numbers in state races than national races, because local legislators usually wielded more power over the lives of ordinary citizens than politicians in

Washington. Jackson captured 42 percent of the national popular vote, followed by Adams at 32 percent, with Crawford and Clay far behind at about 13 percent each.[38]

The electoral vote totals suggested a similar narrative, but with one critical difference. Jackson claimed the most electors at 99, and Adams was again second at 84, but Crawford bested Clay. Though the Speaker had slightly outpolled the treasury secretary in popular elections, Crawford's influence with state legislatures provided him with 41 electors to Clay's 37. Since no candidate had achieved a majority of electoral votes, following the Twelfth Amendment to the Constitution, the election would be decided by a vote in the US House of Representatives among the three candidates leading the electoral vote count. Given that Crawford had edged out Clay in that category, he would join Jackson and Adams in a House election. The candidates' relative finish, unsurprisingly, matched their regional results. Jackson and Adams claimed the top spots because they carried their home regions easily, while making significant inroads elsewhere. Jackson proved quite competitive against Crawford in the South and Clay in the Northwest, with Adams also showing some strength in the latter region. The two leading candidates truly carried the day in the mid-Atlantic states, however, together garnering 86 percent of the electoral vote.[39]

No House election would be required to decide the vice presidency. The candidates' supporters in each state were left up to their own devices to chose a vice presidential running mate for the electoral ticket. With his position on both the Adams and Jackson tickets in several states, Calhoun easily won the office outright with 182 electors to 78. He captured votes in every region, with only five states rejecting him completely. Crawfordite Georgia and Virginia opposed the treasury secretary's archnemesis, of course, with the former casting their votes for Van Buren and the latter anointing North Carolina Radical Nathaniel Macon. Other states decided that their second choice for president should be vice president. Clay received the majority of Delaware's vice presidential electoral votes, while Connecticut and Missouri, joined by a few minority electors from New Hampshire and Maryland, opted for Jackson. Former New York senator Nathan Sanford had been Clay's running mate on several tickets; he received thirty electoral votes from New York, Kentucky, and Ohio. As Calhoun had planned since his abrupt departure from the presidential race, he was now poised to exert influence over any incoming administration.[40]

For the two biggest losers in the presidential race, the election had clearly not gone according to plan. By any traditional measure, Crawford had assembled the strongest campaign by far. His weighty organization, spirited newspaper network, influence over elected officials, well-oiled congressional party, and caucus nomination would have delivered an overwhelming victory in 1816, but unfortunately for Crawford, it was 1824, and the old rules no longer applied. Crawford and his allies correctly believed that he had been attacked more vigorously than any candidate since Jefferson. The decline of Federalism encouraged Republican factionalism, effectively meaning that the party no longer needed to consolidate behind a single candidate. The multiple Republican campaigns both increased and intensified attacks against the front-runner. The rejection of Virginia/New York domination tainted any candidate that either state supported. The growing disgust with corrupt politics doomed the scandal-beleaguered caucus nominee. Each of these changes dramatically undermined the power of Crawford's giant organization, one he had so painstakingly built over more than eight years. Even if Crawford recognized the ground shifting under his feet, he had been committed for so long to his original strategy he simply could not change course at the end of the race. The putative front-runner finished last in the popular vote, winning a popular election only Virginia, but his influence with politicians at least preserved his chance in the House election. Crawford topped Clay by winning in four state legislative elections, amply assisted by Van Buren's ultimate insider machinations in the electoral college. If the House election could be carried by political wheeling and dealing, the treasury secretary remained a viable candidate.[41]

The outcome of Clay's pathetic effort was far more predictable than Crawford's defeat. Demonstrating his ineffectiveness as a strategist in the emerging outdoor mass politics, nearly every decision Clay made throughout the long campaign proved disastrously mistaken. Though the Speaker retained support in Congress, choosing to run without a newspaper network or sizable organization—both staples of successful past and future presidential candidacies—hampered his campaign everywhere except in his home region. Clay squandered his limited resources by focusing myopically on his nearly hopeless cause in the Virginia/New York axis at the expense of other mid-Atlantic and New England states potentially more receptive to his message. While Clay's issues-based campaign pointed to the future importance of issues in president-making, the strategy clearly worked against him in 1824. The other three candidates deliberately obscured their precise views behind vague generalities, allowing Adams's supporters, for instance, to run him as antitariff in the South and Southwest, but protariff in the mid-Atlantic states. "Was not Jackson as much a Tariff man as you were," one Louisiana ally groused to Clay. "His conduct was more covert." Indeed, Clay's visible role as the architect of the Missouri Compromise, the tariff legislation, and the General Survey Bill permitted no evasion, and his national campaign floundered in the face of ardent "local jeolesies [sic]." Even the Speaker eventually grasped his predicament. Correctly claiming that the other candidates had deliberately taken opposing stands on the same issue in different regions, Clay complained that "the difference between them & me is, that I have ever been placed in situations in which I could not conceal my sentiments."[42]

Clay's decision to return to Washington politics proved his greatest mistake of all. His command of indoor maneuvering properly earned him his historical reputation as a shrewd political tactician, but as presidential elections became increasingly democratized, he proved far less adept at the crowd-pleasing required by out-of-doors, mass politics. Clay's reelection to the speakership forced him to take highly visible stands on divisive issues while participating in the sometimes unsavory business of politics. Unfortunately for Clay, as Jackson ratcheted up his attacks on corruption in Washington, he was master of the biggest House in the general's unholy city. In many ways, Clay's campaign was almost the mirror opposite of Calhoun's. While the secretary of war had created and supervised a well-oiled electoral operation, very few ordinary voters favored him. In contrast, Clay attracted a coterie of ardent admirers among the citizenry, but he so poorly managed his campaign at the top that the support never translated into ballot box success.

Adams entered the election with an advantage over his opponents. Controlling three newspaper contracts in every state virtually guaranteed favorable free press coverage across the nation. As the only nonslaveholder in the race, he could also depend upon carrying sectionally minded voters in the North. His edge increased substantially once Clay opted out of New England, which left Adams facing only Crawford, an overtly Southern candidate tainted by scandal. Without much competition in his home region, Adams could focus on his national effort. Unsurprisingly, he ran in more states than any other candidate while fielding the most well-rounded campaign. Where Jackson relied on popular elections and Crawford on state legislatures, Adams successfully mixed both types in his strong second-place finish. For all of his worries about Federalists, they emerged as a non-factor in his campaign. He did not need them in New England to defeat Crawford, and he performed reasonably well with them elsewhere. Adams also padded his vote totals far outside New England with support from the so-called "Universal Yankee Nation," natives from his region who had dispersed into other states.[43]

Not every factor favored the secretary of state. While Adams thoroughly outdueled Jackson in terms of traditional metrics for presidential experience and undoubtedly carried some voters on that basis alone, the general's anticorruption campaign damaged Washington politicians generally, but administration figures especially. Adams had been politically savvy enough to sit back, watch, and reap the benefits as Crawford and Calhoun almost destroyed each other's reputations, but the splatter from their nasty fight stained every cabinet candidate. As a result, Adams generally trailed Jackson in popular elections outside New England. Adams finished far behind Jackson in the South and the Southwest, while performing only marginally better against him in the Northwest. In the all-important Mid-Atlantic, however, Jackson demonstrated how powerfully his campaign message had worked against Adams when he received twice as many popular votes as the secretary of state.

Jackson's outsider candidacy required an insurgent's campaign. Unlike his three rivals, he had no chance of winning a congressional caucus nomination and was less competitive in state legislative elections. With little support from elite politicians, he was forced to turn to other means to win the election. Although it was based on long-standing, local political precedents, his campaign employed the first state caucus nominations for president in 1824 and the first delegate conventions to select electors ever. His supporters also organized more public meetings in a wider array of states than any other candidate. The greater popular involvement in the Jackson effort served both practical and ideological purposes. As outsiders supporting an outsider, Jacksonians almost never controlled the regular levers of power, so they required alternative means of fostering their candidate's campaign. Because they avoided the conventional methods that his opponents employed, however, Jacksonians were free to criticize those methods as illegitimate. The general's greater reliance on a grassroots presidential campaign in 1824, a real break with Early Republic presidential politics, pointed toward future standard practice in presidential mass politics.[44]

Jackson's message proved equally novel. Jackson and his allies carefully cultivated his image as a war hero, veteran of the revolution, westerner, common man, and antipartisan, but above every other qualification, the Jackson campaign stressed his opposition to political corruption. Every candidate insisted that the presidency should be conferred by the people unsolicited, but Jackson repudiated electioneering with far greater consistency and frequency than any contender. Unlike his opponents, he repeated his pledge ad nauseam to an array of correspondents in dozens of letters over several years. Taking the cue from their leader, his followers followed suit, coherently reinforcing Jackson's message against corrupt political practices across every aspect of his campaign, including newspapers, pamphlets, speeches, and toasts.[45]

The congressional caucus served as the most visible sign of corrupt politics as usual, and both the general and his followers stigmatized it unrelentingly. As one of his newspapers colorfully snarled, Jackson "will hang every scoundrel in Washington within five minutes after his inauguration." No presidential candidate had ever run against the capital itself. Clay probably rivaled Jackson in uniform, recurrent messaging, but unfortunately for the Speaker, Jackson's campaign themes simply proved more resonant and less divisive to voters. While Jacksonians differed on specific issues—most

supported internal improvements and defense upgrades, but lacked agreement on tariffs and slavery extension—they united in opposing congressional caucus nominations and Washington insider politics. Jackson's message
attracted diverse blocs of voters, proving quite popular with backcountry
residents in the South and Southwest, urbanites in panic-ravaged cities,
and the Scotch-Irish, Pennsylvania Dutch, and Irish Catholic laborers. Of
all the candidates, the general clearly demonstrated the greatest strength
outside his home base.[46]

Specific circumstances surrounding the 1824 election enhanced the
timeliness of Jackson's message. The War of 1812, the Missouri Compromise, and the Panic of 1819 had each frayed the nation's cohesiveness and
fostered regionalism. Political, economic, and military failures, exacerbated
by nostalgia over the fiftieth anniversary of the revolution and Lafayette's
visit, fed a growing public fear that the United States had betrayed its republican ideals. Instead of solving the nation's problems and reversing the
slide, voters began to believe that corrupt political practices both caused
and contributed to the declension. An increasingly democratized electorate
in presidential elections boosted scrutiny of the candidates, and Jackson's
message against corruption—flexibly encompassing all voters, whatever
their position on specific issues—attracted more ballots than any other
candidate.[47]

Long before Jackson's campaign garnered attention from the public and
the politicians, voters had begun coalescing against Washington insiders,
especially the cabinet secretaries. Clay received letters from every region of
the country denouncing his cabinet opponents simply because they were
department heads. "Abuses have crept in to the administration of the Government," a New Yorker complained, "charged on the present heads of the
different departments." Clay supporters in New England, Ohio, Pennsylvania, Louisiana, and Virginia expressed similar sentiments. Meanwhile,
Maryland's Roger B. Taney, not officially connected to the Jackson campaign in 1824, supported the general nonetheless, noting acerbically, "He is
honest, he is independent, is not brought forth by any class of publicans . . .
I am sick of all Secretary candidates." Jackson's campaign reflected these
beliefs; only Jackson's literature stressed the nation's declension. Many

voters believed that national politics needed an outsider to fix the problems that insiders had created, and Jackson's campaign adroitly capitalized
on their anxieties.[48]

Each candidate offered some version of nationalism to attract voters
outside their home base. Crawford ran as the partisan Jeffersonian in the
hopes of appealing to all Republicans, regardless of their region of residence.
Adams touted his peerless record of public service. His unrivaled diplomatic
background, administrative experience, and negotiation of nationalist treaties certainly branded him the most traditionally qualified candidate in the
race, but also helped him transcend any "geographical considerations."
While Crawford and Adams made generic nationalist appeals that would
not have been out of place in any preceding presidential election, Clay and
Jackson offered specific solutions to contemporary national problems. The
Speaker advanced explicit policies under the overtly nationalist American
System. Jackson countered by aligning voters everywhere against Washington corruption, running an us-versus-them, people-versus-politicians
campaign. From the generic side, Adams's appeal easily trumped Crawford's. The treasury secretary's pose as the "Republican candidate" was
simply unsustainable when faced with a fractured, deeply divided Republican Party. Similarly, Jackson's stance overwhelmed that of Clay. The
Speaker's platform was readily caricatured as a self-serving, regionally biased political ploy by those that it did not directly aid.

Meanwhile, Jackson's message proved quite malleable to any citizen anywhere. Whether a voter was pro- or antislavery, favored or fought tariffs, or
supported or opposed federally funded internal improvements, Jackson's
claim that Washington's intriguing politicos were to blame for the nation's
ills resonated. The general ultimately triumphed over his Washington-based
opponents because they had spent the last four years proving his point.
As some of the nation's problems remained unaddressed, the politicians
turned minor policy disagreements into major political showdowns, rewarded favored friends with coveted patronage positions, engaged in endless rounds of newspaper mudslinging, circulated evil rumors about each
other, and participated in a full-blown political scandal that tarnished every
candidate except Jackson. The practice of politics as usual proved jarring to

many voters, who were anxious that their nation was in decline and that their economic problems remained unsolved. In increasingly democratized presidential elections, these voters tossed a Jackson ballot into the box. As the election moved from the people back to the politicians in the House of Representatives, the politicos would afford the general with even more opportunities to make his case against corruption.

7

→ • ←

Kingmaking behind Closed Doors

A S DECEMBER'S CHILL SETTLED over Washington, Clay prepared to face his own personal winter of discontent. Though he had narrowly defeated Crawford in the popular vote, Clay trailed the treasury secretary by four electoral votes. Since no candidate had achieved a majority of electoral votes, the election would be decided by a vote in the US House of Representatives among the three leading candidates in electoral vote. Clay's fourth-place finish eliminated him from contention. As we have seen in chapter 6, the Speaker had been outmaneuvered by insider trickery. While half the Louisiana legislature had favored Clay, the backroom deal between the Jackson and Adams men denied him any electoral votes whatsoever. Meanwhile, he had departed New York's legislative election with seven electors, but after secret maneuvering by Crawford, Adams, and Jackson supporters, only four voted for Clay when the electoral college convened in December. Finally, Crawfordites in Delaware had improperly granted the treasury secretary two electors. A change of result in Louisiana, New York, or Delaware would, at the least, have tied Clay with Crawford in electoral votes. Instead, the treasury secretary, not the Speaker, would face off against Jackson and Adams. Clay's ouster from the House election benefited all three of his opponents. It removed a western rival to Jackson and a pro-American System rival to Adams, while it prevented Crawford's exclusion from the race. Stymied by insider machinations, the master manipulator had himself been mastered by his competitors. Still, as a high-profile and powerful House Speaker, Clay exerted enormous influence over the legislators responsible for deciding the election. While he could never be king, Clay might yet be the kingmaker.[1]

"I would not cross Pennsylvania Avenue to be in any office under any administration which lies before us," Clay carped about his choices. Still, the three finalists believed the Speaker at least partially controlled their fate, especially through his influence over the delegations from Kentucky, Ohio, and Missouri, the three states he had captured in popular elections. Supporters of each contender pitched their pleas to Clay on different grounds. Jacksonians appealed to Clay as a westerner, Crawfordites as a partisan Republican, and Adamsites to his personal political ambitions. Each candidate's followers cleverly insisted Clay had been their "second choice" from the beginning.[2]

The victorious candidate needed a simple majority of states, meaning thirteen of the twenty-four. Crawford had won only three states, so he had a long climb to overtake his more popular opponents. Unimaginatively, he fell back upon his losing strategy in the general election by appealing to the partisan impulses of elite Republican politicians. Jackson changed tactics. Instead of stressing his fight against corruption, which would have antagonized the very "corrupt" politicos whose votes he now needed, he turned to highlighting his western regionalism. He had won eleven states; if he could hold on to those while adding any two of Clay's western victories, he would come out on top. Adams had triumphed in seven states. He had relied heavily on his social campaign, and he would need every bit of his dealmaking ability to add six more states to his total. Tellingly, Adamsites appealed to Clay's "own future interests" when courting the Speaker, making it the only campaign to suggest overtly that Clay might get a job in their leader's forthcoming administration. To achieve victory, deals would have to be cut, and with 212 representatives to woo, there would be ample opportunities for these partisan, regional, and personal strategies to play out.[3]

Corralling the Representatives: Let's Make a Deal

A sense of frenzied intrigue gripped Washington as each of the three candidates tried to forge a winning coalition of states. Unfortunately for the former front-runner, the tables had turned. In the general election, Crawford had been the man to beat, but as the competition moved into the House, the treasury secretary was widely regarded as the weakest of the three contenders. He had captured only three states in the fall contest, and prospects looked grim for adding any more to his totals in the House election. Georgia and Virginia remained firmly committed to Crawford, of course, while he continued to rely on Delaware. Not only had Crawford taken two of three electoral votes in the diminutive state, but Louis McLane, Delaware's lone representative, admired Crawford personally, disliked Adams intensely, and "would overthrow the Capitol sooner than he would vote for Jackson." Unsurprisingly, Crawford's only true success in the House election came from the same elite politicians that had served as the basis of his entire campaign. Although ordinary voters in North Carolina had opted for Jackson, almost the entire congressional delegation continued to favor Crawford. Elsewhere, the treasury secretary's cause seemed relatively hopeless, but those four states "have nailed their flag, and will sink with the ship," one Georgian noted resignedly. Crawford's health remained a background issue. Although he had largely recovered his speech, vision, and strength, one hand remained paralyzed and persistent rumors exaggerated the severity of his condition.[4]

As Crawford was the least competitive candidate, most coalition rumors naturally centered on him, with gossips suggesting that he would unite with one of the two leaders to gain at least a single presidential term. Such rumors were false. Crawford's managers believed he was every representative's second choice, and they intended to keep their man in the race in the event the two favorites deadlocked. Strategically, they could only prevent Adams or Jackson from achieving a majority, force multiple balloting, and hope that Crawford would eventually emerge as the compromise choice. Martin Van Buren continued to serve as Crawford's chief tactician, counseling New York's pro-Crawford representatives to allow the Adams and Jackson contingents to butt heads just to prevent Adams from achieving a majority of New York's delegation. Meanwhile, Maryland's representatives appeared divided between the two leading aspirants. Van Buren's intelligence suggested that state would vote for Adams on the first ballot, but switch to Jackson on the second. Adams's early failure to seal the deal would only embolden the Jacksonians to fight on, at which point Crawford could be brokered as the candidate suitable to all sides. Van Buren's plan offered the slenderest odds of success, but Crawford's weak position in the general election provided few options. Victory depended on preventing Adams from winning New York on the first ballot, a task seemingly tailor-made for a crafty political fixer like Van Buren.[5]

Despite his lack of support from elite politicians, Jackson and his allies expected to win the House election. The general had triumphed in the popular vote; carried the most states; and, as a westerner, should theoretically have been competitive in the states Clay had won, where he remained quite admired by numerous ordinary citizens. In Jackson's simplistic analysis, the popular vote winner should win the House election. He returned to Washington in December, this time accompanied by his wife Rachel. The hoopla surrounding the impending House vote wearied both Jacksons. "How shall I get through this bustle," Rachel wondered. "There are not less than fifty to one hundred persons calling in a day. My dear husband was unwell . . . and company and business are oppressive."[6]

Oppressive or not, Jackson joined the frenzy to corral the necessary number of representatives, but the general was clearly out of his element. While some of his surrogates pandered to Clay, and some of Clay's allies hinted that the State Department would be the price of the Speaker's support, the general remained deeply opposed to any dealmaking with either Clay or Crawford. "Jackson you well know will not intrigue or trade for any . . . office," John Eaton observed with chagrin, but when "the reverse of his virtues is brought to bear against him . . . it is indeed difficult to conceive how he can maintain his ground & prospects." While Jackson simply hated Clay and Crawford too much to compromise with either, he also believed he had no need to bargain. Combined with the states he had won in the general election, the general required only two more victories. With the states of Ohio, Kentucky, and Missouri ripe for the plucking by the only popular westerner remaining in the race, Jackson believed his triumph an almost foregone conclusion.[7]

In the face of Jackson's rigid opposition to dealmaking, even states that had supported him began to slip from his grasp. Rumors swirled that Clay would nudge several western states to Adams. The lucky general who had sailed along unmolested until late in the campaign endured even more personal attacks. A new pamphlet, composed by his enemies in Tennessee and widely disseminated by Adamsites, contended that Jackson was "illiterate and barbarous . . . vulgar and rude." As a "notorious violator . . . of every law of God and man," the general was simply unfit to serve as president. Even worse for the Jacksons, rumormongers began whispering about Rachel's "immorality." The couple had married before Rachel divorced her abusive first husband, so Washington gossips began spreading tales about the potential First Lady's bigamy. "That they would attempt to disturb the repose of an innocent female in her declining years is a species of wickedness that I did not suppose would be attempted," Jackson observed with cold fury. Surprisingly, however, he dismissed the scandalous chatter as a "plan of my enemies . . . to excite and provoke me," just as they had done during his Senate term. Once Jackson ignored them, the rumors never gained much traction.[8]

While Jackson floundered, Adams proved remarkably adept at the sort of maneuvering required for the second part of the election. He continued courting members of Congress, just as he had done throughout the perpetual campaign. Adams conferred with representatives from at least seventeen states. Ignoring the obvious lost causes such as Crawfordite Georgians and Jacksonians from Tennessee, he focused on New England; the Mid-Atlantic; and, most shrewdly, the states that favored Clay, including Kentucky, Ohio, Missouri, and Louisiana. In a related effort, he and Louisa hosted a well-attended party for yet another high-profile military figure. Lafayette had finally reached Washington on his around-the-country tour, and the Adamses assembled over 180 guests to fete the popular Revolutionary War hero. All this maneuvering required a delicate touch, but as the election shifted from an outdoor spectacle where Jackson's popularity wowed voters to an indoor intrigue where Adams's long experience with social politicking drew in representatives, the secretary of state enjoyed a distinct advantage over the general.[9]

Publicly, Adams maintained his principled opposition to any sleazy deal-making, refusing to speculate about his future cabinet choices. Privately, he displayed an avid willingness to bargain his way into the presidency. With representatives from the states he needed to win over to his cause, Adams openly discussed printing contracts and potential administrative appointments. He promised not to remove any current appointees just because they had supported another candidate in the election. Echoing his campaign pronouncements, Adams also continued offering vague opinions on policy issues. He promised inquisitive southerners that his tariff policy would champion "*conciliation, and not collision.*" While satisfied with current levels of protection, he claimed to be "inclined" to lower tariffs to benefit agricultural and commercial interests. Meanwhile, he declared the constitutionality of federally funded internal improvements a settled question, but the potential for abuse of such enormous power would be controlled by the states and the people through elections. Any representative from anywhere could read almost anything into Adams's deliberately fuzzy policy positions.[10]

Adams set about rounding up the votes he needed for victory. With his success in New York's legislative election, that important mid-Atlantic state appeared as a legitimate target in Adams's House campaign. Countering Van Buren's machinations, he tried to appeal to the anti-Crawford Clintonians in the delegation. General Jacob Brown, disgusted by the "weakness, defeats, and disappointments of the North hitherto," promoted a union between Adams and DeWitt Clinton. Such an alliance would not only block the two southern slaveholders from claiming the executive chair but would also provide Clinton with a victory over Van Buren in their ongoing struggle to control politics in the Empire State. Adams carefully praised Clinton, acknowledged their similar political views, but reminded Brown that Clinton favored Jackson for the presidency.[11]

Clinton's stand demonstrated that succession politics often trumped ideology for representatives in the House. Now that the South's control of the presidency might be broken, the other regional favorites calculated their own future claims on the office. Clay's New York supporters began gravitating toward Adams because they believed that Clay, as a westerner, would be next in line after a northerner. New York's Clintonians made the same calculation; by supporting the westerner Jackson now, they would set up the northerner Clinton to follow the general into the White House. Clinton himself had swayed New Jersey's delegation with similar logic. While Jackson had won the state's popular election, many of its representatives admired Adams. Unfortunately for the secretary of state, Clinton convinced New Jersey's delegation to follow the popular vote and cast theirs for Jackson. While Adams hoped for mid-Atlantic state House votes, convoluted succession politics insured continued murkiness.[12]

Despite his mid-Atlantic state setbacks, Adams's best work occurred in one-on-one meetings with key western legislators. Unknown to the secretary of state, a group of representatives from five western states—Ohio, Kentucky, Missouri, Illinois, and Louisiana—had secretly met and agreed to act in concert to maximize their influence in a House election. Illinois representative Daniel P. Cook had been one of the attendees. As the only congressman from his state, Cook could decide Illinois's presidential choice entirely by himself, which naturally subjected him to enormous pressures from all three candidates. He had previously pledged to support the electoral vote winner in Illinois, which meant that he must vote for Jackson to honor his promise. Yet, he was married to Ninian Edwards's daughter and was still exceedingly grateful that Adams had untiringly supported his father-in-law. At a meeting with Adams, Cook claimed that the split decision in his state "leaves him at perfect liberty to vote in the House as he should think best for the public interest." While he would avoid "standing out alone" for the secretary of state in the West, where many ordinary voters favored Jackson, Cook had discovered—obviously in the secret meeting—that enough representatives from Ohio, Kentucky, Missouri, and Louisiana would join him behind Adams to give him cover in voting for the New Englander. When the Jacksonians explicitly dangled the governorship of the Arkansas Territory to entice Cook to their side, Adams countered with a private dinner for Cook and his wife. His long-term solicitous attention to Cook paid off handsomely when the representative remained loyal to Adams despite the Jacksonians' alluring offer.[13]

Like Cook in Illinois, Missouri's lone representative, John Scott, controlled the presidential vote of his entire state. In a private meeting, Adams agreed to switch Missouri's official printer to one who supported Scott and to oppose a pending petition to remove Scott's brother as a judge in the Arkansas Territory for killing another judge in a duel. Scott ended the meeting by openly lobbying for a cabinet post for Clay. Adams refused to commit on specifics, but tellingly promised that "if I should be elected by the suffrages of the West I should naturally look to the West for much of the support that I should need." Scott's interest in Clay's future only proved what every contender had long expected: Clay increasingly appeared central to a victory in the House election. The key to landing the Speaker's support rested in wooing Kentucky's delegation.[14]

Clay's home state might very well have been Adams's toughest nut to crack. To win Kentucky, Adams needed to overcome the opposition to his victory that was rife within the state. Adams and Clay had not only been rivals in an acrimonious presidential race, they had a long-standing personal dislike for each other that transcended their agreement on various policy issues. The dissimilar pair had never been friendly, but they had truly clashed during the Ghent treaty negotiations, when Adams would rise at 4 a.m. to begin his workday only to discover the card party in Clay's room was just breaking up. Beyond Clay's personal future, many Kentuckians demanded a westerner in the White House and expected their congressional delegation to gratify those wishes by opposing the New Englander and supporting Jackson.[15]

Somewhat surprisingly, then, by early January, Clay had already settled on Adams among his "choice of evils." Publicly, he dismissed Crawford as a result of his health issues and his undemocratic caucus nomination. Clay rejected Jackson because the general "would give to the Military Spirit a Stimulus . . . that might lead to the most pernicious results." The Speaker probably also realized that a President Crawford and his Radical allies would almost certainly block the passage of any American System legislation, while a President Jackson would frustrate Clay's own political hegemony over the West. Clay's move also made immediate political sense. He knew that the secretary of state was generally the second choice in states that favored Crawford, meaning that Adams retained much more maneuverability to win a House election than either of his rivals. Most important of all, three-quarters of Kentucky's delegation already privately supported Adams. Although ordinary Kentuckians favored Jackson for president, their representatives backed the secretary of state solely because they believed "that their kind wishes [regarding Clay] will, in the end, be more likely to be accomplished by so bestowing their votes." Righting an old wrong from 1816, Clay and his fellow Kentucky representatives intended that he would be named secretary of state and thus the presidential heir apparent in the next administration. All this maneuvering occurred behind the scenes; Adams and Clay needed each other but were not yet certain what the other party was thinking.[16]

Accordingly, the secretary and the Speaker carefully commenced a delicate dance aimed at furthering both their political careers. Through intermediaries, Clay informed Adams that he "was much disposed to support [him], if he could at the same time be useful to himself." Meanwhile, Kentucky representative Robert P. Letcher discreetly reminded Adams that his constituents favored Jackson, so he could only back Adams in the House if it benefited Kentucky. "The substance of his *meaning*," Adams noted, "was that if Clay's friends could *know* that he would have a prominent share in the Administration, that might induce them to vote for me," even in the face of opposition from back home. At Letcher's request, Adams readily agreed to meet with the Speaker directly. Though both men had conferred only in general terms, the seeds of a future grand bargain delivering Kentucky's House vote to Adams and the State Department portfolio to Clay had already been sown. Adams himself seemed to grasp the significance of his pending deal with the Speaker. "There is in my prospects and anticipations a solemnity and moment never before experienced," he admitted after his discussions with Letcher.[17]

The adversaries met in Adams's office on January 9, 1825. The secretary of state's normally chatty diary is surprisingly brief and circumspect regarding the details of his fateful encounter with Clay. The two politicos shared "a long conversation explanatory of the past and prospective of the future," Adams noted. They obviously ended their venerable and bitter feud, dismissing over ten years of real animosity in two hours. Probably trying to gauge Adams's level of commitment to the American System, the Speaker insisted that instead of personal concerns, he wanted Adams "to satisfy him with regard to some principles of great public importance." Adams eagerly complied, and Clay left the meeting with "no hesitation in saying that his preference would be for me." Both participants later insisted that Adams never directly offered Clay the State Department in exchange for his backing in the House election. Whether openly declared or not, Adams needed Clay's support to win the House election, and Clay needed Adams's support to be designated next in line for the presidency. While no one except Adams and Clay can ever know for certain what the pair discussed in their meeting, to suggest that two savvy politicians, each with dozens of backroom deals to their credit, would suddenly balk at openly hashing out the most important political bargain either man had made to date simply strains credulity.[18]

New Hampshire representative William Plumer, one of Adams's closest allies, claimed that Adams told him that Clay had agreed to support him, but would need time to win over the rest of Kentucky's delegation. "I did not think it decorous to inquire more particularly," Plumer noted diffidently, "nor did Mr. Adams seem disposed to say anything further of what passed between them." Undeniably, Adams appeared visibly at ease after his meeting with Clay. When Kentucky's legislative instructions demanding their representatives support a westerner in the House vote arrived a few days later, his supporters fretted over this new obstacle to victory. The secretary of state coolly informed them, however, to "see and converse with Mr. Clay." Although one Kentucky state legislator insisted that "he did not wish the vote of Kentucky to be bartered away, or that Mr. Clay should be secretary of State to the exclusion of Jackson as president," a majority of Kentucky's delegation clearly seemed prepared to do just that. A deal had indeed been sealed.[19]

As he had during the campaign, Clay used legislation to further a presidential bid, but this time Adams reaped the benefits of the Speaker's strategy. Eight days after their meeting, Clay introduced a bill in the House to appropriate funding for an extension of the National Road through Ohio, Indiana, Illinois, and Missouri, four western states that Adams had assiduously courted and desperately needed to win in the House election. With the Radicals in control of the Senate, the bill had little chance of passing Congress, but Clay's intent was not to push an expensive new piece of legislation. Instead, his latest bill offered Adamsites a chance to prove their commitment to both the American System and the West. Most of New England's representatives, who had earlier in the year soundly rejected financing Clay's much less expensive General Survey Bill, experienced a sudden change of heart and backed Clay's new bill by a substantial margin. Even more helpfully, Jacksonians from the southern and eastern states unwittingly fell into Clay's trap and voted against the bill, which dramatically illustrated the difference between the potential Jackson and Adams administrations. Clay also sponsored a bill funding the Chesapeake and Delaware Canal. Similar legislation had also failed in the past, but again the New Englanders switched sides, and the bill cleared the House 97–72. If any western representative had qualms that a President Adams and his regional allies would support their internal improvement wish list, Clay's clever legislative gambit erased any doubts.[20]

In histories of the era, Clay and Adams's frequent collaboration and ideological agreement throughout their subsequent careers has overshadowed the shocking nature of their decision to join forces in January 1825. However, historians should not read politicians backward by analyzing their earlier careers based on stances they would later adopt. To their contemporaries, any cooperation between the two severely antagonistic personal enemies, one an enthusiastic proponent of Monroe's policies and the other a tart-tongued critic, was almost inconceivable. About two weeks before the scheduled House election, Clay, joined by majorities of the Kentucky and Ohio delegations, "unequivocally" announced his intention to vote for Adams. The news burst upon the capital with as much fury as the British bombardment in 1814. Recriminations erupted fast and furious, ironically focused mostly on Clay. As the reputed Machiavellian manipulator, the Speaker, rather than the secretary, bore the brunt of the Jacksonian counterattack. The general's followers screeched that Clay had betrayed democracy as well as the West, deliberately blocking the popularly backed

Jackson so that he might subsequently take his place as the first Western president.[21]

Although the general had always distrusted him, even Jackson seemed taken aback by "such an unexpected course" from Clay. "He is greatly fallen, never to rise again in the estimation of the ame[ri]can nation," Jackson insisted. Still, Clay's actions allowed Jackson to reinsert his favorite campaign theme into the House election. "Intrigue, corruption, and sale of public office is the rumor of the day," the general noted with almost evident satisfaction. "It will give the people a full view of our political weathercocks here." Only Crawford, who nursed his own long-running feud with Clay, professed to be unsurprised by the curious turn of events. It "is astonishing every person here except myself," he bragged to Jefferson. "I have long known the principal juggler." Amid the firestorm, Clay could only reiterate the principles that he insisted had supported his unexpected decision. "I should never have selected [Adams] if at liberty to draw from the whole mass of our citizens," the Speaker proclaimed, "but there is no danger in his elevation. . . . Not so of his competitor. . . . I cannot believe that killing 2500 Englishmen at N. Orleans qualifies for the various, difficult, and complicated duties of the Chief Magistracy." Yet, as much as Clay might rationalize his choice, it proved an unpopular stance throughout the West; even in Kentucky, calls to burn Clay in effigy had to be stifled by his friends.[22]

While Jackson carped in private about Clay's decision, the Speaker faced much more serious public charges about his actions. The day after Clay announced his support for Adams, an anonymous House member from Pennsylvania printed an explosive editorial in the Philadelphia *Columbian Observer*. The article blasted "one of the most disgraceful transactions that ever covered with infamy the Republican Ranks." It alleged that Clay's supporters had approached Jackson's men offering to vote for the general in the House election if Jackson promised to make Clay his secretary of state. The Jacksonians had naturally rebuffed this nefarious offer, the editorial alleged, but the fact that Clay now favored Adams only proved that he supported "those who would pay best." These allegations in the *Observer* represented the first occasion that the word "bargain" had publicly been applied to Clay's actions during the House election.[23]

Clay responded furiously in the pages of the *National Intelligencer*. He called the anonymous author "a base and infamous calumniator, a dastard and a liar" and implied that he would challenge the unidentified representative to a duel should he be unmasked. At Clay's behest, the House formed a special committee to investigate the matter. As with the A. B. inquiry, the Speaker maintained a careful political balance on the committee, with four Crawfordites, two Adams men, and one Jacksonian serving. He wisely limited his own supporters' role to ensure public acceptance of the group's findings. There was no danger for Clay in convening an investigation into the charges with a committee composed of the allies of his competitors. Though the Speaker *had* probably entered into this type of bargain with Adams, he knew that neither he nor his followers had ever approached Jackson. Clay simply never intended to promote any westerner other than himself for the presidency and never supported Jackson for high office.[24]

Shortly after Clay's call for an investigation, Pennsylvania representative George Kremer admitted by letter to the committee that he was the author of the article. He claimed that he could "prove, to the satisfaction of unprejudiced minds . . . the accuracy of the statements," agreeing to fully participate in the congressional investigation. Kremer appeared to be the dull-witted front man for a much larger conspiracy to defame Clay. His letter had been ghostwritten by two former Calhounites now supporting Jackson, Samuel Ingham and George McDuffie. In their haste to raise suspicions about Clay, McDuffie had foolishly corrected Kremer's numerous misspellings in his own hand. With his accuser's identity revealed, Clay was shocked. Kremer was an unobtrusive, poorly regarded first-term Congressman with little involvement in the capital's power politics. Favoring a leopard-skin overcoat, his fellow representatives considered him a curious eccentric and a heavy drinker. Kremer was said to be an "intemperate man and that he scarcely knew whether he had written the letter or not," Adams noted. Clay uncharitably dismissed Kremer as an "old vulgar gross drinking half dutchman half irishman of whom I could make nothing."[25]

Kremer began having second thoughts about his intrusion into the divisive House election. He refused to duel with Clay, and the Speaker decided not to pursue an affair of honor with such an inconsequential opponent.

Through intermediaries, Kremer suggested that he would sign an apology acceptable to Clay, "declaring that he knew no fact ascertaining that any bargain had been made." Unwilling to sacrifice the plot besmirching the Speaker, Ingham, McDuffie, and future president James Buchanan, then Kremer's fellow representative from Pennsylvania, dissuaded him from settling the matter. Buchanan had ample reason to prevent Kremer from admitting the truth. He himself had secretly approached Kremer, trying to broker a deal that made Clay secretary of state under Jackson. Kremer believed that Buchanan had come directly from Clay, and his fellow representative allowed this mistaken impression to stand. In fact, Buchanan was freelancing the deal and had never been authorized by Clay or his allies to approach Jackson. Believing that a combined Jackson/Clay administration would most benefit the Keystone State, the ambitious Buchanan extended his clumsy overtures to Kremer as a means of advancing his own political standing in Pennsylvania.[26]

Jackson welcomed the investigation into Kremer's charges. He fervently believed that the Pennsylvania representative had "ample proof" of Clay's corrupt transactions, because Buchanan had also approached him directly with the same unauthorized deal that he had floated to Kremer. Cagily, the general had been noncommittal with Buchanan. Privately, he harshly rebuked the offer. "I would see the earth open & swallow both Mr. Clay & his friends, and myself with them," Jackson thundered, rather than making a deal with his detested enemy. The general admitted that "I did suppose [Buchanan] had come from Mr. Clay; although he used the term Mr. Clay's friends" when suggesting the bargain. For his part, Buchanan misinterpreted Jackson's unrevealing answer as confirmation that Clay would receive the State Department appointment, which he told the Speaker directly.[27]

Jackson's underlings were far less sanguine than the general about a congressional probe into Kremer's accusations. Probably realizing that Clay had called their bluff by convening an investigation into Kremer's likely spurious charges, Eaton sputtered angrily, "What has Congress to do with this: nothing . . . private disputes are for private adjustment, certainly not for the interference of Congress." Jacksonians launched their own congressional counterattack. McDuffie himself submitted a resolution demanding a separate investigation into charges that Adams had bargained with Clay, but the pairs' joint forces in the House successfully quashed the proposal. Jacksonians were irritated because they believed, but could not prove, that Clay had cut a deal with Adams, so Kremer's charges served as a back-handed way of validating the suspected "combination." Clay's openness to investigating his alleged bargain with Jackson, but his unwillingness to sanction scrutiny of his similar dealings with Adams, only further confirmed that Buchanan had peddled fiction, but that the Speaker had indeed concluded an agreement with Adams.[28]

Ultimately, Kremer simply refused to testify to the investigating committee, insisting that "the unequal contest between a humble member on the floor, and the Speaker of the House" was unfair, so "the issue should be left before the American people" to adjudicate. Without their star witness, the committee's report concluded that no further investigation was possible. While Clay appeared to be exonerated by Kremer's obvious obfuscations, his reputation as a corrupt bargainer had already been established before the House had cast a single vote for the next president.[29]

With Clay's official backing, Adams had certainly gained the most important prize in the competition for allies, but Jackson also wrangled his own big-name proponent. Despite his "most solemn asseverations" to remain neutral, Calhoun and his organization had secretly thrown their support to the general. Calhounites Ingham and McDuffie were the principal tormentors pressuring Illinois's Cook to vote for Jackson and the prime movers behind the Kremer fiasco. Meanwhile, Calhoun supporters in Connecticut's delegation were instigating their pro-Crawford fellows to vote for the treasury secretary to deny Adams a New England state that he had long counted in his column. Calhoun had apparently calculated that a politically inexperienced and aged soldier like Jackson might be a more easily manipulated (and possibly one-term) president than a savvy, strong-willed politico like Adams. As Jackson's vice president, Calhoun would likely exert more control over his administration and ensure his place in the succession than he could serving as Adams's junior partner.[30]

Clay and Calhoun supported different candidates, but both for the same personal reasons. While the Speaker also hoped to advance his American

System policies, he backed Adams as a means of securing a stepping-stone to the presidency. Similarly, Calhoun championed Jackson in hopes that playing a major role in the allegedly nonpolitical general's administration would serve Calhoun's own higher political ambitions. Seemingly, both men failed to realize that using a lesser office to win a greater one was exactly the kind of corruption Jackson had long censured. For the general, Clay's actions would help support his future campaign against corruption, with lethal consequences for the impending Adams administration and Clay's own political career. Still, prominent Republicans like Clay and Calhoun were expected to influence the selection of the eventual winner of the one-party election. As the House vote neared, a much-maligned and almost forgotten group of outsiders unexpectedly surfaced. While the Federalists had hovered on the periphery of the 1824 contest throughout the perpetual campaign, they suddenly emerged to play an outsize role in the election's startling finale.

Wooing the Opposition: The Federalists Strike Back

While the Federalists had not fielded their own candidate in 1824, they harbored hopes of influencing the Republican-only election to their benefit. During the election, Clay and Calhoun had expended the greatest effort in courting the opposition party. The Speaker had focused on Federalists in the manufacturing and mercantile communities in New York, while the secretary of war had made a strenuous bid to appeal to nationalist-minded Federalists in Maryland. Comparatively, Crawford and Jackson offered a more restrained approach to winning opposition votes by befriending individual Federalists. Despite their measured efforts, the pair actually outperformed Clay and Calhoun in attracting Federalist supporters. Jackson's pro-Federalist letter portrayed the general as a likely candidate to end the proscription policy, while Crawford attracted many elite Federalist leaders to his cause. Even Timothy Pickering, the Federalist most symbolic of his party, endorsed the treasury secretary, with one political commentator jesting that being a Republican "has not heretofore been a recommendation with Mr. P—— for anything but a gibbet." As we have seen in chapter 1, Adams purposely avoided pursuing the Federalists and received fewer votes from the opposition party than any of his opponents. Many Federalists had never forgiven the secretary of state for leaping off their sinking ship in 1808, and Adams needed to avoid any taint from his Federalist past that might repel Republican voters in the present.[31]

Though some Federalists remained content to vote for their favorite candidate and let the election play out, others plotted a more activist course. Massachusetts representative Daniel Webster championed the latter. He argued throughout the perpetual campaign that his partisan allies should not pursue any specific Republican candidate, but let the Republicans come to the Federalists bearing patronage plums to gain the party's support. Like the various side-switching Republicans that bedeviled the 1824 candidates, Webster continually shifted allegiances during the campaign. Initially he favored Calhoun, but by the time he served on the A. B. investigation committee, he had realigned his support to Crawford and proved a principal defender of the embattled treasury secretary. Once the general election ended and the House decision approached, Webster abandoned the feckless Crawford campaign and tried to position the Federalists between Adams and Jackson so his party could profit regardless of which man triumphed.[32]

Unsurprisingly, Calhoun convinced his Federalist supporters to switch to Jackson. In response, Adams tried to reassure his former party members that their acrimonious relations were over. Claiming he would exclude no person from his administration for their political opinions, Adams insisted that "my great object would be to break up the remnant of old party distinctions, and bring the whole people together." Once Clay joined the Adams campaign, he further encouraged the secretary to reconcile with prominent Federalists. It was perhaps fitting that Clay promoted cooperation between Adams and the Federalists. To political observers in 1824, the secretary of state's reconciliation with his bitter former party appeared almost as improbable as his rapprochement with Clay.[33]

Just as Adams had kept the Federalists at arm's length in the general election so as not to damage his image with Republicans, he now embraced them to prevail in the House vote. Webster deliberately waited until the balloting was less than a week away to meet directly with Adams. With the votes of Maryland and New York still in doubt, the Federalists in those delegations might tip the scales in favor of Adams. Ultimately, Adams overtly promised Webster that he would appoint Federalists to positions in his government. In response, Webster produced a prewritten letter to Henry Warfield, a Federalist congressman from Maryland, that urged Warfield to join Webster in supporting Adams for president. The correspondence stated that Webster's backing of Adams arose "not from any understanding or communication with him," but because Adams would "promote harmony" between the parties. Adams endorsed the document, one that ironically disclaimed dealmaking while he was in the middle of dealmaking.[34]

Webster shared his letter with Warfield, as well as prominent Federalists McLane from Delaware and Stephen Van Rensselaer from New York. He then brokered a meeting between the trio and Adams. The entire affair unreeled almost like a one-act play, since all participants had been briefed ahead of time as to what to expect. Adams directly repeated his pledge to end the proscription of Federalists and, further, to recommended that Monroe name a Federalist as governor of the Arkansas Territory, the same position the Jacksonians were dangling to Cook. Garnering support from his former party only capped an incredible string of social politicking triumphs for Adams. With his gains in Kentucky, Ohio, Missouri, Illinois, New York, and Maryland, he now appeared on the cusp of a come-from-behind victory over Jackson in the House. Belying his reputation as a man lacking in political skills, Adams had performed spectacularly indeed.[35]

Picking a President: Decision Day in the House

Despite Adams's relative confidence in victory, in a political culture based on shifting allegiances, he could never be certain until the votes were counted. When Calhoun predicted that Jackson would sweep the western states and win the election, "he must be either grossly misinformed or too well informed," the secretary of state lamented wryly. Surveying the uncertainty, Webster chuckled that "there were persons who pretended to know how a member would vote by the manner in which he put on or took off his hat." Still, Adams had apparently locked down the six New England states; his bargaining with the Federalists had extinguished some restive murmurings against his candidacy in the Connecticut and Vermont delegations. With five additional western states potentially delivered by Clay coupled with the Federalists possibly tilting New York, Maryland, and Delaware his way, Adams seemed poised to realize his long-held presidential dreams.[36]

For Jackson's men, their early overconfidence had evaporated in the face of Clay's shocking determination to vote for Adams. Despite their doubts, Eaton expected Jackson to carry six western states—he only conceded Kentucky, Ohio, and Illinois to Adams—plus Pennsylvania, New Jersey, Maryland, and South Carolina. With a solid ten states behind him after an initial vote, surely Virginia, North Carolina, and Georgia would abandon Crawford's hopeless cause on subsequent ballots and hop aboard the Jackson bandwagon. Still, Eaton refused to believe that any western state would not vote for the western candidate, especially one that had received a popular vote mandate. "I think in the end the West will break and come right," he predicted hopefully, but with a whiff of desperation.[37]

The House election was scheduled for shortly after noon on February 9, 1825. Although the weather outside was cold and stormy, the galleries, lobbies, and floor were so crowded with congressmen and onlookers that the atmosphere inside was stifling. In the presence of the entire Congress, the president of the Senate, John Gaillard of South Carolina, read the certificates of electors submitted by the states. After declaring Calhoun the vice president–elect, Gaillard announced that no candidate had received a majority for the presidency, and the Senate retired from the room. Representatives divided into state delegations to poll their groups, with a teller reporting the state's decision to the Speaker. As everyone suspected, only four states voted for Crawford. Despite Webster's pressure, Delaware's McLane stuck by the treasury secretary as he had promised all along, and his state was joined by Georgia, Virginia, and North Carolina. Jackson unsurprisingly snared Pennsylvania, New Jersey, and South Carolina, but as the western votes began trickling in, the effectiveness of Adams's social politicking and avid dealmaking became painfully obvious to the general's forces. The popular western hero captured only four states from the region. Illinois, Ohio, Kentucky, Missouri, and Louisiana all cast their lot with Adams instead. The secretary of state's last-minute dalliance with the Federalists proved equally fruitful. In Maryland's delegation, Warfield voted for Adams. After a Jacksonian representative unexpectedly switched to him because Adams had carried his district by a substantial margin, Adams captured Maryland's vote on the first ballot. With the six New England states remaining true to him, Adams had won twelve states, only one shy of success.[38]

As if on cue, New York suddenly emerged as the linchpin to victory, as it seemingly had been throughout the election of 1824. Thanks to Van Buren's exhaustive exhortations, his state's delegation remained almost evenly divided, with seventeen representatives supporting Adams and sixteen opposed. The one remaining vote would decide the outcome of the election. If the representative voted for Crawford or Jackson, New York would deadlock, denying Adams a first-ballot victory, heartening the Jacksonians, and preserving Crawford's long-shot bid for redemption. If the representative voted for Adams, however, the election would be over. To almost everyone's surprise, including his own, the outcome of an election that only Republican candidates had contested rested with a Federalist representative, Van Rensselaer, the same man that Adams had been assiduously courting for a week.[39]

The tenuousness of Van Rensselaer's support must have unnerved the Adamsites. Van Rensselaer had swapped presidential favorites with greater avidity than even Webster. He had supported Calhoun in 1823, but upon developing a close friendship with Van Buren once Van Buren arrived in the Senate, Van Rensselaer switched to Crawford. By January 1825, Van Rensselaer publicly declared himself to be leaning Jackson only a month after promising to support Clay's choice. Meanwhile, Van Buren and McLane believed that Van Rensselaer had promised them *not* to vote for Adams under any circumstances. On the morning of the vote, Clay and Webster put the final screws to Van Rensselaer in the Speaker's office, threatening "dire consequences" from the "disorganization of government" if he failed to back Adams and the House election ended in a stalemate. Beset by all sides, Van Rensselaer cast his ballot with "obvious agitation and distress." In the final ironic act of the completely unpredictable election, a patrician Federalist voted for John Quincy Adams, tipping New York into his column and electing him the sixth president of the United States. Adams's strategic insider dealmaking proved absolutely essential to winning the House election and was another key development determining the outcome of the election of 1824 (see table 3).[40]

TABLE 3. Vote totals for the House election of 1825

STATE	WINNER	VOTES PER CANDIDATE		
		ADAMS	JACKSON	CRAWFORD
NEW ENGLAND				
Connecticut	Adams	6	0	0
Maine	Adams	7	0	0
Massachusetts	Adams	12	1	0
New Hampshire	Adams	6	0	0
Rhode Island	Adams	2	0	0
Vermont	Adams	5	0	0
MID-ATLANTIC				
Delaware	Crawford	0	0	1
Maryland	Adams	5	3	1
New Jersey	Jackson	1	5	0
New York	Adams	18	2	14
Pennsylvania	Jackson	1	25	0
SOUTH				
Virginia	Crawford	1	1	19
North Carolina	Crawford	1	2	10
South Carolina	Jackson	0	9	0
Georgia	Crawford	0	0	7

(continued)

TABLE 3. Vote totals for the House election of 1825 (*continued*)

STATE	WINNER	VOTES PER CANDIDATE		
		ADAMS	JACKSON	CRAWFORD
SOUTHWEST				
Alabama	Jackson	0	3	0
Mississippi	Jackson	0	1	0
Louisiana	Adams	2	1	0
Tennessee	Jackson	0	9	0
NORTHWEST				
Missouri	Adams	1	0	0
Kentucky	Adams	8	4	0
Ohio	Adams	10	2	2
Indiana	Jackson	0	3	0
Illinois	Adams	1	0	0
Total votes	**Adams**	**87**	**71**	**54**
Total states won	**Adams**	**13**	**7**	**4**

Sources: *Rhode Island American*, "Election of President," February 18, 1825, 3; *Rhode Island American*, "Presidential Election," February 22, 1825, 2.

"Well, Mr. Van Buren, you saw that I could not hold out," Van Rensselaer told the New York senator sheepishly as he returned to his desk. Van Buren later claimed that the pious Van Rensselaer, after praying for divine guidance, opened his eyes and spied an Adams ballot on the floor, which he picked up and tossed in the ballot box. Van Buren's colorful tale could not conceal a hard truth. The supposedly nonpolitical Adams had bested the crafty New Yorker *twice*—once in the New York legislative vote and now in the House. Van Rensselaer later claimed publicly that he had indeed felt committed to Clay, so once Clay backed Adams and Adams promised not to proscribe Federalists, Van Rensselaer decided he had little choice except to vote for the secretary of state. Like any good Federalist, in the end, he opted to go with the winner in the hope of extracting the maximum patronage return for his party. Still, Van Rensselaer had never expected Adams to win on the first ballot or that he himself would determine New York's

choice, so he was truly mentally anguished when the entire election ultimately turned on his decision.[41]

"May the blessing of God rest upon the event of this day!" Adams exclaimed upon hearing the news that he had been elected. Even he proved
somewhat surprised that he had won on the first ballot. Perhaps less thrilled
than the man for whom he had voted, Clay simply declared that "the 'long
agony' was terminated." His allies could not help celebrating the downfall
of the inexperienced brute whom they deemed primarily responsible for
Clay's loss. "It is something that he who defeated your election, should
himself be defeated," one Clayite noted with satisfaction about Jackson's
collapse. With the Speaker in tow, the president-elect attended Monroe's
customary Wednesday evening drawing room gala. The pair somewhat
tremulously encountered Jackson at the party, but the general was "alto-
gether placid and courteous," and he readily shook hands with both men.
Adams returned to his own home late; after midnight "a band of musi-
cians came and serenaded me." Although Adams's victory pleased and excited him, his father may have been even more moved. "Never did I feel
so much solemnity as upon this occasion," the elder John Adams told
his son. "The multitude of my thoughts and the intensity of my feelings are
too much for a mind like mine, in its ninetieth year." Despite distancing
himself from his past, Adams's victory was a family affair indeed.[42]

Crawford awaited the results at home with his wife and friends. He had
long since resigned himself to defeat, and while some of his cronies were disconsolate, he appeared almost relieved. "Most sincerely do I wish we may go
to Woodlawn [his estate in Georgia] instead of the White House," Crawford
told one visitor. "I am sure we shall be far happier." When word arrived that
Adams had triumphed, the treasury secretary appeared almost stunned. "Is
it possible!" Crawford exclaimed, "I thought it would have been Jackson.
Well, I am glad it is over." The perpetual campaign had probably taken the
greatest toll on Crawford compared to the other competitors. While some
of his supporters cried when the results were announced, a jaunty Crawford ordered the card and chess tables set up, and his party lasted well into
the night. His long political nightmare was finally over. Though himself an
ambitious political schemer, the treasury secretary had been overmatched

against the multiple attacks coming from the equally cunning politicos running against him. Facing more democratized presidential elections, Crawford's commitment to the elitist rules of traditional presidential politics proved less competitive than the strategies of his rivals.[43]

Jackson adopted a carefully nurtured facade of cordiality to prove that he harbored no "feelings of complaint" about the outcome. Privately, the general was furious, though not surprised, at the corruption he believed evident in the results. "Thus you see here, the voice of the people of the West have been disregarded," Jackson bellowed, "and demagogues barter them as sheep in the shambles, for their own views, and personal agrandisement [sic]." Many of his supporters demonstrated similar wrath, especially in Pennsylvania, where voters had favored Jackson overwhelmingly. In Pittsburgh, some Jacksonians burned Adams in effigy, while others paraded a life-size Clay mannequin through the streets with a "For Sale" sign hanging from its neck. Another rowdy bunch who had been copiously drinking whiskey out of a large cask announced their intention to "roast a Kentucky gambler over a burning tar barrel." Simpson's *Columbian Observer* ran a huge black-bordered headline that screamed, simply, "SHAMEFUL." Adams's and Clay's long political nightmare had just begun.[44]

Birth of a Legend: Bargaining and the Politics of Corruption

Adams may have enjoyed the shortest presidential honeymoon on record. His unexpected upset of Jackson in the House election sparked a torrent of criticism in the capital and beyond from the moment the results were announced. While the general may have been publicly civil to Clay, his followers were visibly outraged at the Speaker. "We owe all of our confusion to Clay," Eaton howled. "Had he regarded the wishes of the people, or even stood silent (voting as he pleased) and such surely was the course for one who had himself been a candidate, all things . . . would have moved on harmoniously and well." Ironically, the Speaker bore the brunt of blame for all of the western losses; most Jacksonians ignored the Adams deals that had been largely responsible for denying Missouri and Illinois to the general.[45]

Jacksonians accused the Speaker of clearly subverting the will of his constituents. The Speaker parried that he had received conflicting advice from citizens in his home state. "I could not comply with their wishes unless, at the same time, I were to vote for all three of the Candidates," he insisted, so he felt liberated to follow his conscience and back Adams. He vehemently dismissed Kentucky's legislative instructions. The resolution's supporters had claimed to represent "the wish of the people," but how could they even know what the people wished, Clay demanded? He had defeated Jackson by over ten thousand votes in Kentucky. "I could not see how such an expression *against* him, could be interpreted into that of a desire *for* his election," the Speaker argued hotly.[46]

The Washington *Gazette* turned Clay's own words against him, arguing that "a thousand 'military chieftains' could not have done so much harm to our constitutional principles." These claims forced the Adams men to counter that the framers would not have included a contingent House election in the Constitution if the popular victor were simply to be crowned president. Clay and Adams certainly believed that they had not violated any republican tenets, but both men had clearly missed the changes in the political culture. Thomas Hart Benton cogently argued that while Adams's election had been "perfectly constitutional" it violated "democratic principles." With presidential elections becoming increasingly more democratic, voters expected their will to be reflected in the choices made by Washington politicians. Jackson had not only won the popular vote, he was undoubtedly the second choice of voters in most of the states Crawford and Clay had carried. The general's dominant position had been conveniently ignored by Adams and his congressional allies.[47]

Beyond criticizing the election itself, threatening rumors swirled about the "determined opposition" to Adams's potential appointment of Clay to the State Department. "The object was to intimidate me, and deter me from the nomination," Adams bristled. The president-elect did not give the critics much time to ponder the matter. The day after his House election, Adams privately admitted that he would offer Clay the State Department portfolio in his cabinet, making it official two days after that. Adams argued that Clay was more than qualified for the post, that the "western section" was long overdue for a cabinet appointment, and that he owed a political debt to the region for "the confidence in me manifested by their delegations." The president-elect's assertions were certainly correct. Clay had sufficient experience in foreign affairs to merit the post, no westerner had ever served in any president's cabinet, and the House votes of five western states had boosted him into the White House.[48]

Avoiding any appearance of a planned quid pro quo, Clay did not immediately accept the State portfolio. Both he and Adams were aware of the simmering fury over the appointment, but Clay "made light of the threatened opposition," Adams observed. The Speaker made a pretense of consulting with his friends, and they almost universally insisted that he take the position. Many suggested that hysterical talk about "horrible conspiracies" only aimed at frightening Clay out of accepting the portfolio. Others openly acknowledged that he would be far closer to becoming president from the State Department post than the Speaker's dais. Naturally, Adamsites also urged Clay to accept, but surprisingly, even some Crawfordites strongly encouraged him to join the new administration. Opposition emanated from disgruntled Jacksonians and from Calhounites determined that their man would be the next in line for the presidency.[49]

Clay carefully weighed the pros and cons of becoming Adams's secretary of state. He acknowledged that accepting the position would be deemed "conclusive evidence" that he had engaged in a shady bargain with Adams, but he then decided that he would be similarly accused even if he refused. "It will be said that the patriotic Mr. Kremer, by an exposure of the corrupt arrangement, had prevented its consummation," Clay insisted. He opined that he might better serve the new administration from "my theater" in the House, but then countered that he must accept direct responsibility for the success of a government that he had helped create by working directly in its cabinet. If he avoided joining Adams, critics would contend that "I thought so ill of him that I would not take the first place under him," Clay reasoned. Ultimately, he resolved to set aside his "personal objections" and accept the appointment as Adams's secretary of state. Clay also harbored unstated intentions, of course. He planned to use his new influence over Adams to further the American System, as many of his supporters avidly desired, while also positioning himself to become the next president, just as the last four secretaries of state had done. Accordingly, he willingly accepted the short-term political damage for the long-term political benefit. Clay believed the fallout from his decision would quickly fade, while his honor would be permanently scarred if he allowed his enemies to intimidate him out of accepting a job he both wanted and needed. As had so often occurred during the election, Clay's political instincts proved quite mistaken.[50]

When Clay's appointment was announced, the roars of disapproval exceeded the volume of complaints surrounding his initial declaration that he planned to vote for Adams. Critics insisted that a "corrupt bargain" had occurred in which Adams and Clay had traded the State Department appointment in exchange for House votes from the western states. Jacksonians shrieked the loudest, led privately by the general himself. "So you see the *Judas* of the West has closed the contract and will receive the thirty pieces of silver," Jackson snarled, insisting that the pair would be turned out of office after one term. Indeed, Jackson exploited the corrupt bargain charges to lay down a marker for future elections. Only the voters could correct these abuses, the general warned, and "if they do not in less than 25 years, we will become the slaves, not of a 'military chieftain' but of such ambitious demagogues as Henry Clay." Later in life, several Jacksonians, including Van Buren and Benton, conceded that the charges had been overwrought and unfair. Benton admitted that Clay had informed him in mid-December that he planned to vote for Adams and that he did not support Jackson "for the reasons afterward averred to in his public speeches." Though fourteen senators voted against him, Clay was confirmed as secretary of state. Still, the short- and long-term injury to his reputation could not be undone.[51]

Many critics of the Adams/Clay alliance truly believed their bargain had been corrupt simply because the pair had seemed to be irreconcilable adversaries. "When we behold two men political enemies, and as different in political sentiments as any men can be, so suddenly unite, there must be some unseen cause to produce this political phenomena," Jackson theorized. Indeed, the ideological closeness that Clay and Adams would demonstrate in Whig party politics lay in the future; to their contemporaries, the pair stood on opposite sides of the Monrovian-era ideological struggles. Several

Jacksonians had also overheard some loose-lipped Kentucky representatives vowing to vote for Adams because he planned to make Clay secretary of state, while Jackson did not. Kentucky's delegation clearly understood that most of the state's citizens wanted a western president, but they gambled that many would be able to forego a generic regional victory in 1824 in favor of the particular victory of their home state hero at a later date. They believed that Adams's designation of Clay as his heir apparent "will reconcile the State to Adams's elevation" over Jackson.[52]

The bargainers also had their defenders. Supreme Court Associate Justice Joseph Story recognized the ideological connection between Adams and Clay despite their positions on opposite sides of the Monroe administration. "If your vote had been other than it was, I would have found it somewhat difficult to have reconciled it with your known public opinions on subjects intimately connected with executive duties," Story reassured the Speaker. Crawford himself, though he believed that Clay had been politically foolish, understood the reasoning behind Clay's support for Adams; he even conceded that he would have picked Adams over Jackson. Van Buren, who actually voted to approve Clay's nomination as secretary of state, echoed his chief. He insisted that the corrupt bargain charge was not "justified by the proofs affixing such a stigma," but he still presciently believed that Clay had signed his "political death warrant."[53]

Charges of a corrupt bargain were politically useful to 1824's losers, of course. Calhoun, who had been conspiring secretly to defeat Adams throughout the House election process, publicly broke with the new president using Adams's deal with Clay as a justification for his opposition. The corrupt bargain "was the most dangerous stab, which the liberty of this country has ever received," Calhoun screeched dramatically. His followers had also been planning to coalesce against Adams and Clay before the House election had even occurred. Although Crawford and Van Buren dismissed the corruption charges, many of the treasury secretary's erstwhile supporters joined Calhoun in exploiting them for political gain against an administration they hoped to strangle in its cradle. Several Crawfordite senators, although they clearly lacked the numbers to derail Clay's appointment, deliberately voted against him to lend credence to the "corrupt bargain" charges. As a proven vote magnet, Jackson naturally benefited from this resistance. Oddly, just as Jackson's men blamed Clay more than Adams for the general's defeat, Adams condemned Calhoun more than Jackson for the emerging alliance against his incipient administration. Undervaluing Jackson's political skills, as usual, and knowing Calhoun's propensity for political intrigue, Adams insisted that all the carping boiled down to a plot "to bring in General Jackson as the next president, under the auspices of Calhoun."[54]

Since many Jacksonians truly believed Adams and Clay were guilty, but the two men vociferously denied the charges, historians have wrestled with the truth of the accusations. Most historians have suggested the pair reached an implicit understanding without any open deal or that the entire charge was a Jacksonian falsehood. Instead, the circumstantial evidence suggests that Adams and Clay did indeed conclude an explicit bargain to trade the State Department appointment for House votes. Both men were certainly political veterans accustomed to horse-trading. Clay had negotiated the Missouri Compromise with much more subterfuge than his support for Adams's presidential bid ever entailed, and Adams had cut deals with Cook, Scott, and the Federalists that were far more questionable than any bargain with Clay. Kentucky's representatives openly stated that to defy their constituents, they needed assurances that Clay would receive the appointment. Adams needed their votes, or he would lose the presidency to Jackson. Clay needed to be Adams's secretary of state to be positioned as the front-runner for the next presidency. Both men, with the concurrence of Kentucky's House delegation, broadly agreed on Clay's American System policies. An alliance with Clay offered Adams exactly what he had sought in his attempt to draft Jackson as his vice presidential running mate—a slaveholding westerner to balance his administration. The deal made ideological, regional, and political sense for all parties involved. The bargaining that occurred between Adams and Clay was routine, although not flaunted, practice in early nineteenth-century politics.[55]

If Clay and Adams explicitly bargained, as the circumstantial evidence suggests, their deal could hardly be called corrupt, however. A dishonest deal would have involved either two ideologically opposed parties cooperating merely for political advancement or one or both of the parties receiving an office for which they were not qualified. The bargain between Clay and Adams does not meet either of these criteria. The pair broadly agreed on the specifics of Clay's American System and the role of government in domestic policy. Both men were also eminently qualified for the positions they received. Unfortunately for Adams and Clay, historians did not control the public's perception of their dealmaking. Whether the paired had, corruptly or cleanly, bargained or not bargained, most voters rejected any sort of backroom alliance between politicians and especially one that overturned the victory of the man who received a plurality of their ballots. Unfortunately for Adams and Clay, their routine political bargain had validated Jackson's campaign message against Washington corruption in the public's mind. Their deal seemed to authenticate the lurid warnings expressed in the *Letters of Wyoming* that politicians routinely bartered and sold high offices for their own benefit rather than for the good of the nation.

Ambitious partisans of Calhoun and Crawford, with the vice president–elect himself leading the pack, eagerly seized on Jackson's vote-getting abilities to place him at the head of a coalition of 1824's losers against the less popular alliance of 1824's winners. Dismissing Jackson as a celebrity soldier, Adams and Clay had never understood the true nature of his appeal. Unwittingly, they handed the general the perfect political bludgeon, one that dramatically corroborated every single charge he had ever leveled against corrupt political practices in the capital, and Jackson gleefully began using it to beat them to their political deaths. The *Nashville Gazette* proclaimed the general a candidate for the next presidential election before Adams had even been inaugurated. A mere seven months after Adams took office, the Tennessee state legislature nominated Jackson for the second time. For weary voters, 1828's perpetual campaign had already begun. For presidential politics, the transition from the elite-centered elections in the Early Republic to the more democratically based contests of the Jacksonian era was also in full swing.[56]

→ • ←

Winners and Losers

A DAMS WAS INAUGURATED ON March 5, 1825. "After two succes-
sive sleepless nights" and with a "supplication to Heaven," the
president-elect traveled to the Capitol in a carriage accompanied
by Secretary of the Navy Samuel Southard and Attorney General William
Wirt, with Monroe trailing behind in his own coach. "Several companies
of militia and a cavalcade of citizens" conducted the high officials and listened in as Adams read his inaugural address and recited the oath of office.
A defeated adversary also in attendance could not resist criticizing the
new president. Adams had "been escorted to the capitol with a pomp and
ceremony of guns and drums not very consistent, in my humble opinion,
with the character [sic] of the occasion," Jackson noted disparagingly.
Despite the general's carping, Adams had earned a little pageantry on his big
day. The sixth president had expertly navigated 1824's convoluted political
currents. Demonstrating a true talent for political maneuvering, Adams
claimed the most significant prize available. While opposition to his administration had already begun to coalesce, Adams emerged as the clearest
winner in the election of 1824. Most of the other participants were not as
fortunate as the new president.[1]

The Harder They Fall: The Fickle Fortunes of Political Giants

On the surface, Adams's secretary of state appeared to be as much a winner in the election of 1824 as the president himself. After years of trying, Clay had finally claimed the coveted cabinet position that he believed designated him the front-runner to succeed Adams. Unfortunately for the former Speaker, his bargain with Adams also proved the most disastrous political decision in a string of questionable choices that Clay had made during the course of the election. Despite his reputation as a master political strategist, Clay only demonstrated superior skills at indoor politicking when passing tariff and internal improvement legislation; he demonstrated inferior skills at outdoors politicking in running an ineffectual presidential bid. From his slow-moving campaign to his lack of a newspaper network and organization, through his overt focus on divisive issues, Clay had sabotaged his own chance for victory in 1824. His bargain with Adams had even more far-reaching consequences. "He has not only fallen," Calhoun chortled, "but has fallen under such circumstances, as will make him miserable for life." While corruption charges would bedevil Adams during his term in office, he at least had the chance to serve as president. For Clay, the charges of corruption would cling to him long beyond the star-crossed Adams administration, discoloring his political reputation for the remainder of his life. He would *still* be defending his twenty-year-old decision when running for president in 1844. Though it was not solely responsible for his various electoral defeats, Clay's deal with Adams would help frustrate his presidential ambitions.[2]

While the damage to Clay affected his future presidential runs, 1824's former front-runner bore the deepest immediate political scars from the brutal contest. Though Crawford lived up to his reputation for political intrigue during the 1824 election, he was no more devious than the other contenders. Attacked from all sides, however, Crawford's eight-year bid ended in ignominious failure, and he returned to Georgia after the House election. With his health fully recovered by 1827, Crawford remained active in state politics as a superior court judge for the rest of his life. He continued to correspond with his national political network and remained quite popular with his devoted followers. Martin Van Buren courteously informed him in person that he had decided to back Jackson and not Crawford in the 1828 presidential election. He flirted with running for president in 1832, but ultimately decided against another nasty confrontation with Jackson. Never again would Crawford get as close to the presidency as he had been in 1824. In 1834, he died of heart failure at the age of sixty-two.[3]

Crawford managed to mend some political fences before his departure for Georgia. Despite eight years of unrelenting criticism of Crawford's character and capabilities, Adams surprisingly asked the treasury secretary to remain at his post. Crawford praised the "personal respect and regard" that Adams had demonstrated, both in offering the treasury portfolio and in Adams's unsolicited proposal to purchase Crawford's dishware and wine before he left Washington.[4]

His relationships with his other antagonists proved less amenable to improvement. Crawford's association with Monroe ended as acrimoniously as it had begun during the 1816 nomination fight. At a meeting in Monroe's office just before the expiration of his term, the two men nearly engaged in a physical confrontation. Crawford pressed the president to appoint some of Crawford's cronies to patronage positions. When Monroe delayed, ostensibly to consult the Senate, Crawford snarled, "I wish you would not dilly-dally . . . but have some mind of your own and decide it so that I may not be tormented with your want of decision." Monroe rebuked Crawford, "demand[ing] to know if he came there to treat him with disrespect." Crawford, who was still walking with a slight limp, raised his cane and shrieked, "You damned infernal old scoundrel!" Monroe brandished the fireplace tongs to ward off Crawford's attack and ordered the secretary out of his office. Crawford apologized at the door, and the two men agreed to "let it pass," but they never spoke to each other again.[5]

Crawfordites had initiated an even more damaging assault on Monroe than their chief. When Samuel Lane, the commissioner of public buildings, died in 1822, Congress discovered serious arrearages in his accounts. Unfortunately for Monroe, Lane had also managed his personal funds. Congressional investigators turned up evidence that Lane had improperly charged Monroe's private bills to the White House furniture account. In an even more eyebrow-raising transaction, Monroe had "sold" his personal furniture to the government, borrowed money from the furniture account on the sale to help defray expenses for his tour of New England, and then recovered his property when he paid off the loan. To make matters worse, the deal had been handled privately between Lane and Monroe, with the commissioner mysteriously omitting the affair from official treasury records until 1821. Compounding his shady dealings with Lane, Monroe was seeking reimbursement from the government for expenses incurred while performing his official duties. Totaling $53,000, some of Monroe's claims went as far back as his service as minister to France in 1794.[6]

Just as the A. B. scandal began to break anew in 1824, which Crawfordites had blamed on Calhoun and his secret supporter in the White House, Congress convened two separate committees to investigate both of Monroe's accounting issues. Gleeful Crawfordites accused the president of embezzling government monies and turned their inquisitorial screws into every aspect of Monroe's personal finances. Adams sympathetically compared Monroe's ordeal to forcing "a blooming virgin to exhibit herself naked before a multitude." The president himself complained about Congress's "malignant & systematic persecution," insisting that the fraud charges were "the most mortifying incident of my whole life." Ultimately, Congress accepted Monroe's explanation of the furniture budget irregularities, but—led by Crawfordites and Jacksonians—they refused to reimburse his expenses. Nearly destitute, a humiliated Monroe sold his Albemarle plantation to discharge his debts to the BUS and moved in with his daughter in New York City. Congress finally settled with the former president, making two payments of almost $30,000 each in 1826 and 1831. Monroe barely had time to enjoy his victory, dying shortly after the second installment was remitted. The president had paid a steep price indeed for meddling in the hypercharged election to determine his successor.[7]

Calhoun fared little better than Monroe. Much like Clay, he appeared poised to be a credible contender in a future presidential election, but his apparent success in 1824 proved just as illusory. Reelected vice president on the victorious Jackson ticket in 1828, Calhoun became immediately enmeshed in a struggle with Van Buren, the new secretary of state, to control

Jackson's administration. Van Buren used Crawford, his old ally, to outmaneuver Calhoun. The general had always regarded Calhoun to be one of his most vocal supporters in Monroe's cabinet. In fact, Calhoun had been as sharply critical as Crawford of Jackson's military activities in Florida during the Seminole War. Crawford helpfully supplied Van Buren with one of his own 1818 letters that documented Calhoun's criticism of Jackson. The general broke with Calhoun after reading the letter, and Van Buren won the battle of influence. Responding to an irate Calhoun, Crawford blisteringly informed the vice president that since the election of 1824 "I considered you a degraded, a disgraced man for whom no man of honor and character could feel any other than the most sovereign contempt." If revenge is a dish best served cold, Crawford probably enjoyed seeing his primary 1824 tormentor receive his just deserts in 1830. After his break with Jackson, Calhoun never realized his fervent presidential ambitions.[8]

The Federalists continued their long decline after the 1824 contest. While their timely support had helped push Adams over the finish line, ironically, backing their former colleague weakened the party. They received only a handful of appointments from the new president, and Adams never even named Daniel Webster his minister to Britain as the Massachusetts representative had so eagerly hoped. The Federalists spent the Adams years grumbling that they had little to show for their assistance, with the party deeply fractured over the controversial decision to back Adams in the first place.[9]

Several of the western representatives who had supported Adams over Jackson in the House election against their constituents' wishes were swept aside in an reelectoral bloodbath. Missouri's John Scott and Illinois's Daniel Cook were both turned out of office in the next election, while half the Adams advocates in Clay's home state paid the price at the ballot box for following the Speaker's lead. Of the seven Kentucky representatives who voted with Clay in favor of Adams, two chose not to face the voters again, and two more were soundly defeated for reelection. "I will only remark that Mr. Adams is more unpopular in this State, than I had supposed him to be," one of Clay's Kentucky allies observed sardonically.[10]

While the election of 1824 produced a plethora of losers, Adams was not the only winner in the contest. Though the popular and electoral vote victor had ultimately fallen to Adams in the House, Jackson was well positioned for an even more successful rematch against the president in 1828. He had proven to the defeated Crawfordites and Calhounites that his name at the top of the ticket attracted a host of voters across the Mid-Atlantic, West, and South. Meanwhile Adams and Clay's "corrupt bargain" had validated the central message of Jackson's campaign against corruption, galvanizing his own followers into fighting the new administration at every turn. The general would spend four years highlighting for voters the corrupted political process that he claimed the Adams/Clay alliance had nurtured. Since Jackson had demonstrated his formidable campaign skills, he would not sail comfortably above the fray in 1828, as he done for most of the 1824 election. Assuming Jackson's precarious health held out, 1824's victors would still face a strenuous challenge from the man they defeated.[11]

We're Having a Party: The Birth of the Democrats and the Whigs

While the election of 1824 certainly affected the fortunes of individual politicians, it also changed American parties. Already in decline courtesy of the fading competitiveness of the Federalists, the Republican Party sustained even more damage in the bitterly fought contest. Though the ink of Adams's inaugural address had barely dried, Jacksonians were already planning to attack the new administration. For many of Jackson's followers, defeating the corrupt combination of Clay and Adams trumped even supporting the general. "My first purpose is to pull down the tyranny, and overset the usurpation upon public liberty lately made by Adams & Clay, by their expulsion from office & power," one Jacksonian adamantly revealed. While the general would be his first choice to overturn the results of 1824, this supporter planned to back the candidate in 1828 with the best chance of defeating Adams's reelection.[12]

Meanwhile Crawfordite Radicals observed the Adams administration's ideological bent with growing alarm. Van Buren, already livid over the outsize role the Federalists had played in resolving the Republican-only election, excoriated Adams's inaugural address, criticizing the new president's minimization of the philosophical differences between the two parties as well as his ardent promotion of Federalist-style activist government. The factional and ideological cracks in the Republican Party that 1824's perpetual campaign had exposed widened into insurmountable fissures once Adams and Clay joined forces. Ironically, the 1824 election would help revitalize a two-party system, but the Republicans would not be one of those parties.[13]

Some historians have suggested that presidential elections can produce new parties; the 1824 contest proved this to be true. With the Republican Party unable to salve the wounds the divisive election had produced, two new parties began to emerge. The contest of 1824 produced two winners, one in the popular election and the other in the House. Two new parties were eventually cobbled together around those two figures. The forces of Adams and Clay quickly consolidated in defense of the new administration, while the allies of the losing candidates just as rapidly coalesced under the banner of the popular vote champion, presaging the future Democratic and Whig parties. Clay served as the focal point for the realigning alliances. Adamsites needed Clay and his western supporters to sustain the new administration. Meanwhile, each faction opposing the Adams administration gained politically from undermining Clay. By attacking Clay, Jacksonians blocked the general's principal competitor for western votes, Calhounites undercut a similarly aged rival to Calhoun, and Crawfordites thwarted any alliance between Clay's allies and Clintonians in New York.[14]

The propensity of Republican politicians readily to shift their political alliances between candidates during the 1824 presidential election facilitated the creation of new parties. "This species of duplicity pervades the conduct of so many public men in this country," Adams complained, "that it is scarcely possible to know upon whom any reliance can be placed." Such "duplicity" proved essential to party building. For instance, Tennessee lawyer Alfred Balch, who detested Jackson, admired Van Buren, and had supported Crawford in 1824, seamlessly reconciled with the general and served on his 1828 presidential Committee. The candidate organizations also helped midwife the new parties. Jacksonians, who had generally been political outsiders, would assume greater insider roles in this latest coalition. "Your election will create new leaders of as much consequence as . . . [the present] leading men in Pennsylvania," one of the general's followers presciently predicted.[15]

The ideological fault lines uncovered in 1824 also nudged the political system toward the new Jacksonian era parties. The election represented the triumph, albeit subdued, of states' rights over state planning. States' rightists believed that concentrating power in a remote center invited tyranny, while nationalists needed power in the center to implement the domestic and international policies that they deemed vital to the nation's welfare. In the election of 1824, the issue had been tangential to the main streams of debate about the candidates. Voters regarded Crawford as a moderate states' rightist at best, while Adams and Calhoun had run as restrained nationalists. Only Clay had offered an activist presidency to the electorate. His campaign demonstrated that voters, unsurprisingly, favored tariffs or internal improvement projects that benefited them directly, while rejecting grandiose national projects seemingly beneficial to citizens or regions elsewhere. Jackson's 1824 campaign had not directly engaged the issue at all, but his run aided the cause of states' rights nonetheless. Most states' rightists equated power in the center with corruption, and the general's vigorous denunciation of corruption only strengthened this association. The Jacksonians' rejection of the Adams/Clay bargain proved the essential point of agreement with the Crawfordites and smoothed the way toward their future alliance in the Democratic Party. In turn, the Radical Crawfordites converted many Jacksonians to the states' rights cause.[16]

Much of the organizational machinery that Jacksonians had created to sustain the general's 1824 campaign was maintained during Adams's term and revived for the 1828 election. The desire to beat Adams at the polls certainly fueled the development of the future Democratic Party. The creation of both Whigs and Democrats transcended simple mechanical expediency, however. Adams, Clay, and their allies were obviously the primary supporters of American System policies, and just as clearly, Jacksonians, Calhounites, and Crawfordites became the principal detractors of Clay's brainchild. Policy-related disagreements proved coequal with winning elections in the formation of new parties. Both the partisan machinery and partisan issues bridged the gap between traditional elitist politics and future democratized president making, with the election of 1824 as the hinge between them. Considering the venerable objections to the congressional caucus and the slow-but-relentless democratization of presidential elections, traditional practices had begun dissolving during the Early Republic elections that preceded 1824. However, certain tools introduced in 1824, such as Jackson's organization and Clay's American System polices, proved crucial to future president making. In a fluid process, traditional aspects of presidential campaigning, such as public meetings, press networks, and dirty attacks, were enhanced for use in Jacksonian era politics.

Transitional Elections: A Changing American Political Culture

While the states' rights position had enjoyed a moderate victory in the election of 1824, democratization of presidential elections took a much larger step forward. Though the selection of presidential electors had been trending toward popular over state legislative control for some time, Jackson's controversial rejection in the House election pushed the movement even further. Six state legislatures picked presidential electors in 1824; in 1828, only two—Delaware and South Carolina—would do so, a development directly connected to the public's dissatisfaction with the House for disregarding the popular vote winner. Most dramatic, Van Buren and his Albany Regency suffered a devastating repudiation at the polls after they thwarted efforts to allow ordinary voters to pick the presidential electors. Although he was a wily insider, even New York's Wizard acknowledged his mistake and switched sides on the issue. Meanwhile Kentucky's legislature invoked the hallowed "wishes of the people" when instructing their congressional representatives to vote for Jackson in the House election. While it may have been empty rhetoric coming from politicians who favored Jackson over Adams, several congressmen who flouted this reputed popular will found themselves voted out of office in the next midterm elections. Indeed, the "wishes of the people" had become so critical in electing presidents that proto–straw polls gauging public opinion, a direct antecedent of modern polls, were another 1824 innovation.[17]

Jackson's popular victory also doomed several other elitist hallmarks of traditional presidential politics. The Virginia Dynasty, the Virginia/New York axis controlling the two highest offices, and the secretary of state as the heir apparent had each been accepted as unwritten rules governing presidential politics, but all were quickly jettisoned by elite politicians once ordinary voters rejected them with their ballots. Collectively, these changes dramatically democratized American presidential elections.[18]

Replacing the congressional caucus with state nominations to select presidential candidates most visibly signaled the move toward democratized presidential contests. In 1824, power over presidential nominees shifted from political elites in Washington toward statehouse politicos or, in the case of Jackson especially, meetings of local citizens. This move would directly lead to even more popular involvement with the first national conventions for nominating prospective presidents, organized in 1832. Jacksonian opposition had not doomed the caucus as much as Crawford's poor showing. Congressional caucuses had always been criticized, but when the voters overwhelmingly rejected the caucus choice in 1824, politicians prudently ceased nominating presidents in the national legislature. "The friends of that candidate who find themselves the most numerous in Congress will hold caucuses so long as the people will bear them out in it by electing him whom they recommend," Adams perceptively predicted in 1823. "Nothing will put it down but the failure of success." Crawford's abject failure then successfully "put down" congressional caucus nominations forever.[19]

Jacksonian tactics also supported the democratization of presidential politics. Because the general's followers lacked access to the patronage and congressional powers that the other candidates enjoyed, they resorted to popular involvement in their campaign out of simple necessity. Still, the public meetings and state delegate conventions that the Jacksonians employed incorporated more ordinary people in the process of picking a president than any previous presidential campaign. These techniques had a long history in politics, but they had only been sparingly deployed in presidential contests prior to Jackson's effort. Their routine usage in future presidential elections stemmed directly from the general's groundbreaking 1824 bid. In the election of 1824, Crawford had run the strongest, most powerful—though most conventional and elitist insider campaign—and finished a distant fourth in the popular election. Contrarily, Jackson ran the most innovative, democratized, and untraditional outsider campaign and unexpectedly finished first. The writing was on the wall for every elite politician to see. Presidential elections were in transition from the elitist Early Republic contests. Future presidential elections would be increasingly Jacksonian rather than Crawfordite.[20]

Voter turnout dramatically demonstrated the increasingly populist bent of presidential elections and, once again, the 1824 contest served as the hinge. Even discounting the inclusion of four additional state popular elections, voter participation increased a dramatic 133 percent in 1828 over 1824. More than 600,000 more citizens went to the polls, representing an increase from 27 percent to 57 percent of eligible voters casting a ballot. Yet, 1824's turnout had also increased by 130 percent over 1820. Along with Adams and Jackson, democratization had also emerged as a "winner" in the transitional 1824 election. The people had spoken.

Insiders versus Outsiders: The Politics of Corruption

The peoples' increasingly prominent voice sounded the death knell of the Early Republic's elitist presidential politics. Where once the candidate's reputation had been the sole purview of one's fellow politicians, now, ordinary citizens had become judge, jury, and sometimes executioner. As the election of 1824 unfolded, the people had numerous opportunities to assess the candidates' characters. The cabinet's insider machinations fueled acrimonious congressional debates, dominated nasty newspaper wars, and ultimately reached the ears of an engrossed public. Almost every action in ordinary national politics became enmeshed in the succession question, creating one perpetual campaign for the presidency. This continuous campaign unsurprisingly favored sullying an opponent's reputation over burnishing one's own positive image; mudslinging became indispensable to the practice of presidential politics.

Ironically, when insiders criticized insiders, their political slurs repelled the very voters the candidates needed to win the election. While schmoozing and dealmaking might be respected by one's by one's peers and even essential to good governance, the public often deemed such practices unsavory. This tendency proved easily exploitable by outsider candidates. Characterizing normal insider political practices as corruption, Jackson promised to sweep clean the "Giant Augean stable" in the nation's capital. Adroitly capitalizing on the public appeal of his favorite subject, the general marched to a popular and electoral vote majority in 1824 and an outright victory in 1828.

Running as a virtuous outsider against corrupt insiders not only proved useful in the 1824 and 1828 election cycles, it also served as a successful strategy for several presidential candidates across diverse electoral landscapes in future contests. Despite his wealth and education, in 1840, William Henry Harrison posed as an outsider common man of the people, living in a log cabin and drinking hard cider, in opposition to Van Buren, whom Harrison caricatured as a moneyed insider lavishly living at public expense. In the campaigns of 1872 and 1876, outsider Democratic candidates Horace Greeley and Samuel Tilden castigated the corrupt Ulysses S. Grant administration, demanding civil service reform as a corrective for insider abuses. The outsider-versus-insider theme proved effective into the twentieth century and beyond, with Harry Truman's bludgeoning of the "do-nothing" Republican Congress in 1948, Ronald Reagan's insistence in 1981 that "government is not the solution to our problem; government is the problem," or Donald Trump's promise to "drain the swamp" in 2016. As outsiders gleefully pillory insiders in an all-too-common theme in US presidential politics, the election of 1824 casts a long shadow indeed.

NOTES

Abbreviations

Adams Memoirs 5 — Adams, Charles Francis, ed. *Memoirs of John Quincy Adams: Comprising Portions of his Diary from 1795 to 1848.* Vol. 5 (Philadelphia: J. B. Lippincott, 1875)

Adams Memoirs 6 — Adams, Charles Francis, ed. *Memoirs of John Quincy Adams: Comprising Portions of his Diary from 1795 to 1848.* Vol. 6 (New York: AMS Press, 1970)

Calhoun Papers 7 — Hemphill, W. Edwin, ed. *The Papers of John C. Calhoun.* Vol. 7, *1822–1823* (Columbia: University of South Carolina Press, 1973)

Clay Papers 3 — Hopkins, James F., and Mary W. M. Hargreaves, eds. *The Papers of Henry Clay.* Vol. 3, *The Presidential Candidate, 1821–1824* (Lexington: University of Kentucky Press, 1963)

Clay Papers 4 — Hopkins, James F., Mary W. M. Hargreaves, Wayne Cutler, and Burton Milward, eds. *The Papers of Henry Clay.* Vol. 4, *Secretary of State, 1825* (Lexington: University of Kentucky Press, 1972)

Jackson Papers 5 — Moser, Harold D., David R. Hoth, and George H. Hoemann, eds. *The Papers of Andrew Jackson.* Vol. 5, *1821–1824* (Knoxville: University of Tennessee Press, 1996)

Jackson Papers 6	Moser, Harold D., J. Clint Clifft, and Wyatt C. Wells, eds. *The Papers of Andrew Jackson*. Vol. 6, *1825–1828* (Knoxville: University of Tennessee Press, 2002)
Monroe Writings 6	Hamilton, Stanislaus Murray, ed. *The Writings of James Monroe*. Vol. 6 (Putnam, 1902; reprint, Lexington, KY: Elibron Classics, 2007)
Van Buren Autobiography	Fitzpatrick, John C., ed. *The Autobiography of Martin Van Buren*. Vol. 2 (Washington, DC: Government Printing Office, 1920)

Introduction

1. Virginius, "For the Enquirer," 3.
2. Balogh, *Government Out of Sight*, 379.
3. Nord, *Communities of Journalism*, 2, 13.
4. Holt, *Rise and Fall of the American Whig Party*, xi.
5. Heale, *Presidential Quest*, 61–62; Parsons, *Birth of Modern Politics*, 41, 43, 88; Ratcliffe, *One-Party Presidential Contest*, 4–5; Peart, *Era of Experimentation*, 9, 109, 137.

1. The Big Five

1. Chase, *Presidential Nominating Convention*, 21–22; Shipp, *Giant Days*, 140–44.
2. Mooney, *William Crawford*, 3–17, 27–40; Shipp, *Giant Days*, 66–97.
3. Thomas Jefferson to William Crawford, February 15, 1825, in Shipp, *Giant Days*, 163, 192; Mooney, *William Crawford*, x, 126, 342; White, *The Jeffersonians*, 165–77.
4. Sellers, *Market Revolution*, 131–37.
5. Sellers, *Market Revolution*, 131–37; Torre, "Financial Panics in the Early American Republic," 440–44; Hammond, *Banks and Politics in America*, 246–73.
6. Dangerfield, *Era of Good Feelings*, 103–4; Sellers, *Market Revolution*, 119, 125; Joseph Gist's Circular, February 6, 1823, in Hay, "Unpublished Calhoun Letters, II," 495; Unknown [James Gadsden?]to Andrew Jackson, April 10, 1822, in *Jackson Papers*, 5:167.
7. Peter Porter to Henry Clay, May 26, 1823, Porter to Clay, November 17, 1823, in *Clay Papers*, 3:421, 523; Jackson to John C. Calhoun, c. August 12, 1823, in *Jackson Papers*, 5:287; *Adams Memoirs*, 5:108; Calhoun to V[irgil] Maxcy, August 2, 1822, in *Calhoun Papers*, 7:231; Peart, *Era of Experimentation*, 112–15.

8. Mooney, *William Crawford*, 225; Chase, *Presidential Nominating Convention*, 92; Ratcliffe, *One-Party Presidential Contest*, 25.

9. *Adams Memoirs*, 5:20; *Adams Memoirs*, 6:278; Calhoun to Charles Fisher, August 1, 1823, in Newsome, "Correspondence of Calhoun, McDuffie, and Fisher," 481; Jackson to John Coffee, March 1, 1821, Jackson to Gadsden, December 6, 1821, in *Jackson Papers*, 5:15, 121; Clay to Francis Brooke, February 26, 1823, in *Clay Papers*, 3:387.

10. *Van Buren Autobiography*, 121–22; James Monroe to Jefferson, February 13, 1817, in *Monroe Writings*, 6:2–4; Hecht, *John Quincy Adams*, 268.

11. John Quincy Adams to Joseph Hopkinson, January 23, 1823, in *Adams Memoirs*, 6:114–15, 134–35; Livermore, *Twilight of Federalism*, 96–97.

12. Adams to Hopkinson, January 23, 1823, in *Adams Memoirs*, 6:136, 415; John Eaton to Jackson, January 11, 1823, in *Jackson Papers*, 5:236; Adam Beatty to Clay, June 30, 1823, in *Clay Papers*, 3:446.

13. Livermore, *Twilight of Federalism*, 6, 11, 80–84, 265.

14. Livermore, *Twilight of Federalism*, 14–15, 23, 56, 265; *Van Buren Autobiography*, 116; Appleby, *Inheriting the Revolution*, 31.

15. Hofstadter, *Idea of a Party System*, 23; Livermore, *Twilight of Federalism*, 70–77, 140–41; Nagel, *John Quincy Adams*, 288; Henry Shaw to Clay, April 4, 1822, in *Clay Papers*, 3:185; Adams to Hopkinson, January 23, 1823, in *Adams Memoirs*, 6:136.

16. Bemis, *Adams and Foreign Policy*, 50, 88, 159, 188, 223, 338–39, 394, 418; Heale, *Presidential Quest*, 42–50.

17. Henry Warfield to Clay, December 18, 1821, in *Clay Papers*, 3:148; *Adams Memoirs*, 5:298; *Adams Memoirs*, 6:46, 407; Nagel, *John Quincy Adams*, 236, 241, 268.

18. Brown, *Life of Rufus Choate*, 417.

19. Niven, *John C. Calhoun*, 62–66, 88–91; John, "Affairs of Office," 53.

20. Ammon, *James Monroe*, 368.

21. Niven, *John C. Calhoun*, 80–96; *Calhoun Papers*, 7:xxxix.

22. Monroe to Trench Ringgold, May 8, 1826, in *Monroe Writings*, 6:81–82; *Van Buren Autobiography*, 306; *Adams Memoirs*, 6:8; Charles Miner to Clay, June 19, 1823, in *Clay Papers*, 3:436.

23. Calhoun to N[inian] Edwards, August 20, 1822, in *Calhoun Papers*, 7:248; Hickey, *War of 1812*, 2, 168, 300–309; Niven, *John C. Calhoun*, 31–57.

24. Monroe to James Madison, May 10, 1822, Monroe to Jackson, May 30, 1822, in *Monroe Writings*, 6:286, 292; Niven, *John C. Calhoun*, 66–67; Calhoun to N[inian] Edwards, August 20, 1822, in *Calhoun Papers*, 7:xxiii–xxvi.

25. Calhoun to Swift, August 5, 1823, in Hay, "Unpublished Calhoun Letters," 88.

26. Calhoun to Joseph G. Swift, April 29, 1823, Calhoun to Swift, May 10, 1823, Calhoun to Swift, August 5, 1823, in Hay, "Unpublished Calhoun Letters," 84–88; Calhoun to Maxcy, January 20, 1823, Calhoun to Maxcy, March 13, 1823, Calhoun to M[icah] Sterling, March 27, 1823, in *Calhoun Papers*, 7:432, 519, 547.

27. Calhoun to Sterling, January 5, 1824, in Hay, "Unpublished Calhoun Letters, II," 288; Calhoun to Maxcy, March 25, 1823, in *Calhoun Papers*, 7:542; Calhoun to Swift, August 24, 1823, Calhoun to Swift, September 27, 1823, in Hay, "Unpublished Calhoun Letters," 89, 92–93.

28. Calhoun to Fisher, August 1, 1823, in Newsome, "Correspondence of Calhoun, McDuffie, and Fisher," 482; H. Johnson to Edwards, August 10, 1823, in Edwards, *History of Illinois*, 504; Calhoun to Sterling, March 27, 1823, in *Calhoun Papers*, 7:547.

29. Remini, *Henry Clay*, 48, 77–82.

30. Remini, *Henry Clay*, 72–100.

31. Remini, *Henry Clay*, 132–70; *Adams Memoirs*, 5:52, 90; Lewis, *American Union and Neighborhood*, 158, 169.

32. Howe, *What Hath God Wrought*, 204–5; Remini, *Henry Clay*, 227, 252; Heale, *Presidential Quest*, 45; Shaw to Clay, April 4, 1822, Benjamin Tyler to Clay, June 24, 1822, Hezekiah Niles to Clay, July 1, 1822, John Norvell to Clay, November 14, 1822, Miner to Clay, November 16, 1822, George McClure to Clay, July 23, 1823, in *Clay Papers*, 3:185, 241–42, 246, 321, 325, 462–63; *Adams Memoirs*, 5:58.

33. McManus, "Monroe's Domestic Policies," 446–51; Remini, *Henry Clay*, 182–92; 37 Annals of Cong. 1830 (1821) (1830); *Adams Memoirs*, 5:4–6, 199, 208; Benton, *Thirty Years' View*, 8.

34. *Adams Memoirs*, 5:58, 326; Clay to John Godman, August 9, 1823, Clay to Charles Hammond, October 25, 1824, in *Clay Papers*, 3:464, 870.

35. Clay to Thomas Dougherty, December 7, 1821, Clay to Porter, April 14, 1822, Clay to Brooke, January 31, 1823, Clay to Porter, February 2, 1823, Clay to Richard Bache, February 17, 1824, Clay to Josiah Johnston, August 31, 1824, in *Clay Papers*, 3:145, 191, 358, 362–63, 645, 822.

36. Remini, *Henry Clay*, 239.

37. Remini, *Life of Andrew Jackson*, 4–13, 19–22, 29–39; Jackson to Rachel Jackson, March 16, 1824, in *Jackson Papers*, 5:376; Coens, "Formation of the Jackson Party," 11–15.

38. Warshauer, "Jackson and New Orleans," 81–82.

39. Warshauer, "Jackson and New Orleans," 81–82; *Adams Memoirs*, 6:340.

40. Warshauer, "Jackson and New Orleans," 79–80; Ward, *Andrew Jackson*, 5–6; Remini, *Life of Jackson*, 117–27; Monroe to Jefferson, July 22, 1918, Monroe to Madison, February 7, 1819, in *Monroe Writings*, 6:63, 88; *Adams Memoirs*, 5:359–73, 460–68; Parsons, *Birth of Modern Politics*, 118–22; Jackson to Monroe, March 19, 1822, Jackson to Andrew Jackson Donelson, August 6, 1822, Jackson to William Fulton, April 4, 1823, in *Jackson Papers*, 5:162, 213, 268.

41. Remini, *Life of Jackson*, 129–47; Warshauer, "Jackson and New Orleans," 79–89; Jackson to Philip Barbour, January 22, 1822, James Bronaugh to Jackson, February 8, 1822, Thomas Mera to Jackson, December 7, 1824, in *Jackson Papers*, 5:137–38, 145, 451; Clay to Francis Blair, January 29, 1825, in *Clay Papers*, 4:47; Coens, "Formation of the Jackson Party," 11–15; Howe, *What Hath God Wrought*, 205.

42. Opal, *Avenging the People*, 2, 143; Remini, *Life of Jackson*, 141–47; Jackson to Barbour, January 22, 1822, Jackson to Donelson, March 21, 1822, Jackson to Richard Call, June 29, 1822, in *Jackson Papers*, 5:138, 161, 198.

43. *Adams Memoirs*, 5:128–29; Peart, *Era of Experimentation*, 139; Somkin, *Unquiet Eagle*, 135–69; Murphy, "Jackson's Rise," 267; Parsons, *Birth of Modern Politics*, 91.

44. Samuel Overton to Jackson, August 1, 1821, Gadsden to Jackson, April 13, 1822, Samuel Houston to Jackson, August 3, 1822, Gadsden to Jackson, July 30, 1823, in *Jackson Papers*, 5:89, 171–72, 212, 286; *Van Buren Autobiography*, 232–44.

45. *Van Buren Autobiography*, 239; Meyers, *The Jacksonian Persuasion*, 3–17; Pleasant Miller to Fisher, January 3, 1824, in Hay, "Unpublished Calhoun Letters, II," 498; Heale, *Presidential Quest*, 58–59; Jackson to Donelson, February 6, 1824, in *Jackson Papers*, 5:367.

2. Electioneering without Electioneering

1. Pocock, "The Classical Theory of Deference," 516–23; Formisano, "The Early Republic's Political Culture, 1789–1840," 473–87; Robertson, "Voting Rites and Voting Acts: Electioneering Ritual, 1790–1820," 58–65; Altschuler and Blumin, *Rude Republic*, 15–17.

2. Formisano, "The Early Republic's Political Culture, 1789–1840," 473–87.

3. Hargreaves, *Presidency of Adams*, 45; Saltman, *Voting Technology*, 59–63.

4. McCormick, *Second American Party System*, 29; Saltman, *Voting Technology*, 61–63; Appleby, *Inheriting the Revolution*, 28–32.

5. James Jackson to Jackson, July 24, 1822, in *Jackson Papers*, 5:204; Clay to Hammond, October 25, 1824, in *Clay Papers*, 3:870; Heale, *Presidential Quest*, 4; Formisano, "State Development in the Early Republic," 20; Coens, "Formation of the Jackson Party," 23; McCormick, *Presidential Game*, 142; Balogh, *Government Out of Sight*, 3, 379.

6. *Van Buren Autobiography*, 191; Crawford to Charles Tait, September 4, 1821, in Shipp, *Giant Days*, 149; *Adams Memoirs*, 6:132; Clay to Porter, April 14, 1822, Clay to Hammond, October 25, 1824, in *Clay Papers*, 3:191, 870; Calhoun to Edwards, July 3, 1821, in Edwards, *History of Illinois*, 489; Jackson to Call, June 29, 1822, Jackson to James Bronaugh, August 1, 1822, in *Jackson Papers*, 5:197, 210–11.

7. Heale, *Presidential Quest*, 50; Kresson, *James Monroe*, 458.

8. *Adams Memoirs*, 5:212; Crawford to Tait, October 2, 1820, in Shipp, *Giant Days*, 161–62, 229; Jackson to Coffee, September 23, 1824, Jackson to William Carroll, November 2, 1824, in *Jackson Papers*, 5:441, 449–50; Calhoun to Swift, May 10, 1823, Maxcy to Swift, October 5, 1823, in Hay, "Unpublished Calhoun Letters," 93.

9. Clay to Hammond, October 29, 1823, in *Clay Papers*, 3:505; Jackson to William Lewis, March 31, 1824, Jackson to Donelson, April 4, 1824, Caleb Atwater to Jackson, June 24, 1824, William Johnson to Jackson, September 22, 1824, in *Jackson Papers*, 5:388, 389, 421, 441; Remini, *Life of Jackson*, 146–47; Heale, *Presidential Quest*, 57–59.

10. Heale, *Presidential Quest*, 50–52; *Clay Papers*, 3:183; Jackson to Donelson, April 4, 1824, in *Jackson Papers*, 5:389.

11. Cohen, "Sport for Grown Children," 1301–10; Mooney, *William Crawford*, 238–39; Miner to Clay, June 19, 1823, in *Clay Papers*, 3:147.

12. Smith, "First Straw?," 21–31; Madonna and Young, "First Political Poll," 1–3.

13. Smith, "First Straw?," 27–29.

14. *Adams Memoirs*, 5:297; *Adams Memoirs*, 6:44; Calhoun to Swift, November 16, 1823, in Hay, "Unpublished Calhoun Letters, II," 287; Peart, *Era of Experimentation*, 146.

15. Clay to Josephus Stuart, June 14, 1824, William Ingalls to Clay, June 5, 1824, Clay to Porter, February 15, 1824, in *Clay Papers*, 3:641, 774, 776; *Adams Memoirs*, 6:469; Calhoun to Maxcy, June 25, 1822, Calhoun to Unknown, March 18, 1823, Calhoun to Edwards, October 5, 1822, in *Calhoun Papers*, 7:182, 531, 295.

16. Peart, *Era of Experimentation*, 118; Jackson to Samuel Swartwout, March 25, 1824, John McFarland to Jackson, August 14, 1824, in *Jackson Papers*, 5:381–82, 436; Calhoun to Maxcy, June 25, 1822, in *Calhoun Papers*, 7:182; *Adams Memoirs*, 6:363; *Adams Memoirs*, 5:468.

17. *Adams Memoirs*, 6:61; Mooney, *William Crawford*, 234, 269–76, 280–89.

18. Niven, *Martin Van Buren*, 143; Chase, *Presidential Nominating Convention*, 47; Porter to Clay, September 30, 1822, in *Clay Papers*, 3:290.

19. Calhoun to Maxcy, August 2, 1822, in *Calhoun Papers*, 7:231.

20. *Adams Memoirs*, 6:64; Jefferson to Crawford, February 15, 1825, in Shipp, *Giant Days*, 168, 192.

21. *Adams Memoirs*, 6:44, 361; *Adams Memoirs*, 5:469; Bemis, *Adams and the Union*, 22–24; Hargreaves, *Presidency of Adams*, 20–32; George Dangerfield, *Awakening of American Nationalism*, 218.

22. *Adams Memoirs*, 6:44, 131.

23. Calhoun to Maxcy, April 12, 1822, Calhoun to Maxcy, June 25, 1822, Calhoun to Maxcy, August 2, 1822, in *Calhoun Papers*, 7:lii, 30, 181–82, 232; Niven, *John C. Calhoun*, 81, 98; B. B. Smith to Fisher, January 24, 1824, in Newsome, "Correspondence of Calhoun, McDuffie, and Fisher," 499; Ammon, *James Monroe*, 499; Peterson, *Great Triumvirate*, 118; Hay, "Calhoun and the Presidential Campaign of 1824," 26–36; Remini, *Henry Clay*, 207–8; Calhoun to Swift, April 29, 1823, Calhoun to Swift, September 27, 1823, in Hay, "Unpublished Calhoun Letters," 86, 93; Jeffrey, *State Parties*, 22.

24. Hay, "Calhoun and the Presidential Campaign of 1824," 27–31.

25. *Adams Memoirs*, 6:7, 191; Calhoun to Maxcy, October 28, 1822, in *Calhoun Papers*, 7:319; Crawford to Tait, June 3, 1822, in Shipp, *Giant Days*, 232; Langdon Cheves to Clay, November 9, 1822, in *Clay Papers*, 3:314; *Adams Memoirs*, 5:99, 203, 428, 514, 525.

26. Shaw to Clay, April 4, 1822, Clay to Porter, April 14, 1822, Beatty to William Rochester, April 18, 1822, Porter to Clay, July 8, 1822, Porter to Clay, September 30, 1822, Clay to Johnston, October 2, 1824, in *Clay Papers*, 3:185, 192, 194, 252, 290, 855.

27. Tyler to Clay, June 24, 1822, Brooke to Clay, August 14, 1823, Clay to Porter, February 15, 1824, Clay to Porter, February 19, 1824, Clay to Brooke, February 23, 1824, Brooke to Clay, July 12, 1824, Asher Robbins to Clay, August 5, 1824, Johnston to Clay, September 11, 1824, Clay to Robert Henry, September 14, 1824, in *Clay Papers*, 3:241, 468–69, 641, 653, 656, 793–94, 804, 836–38; Henry Somerville, "To the Voters of the Fifth District," 2.

28. Jackson to Coffee, December 27, 1824, William Johnson to Jackson, August 16, 1824, John Rhea to Jackson, February 10, 1822, Jackson to Lewis, May 7, 1824, in *Jackson Papers*, 5:458, 437, 148, 404.

29. McFarland to Jackson, August 14, 1824, in *Jackson Papers*, 5:436; Coens, "Formation of the Jackson Party," 37–38; Heale, *Presidential Quest,* 60.

30. Porter to Clay, October 6, 1824, Johnston to Clay, June 27, 1824, Johnston to Clay, September 4, 1824, in *Clay Papers,* 3:859, 787, 829; Clay to Maxcy, June 25, 1822, in *Calhoun Papers,* 7:183; George McDuffie to Unknown, December 12, 1823, in Newsome, "Correspondence of Calhoun, McDuffie, and Fisher," 489; Atwater to Jackson, June 24, 1824, in *Jackson Papers,* 5:421.

31. Clay to Benjamin Leigh, October 18, 1823, Clay to Hammond, October 29, 1823, in *Clay Papers,* 3:500, 505; McDuffie to Unknown, December 12, 1823, in Newsome, "Correspondence of Calhoun, McDuffie, and Fisher," 489; Jackson to Donelson, April 17, 1824, in *Jackson Papers,* 5:396; *Adams Memoirs,* 6:158, 176–77.

32. Hay, "Calhoun and the Presidential Campaign of 1824," 31.

33. Jackson to Donelson, August 6, 1822, Jackson to Donelson, April 17, 1824, in *Jackson Papers*, 5:213, 396; McDuffie to Unknown, January 13, 1823, in Newsome, "Correspondence of Calhoun, McDuffie, and Fisher," 487.

34. Clay to Hammond, October 29, 1823, in *Clay Papers,* 3:505; *Adams Memoirs,* 6:403; Calhoun to Swift, undated [summer 1823?], in Hay, "Unpublished Calhoun Letters," 88; Clay to George Featherstonhaugh, February 26, 1825, in *Clay Papers,* 4:83.

35. Jackson to Chandler Price, January 20, 1824, in *Jackson Papers,* 5:342; Clay to Brooke, February 4, 1825, in *Clay Papers,* 4:55; Ratcliffe, *One-Party Presidential Contest,* 261.

36. John, *Spreading the News,* 4, 15, 36–41; Starr, *Creation of the Media,* 86; Calhoun to Maxcy, June 25, 1822, in *Calhoun Papers,* 7:160, 182.

37. Amos Kendall to Clay, February 9, 1825, in *Clay Papers,* 4:78; *Adams Memoirs,* 5:117–18; Pasley, *Tyranny of Printers,* 9–15.

38. *Adams Memoirs,* 6:56, 61; Starr, *Creation of the Media,* 85, 87, 189; *Adams Memoirs,* 5:16, 266.

39. *Adams Memoirs,* 6:47, 291; *Calhoun Papers,* 7:xli; William Hayden to Jackson, March 29, 1824, Jackson to Hayden, March 30, 1824, in *Jackson Papers,* 5:385–86.

40. Starr, *Creation of the Media,* 87, 189; Jonathan Russell to Clay, August 7, 1822, in *Clay Papers,* 3:271; Calhoun to Maxcy, June 9, 1822, Calhoun to Edwards, June 12, 1822, in *Calhoun Papers,* 7:xliv, 153, 160; *Adams Memoirs,* 6:47, 57, 59, 66, 94–95.

41. Hay, "Unpublished Calhoun Letters," 85; Calhoun to Maxcy, March 13, 1823, in *Calhoun Papers*, 7:519; *Jackson Papers*, 5:123; Samuel H. Williamson, "Seven Ways to Compute the Relative Value of a U.S. Dollar Amount, 1790 to Present," MeasuringWorth.com, accessed September 21, 2021.

42. Calhoun to Maxcy, June 9, 1822, Calhoun to Thomas Rogers, June 9, 1822, Calhoun to Edwards, June 12, 1822, Calhoun to John Colhoun, July 1, 1822, in *Calhoun Papers*, 7:153, 155–56, 161, 196; McDuffie to Unknown, December 26, 1823, in Newsome, "Correspondence of Calhoun, McDuffie, and Fisher," 493; Jackson to George Nashee, December 17, 1822, Whitman Mead to Jackson, May 10, 1824, in *Jackson Papers*, 5:227, 405; Stephen Simpson to Jackson, November 3, 1825, in *Jackson Papers*, 6:120; Calhoun to Swift, August 5, 1823, in Hay, "Unpublished Calhoun Letters," 88; Cheves to Clay, November 9, 1822, in *Clay Papers*, 3:316; Monroe to Madison, March 31, 1821, in *Monroe Writings*, 6:174; *Adams Memoirs*, 6:18, 56, 244.

43. Jackson to George Wilson, August 13, 1824, in *Jackson Papers*, 5:433–34; Jackson to Henry Lee, October 7, 1825, Simpson to Jackson, November 3, 1825, in *Jackson Papers*, 6:104, 119; Calhoun to Maxcy, June 9, 1822, Calhoun to Edwards, June 12, 1822, in *Calhoun Papers*, 7:154, 161; *Adams Memoirs*, 6:17–18.

44. Richard Easter to Jackson, May 10, 1821, Jackson to Lewis, May 7, 1824, in *Jackson Papers*, 5:41, 404; Jackson to Lewis, February 27, 1825, in *Jackson Papers*, 6:43; Calhoun to Maxcy, May 31, 1822, Calhoun to Maxcy, June 25, 1822, Calhoun to Maxcy, August 2, 1822, Calhoun to Maxcy, December 15, 1822, in *Calhoun Papers*, 7:137, 182–84, 231, 387; *Adams Memoirs*, 6:59, 136, 302; Hay, "Unpublished Calhoun Letters," 89; Newsome, "Correspondence of Calhoun, McDuffie, and Fisher," 500.

45. Adams to Hopkinson, January 23, 1823, in *Adams Memoirs*, 6:47, 56, 61, 136, 403.

46. Calhoun to Swift, August 5, 1823, Maxcy to Swift, October 5, 1823, in Hay, "Unpublished Calhoun Letters," 88, 93.

47. Hopkinson to Louisa Adams, January, 1823, in *Adams Memoirs*, 6:56, 59, 61, 131, 351, 400; J. Wingate Jr. to Clay, March 18, 1825, in *Clay Papers*, 4:121; Calhoun to Fisher, December 2, 1823, in Newsome, "Correspondence of Calhoun, McDuffie, and Fisher," 483, 500, 503; Porter to Clay, September 30, 1822, Cheves to Clay, November 9, 1822, Shaw to Clay, February 11, 1823, Thomas Hart Benton to Clay, July 23, 1823, Daniel Call to Clay, June 30, 1824, Johnston to Clay, August 9, 1824, in *Clay Papers*, 3:290, 314, 374, 460, 790, 807; Niven, *John C. Calhoun*, 96–99; Crawford to Tait, September 17, 1822, in Shipp, *Giant Days*, 234; Thomas McKenney to Calhoun, May 22, 1822, Calhoun to Maxcy, May 31, 1822, Calhoun to Maxcy, June 9, 1822, Calhoun to Maxcy, August 2, 1822, Calhoun to Edwards, August 20, 1822, in *Calhoun Papers*, 7:xli, 120, 137, 153, 231, 248; Mooney, *William Crawford*, 228, 232, 269; *Adams Memoirs*, 5:468; Hay, "Calhoun and the Presidential Campaign of 1824," 27–36; Maxcy to Swift, October 5, 1823, in Hay, "Unpublished Calhoun Letters," 89, 93.

48. Murphy, "Jackson's Rise," 266; Jackson to Fulton, December 21, 1823, Jackson to Thomas Maund, December 27, 1823, Atwater to Jackson, June 24, 1824, in *Jackson Papers*, 5:252, 328, 332, 421, 436; Coens, "Formation of the Jackson Party," 15; Pasley,

Tyranny of Printers, 389; Jackson to Lee, October 7, 1825, in *Jackson Papers,* 6:104; Heale, *Presidential Quest,* 60.

49. Kendall to Clay, June 20, 1822, Godman to Clay, July 1, 1823, Clay to Stuart, December 19, 1823, in *Clay Papers,* 3:183, 236, 447, 545; Remini, *Henry Clay,* 241.

50. Erastus Root to Clay, February 9, 1824, in *Clay Papers,* 3:634.

51. Nord, *Communities of Journalism,* 83–84; Pasley, *Tyranny of Printers,* 4; John, *Spreading the News,* 13; Robertson, "Voting Rites," 60, 67; Calhoun to Rogers, June 9, 1822, Calhoun to Maxcy, June 25, 1822, Calhoun to Maxcy, October 28, 1822, in *Calhoun Papers,* 7:155, 184, 319

52. Jackson to Wilson, August 13, 1824, in *Jackson Papers,* 5:434; *Adams Memoirs,* 5:469.

53. Peterson, *Great Triumvirate,* 118; Hopkinson to Louisa Adams, January 1823, in *Adams Memoirs,* 6:51, 131, 136, 361, 412; *Jackson Papers,* 5:39, 433–34; Calhoun to Swift, November 16, 1823, in Hay, "Unpublished Calhoun Letters, II," 287; Calhoun to Sterling, March 27, 1823, in *Calhoun Papers,* 7:546–47; Hay, "Calhoun and the Presidential Campaign of 1824," 27; Calhoun to Swift, April 29, 1823, Calhoun to Swift, May 10, 1823, in Hay, "Unpublished Calhoun Letters," 86–87; *Adams Memoirs,* 5:297; Clay to Porter, January 31, 1824, in *Clay Papers,* 3:629–30; Smith, "First Straw?," 30.

54. Coens, "Formation of the Jackson Party," 6, 21; Mooney, *William Crawford,* 287.

3. One-Party Politics

1. Chase, *Presidential Nominating Convention,* 5; Coens, "Formation of the Jackson Party," 14; Livermore, *Twilight of Federalism,* 9.

2. Clay to Porter, April 14, 1822, Clay to Return Meigs, June 8, 1822, in *Clay Papers,* 3:191, 226; Adams to Hopkinson, January 23, 1823, in *Adams Memoirs,* 6:135; Calhoun to Sterling, March 27, 1823, in *Calhoun Papers,* 7:546; Crawford to Boling Hall, November 20, 1821, in Shipp, *Giant Days,* 230.

3. *Jackson Papers,* 5:196–97.

4. Jackson to Bronaugh, August 1, 1822, in *Jackson Papers,* 5:210; Andrew Hynes to Clay, July 31, 1822, Clay to Porter, August 10, 1822, George Thompson to Clay, August 12, 1822, in *Clay Papers,* 3:265, 274, 275; Crawford to Tait, September 17, 1822, in Shipp, *Giant Days,* 234; Calhoun to Swift, August 24, 1823, in Hay, "Unpublished Calhoun Letters," 89.

5. Shaw to Clay, April 4, 1822, Clay to Meigs, June 8, 1822, Kendall to Clay, June 20, 1822, Clay to Kendall, June 23, 1822, John Wright to Clay, November 2, 1822, John Sloane to Clay, December 19, 1822, in *Clay Papers,* 3:185, 226–39, 308, 341; "Another State Nomination," *Easton (MD) Gazette,* December 21, 1822; "The Presidency," *Essex Register* (Salem, MA), February 1, 1823.

6. Meigs to Clay, September 3, 1822, Clay to Meigs, September 11, 1822, Sloane to Clay, October 16, 1822, Clay to Porter, October 22, 1822, Wright to Clay, December 4, 1822, Clay to Brooke, January 8, 1823, in *Clay Papers,* 3:285, 294, 301, 331, 350.

7. Beatty to Rochester, April 18, 1822, in *Clay Papers*, 3:194; Isaac Baker to Jackson, May 3, 1823, in *Jackson Papers*, 5:274.

8. *Adams Memoirs*, 5:466; Ratcliffe, *One-Party Presidential Contest*, 36; Calhoun to Maxcy, November 17, 1822, in *Calhoun Papers*, 7:345.

9. Ratcliffe, *One-Party Presidential Contest*, 64–66; "Presidential Election," *Eastern Argus* (Portland, ME), January 28, 1823; "Voice of Maine!," *Augusta Chronicle and Georgia Advertiser*, February 6, 1823; "Voice of Maine," *Columbian Centinel* (Boston), January 21, 1824; "Rhode Island Nomination," *Independent Chronicle and Boston Patriot*, January 24, 1824.

10. "The Caucus," *Delaware Gazette and State Journal* (Wilmington, DE), February 20, 1824; "Nomination of Mr. Crawford," *City Gazette* (Charleston, SC), December 20, 1823; *Clay Papers*, 3:662; *Jackson Papers*, 5:367.

11. Warfield to Clay, May 30, 1822, Albert Tracy to Clay, April 27, 1823, in *Clay Papers*, 3:212; Eaton to Jackson, January 11, 1823, in *Jackson Papers*, 5:235; R. H. Walworth to Azariah Flagg, January 27, 1822, in Hay, "Calhoun and the Presidential Campaign of 1824," 25; *Adams Memoirs*, 6:327–28.

12. *Adams Memoirs*, 6:248, 295; Jackson to Fulton, December 21, 1823, Charles Tutt to Jackson, June 12, 1824, Jackson to Coffee, December 27, 1824, in *Jackson Papers*, 5:329, 414, 458; Calhoun to Fisher, June 11, 1823, McDuffie to Fisher, December 14, 1823, in Newsome, "Correspondence of Calhoun, McDuffie, and Fisher," 481, 491; Calhoun to Maxcy, March 13, 1823, in *Calhoun Papers*, 7:518; Calhoun to Swift, November 9, 1823, in Hay, "Unpublished Calhoun Letters," 96; Clay to Kendall, February 16, 1823, Porter to Clay, May 26, 1823, Thomas Wharton to Clay, August 13, 1823, in *Clay Papers*, 3:382, 422, 467.

13. Calhoun to Swift, May 10, 1823, in Hay, "Unpublished Calhoun Letters," 86; Beatty to Rochester, April 18, 1822, Porter to Clay, September 30, 1822, Clay to Porter, February 2, 1823, in *Clay Papers*, 3:194, 290, 363; Calhoun to Maxcy, March 12, 1823, in *Calhoun Papers*, 7:515.

14. Baker to Jackson, May 3, 1823, Jackson to John McLemore, January 30, 1824, Jackson to Donelson, February 12, 1824, in *Jackson Papers*, 5:275, 351, 356; Calhoun to Maxcy, March 13, 1823, Calhoun to Unknown, March 18, 1823, Calhoun to Samuel Southard, March 19, 1823, in *Calhoun Papers*, 7:518, 530, 532; Calhoun to Fisher, August 1, 1823, in Newsome, "Correspondence of Calhoun, McDuffie, and Fisher," 482.

15. Clay to Johnston, June 25, 1824, in *Clay Papers*, 3:785; Maxcy to Henry Wheaton, December 21, 1823, in Hay, "Unpublished Calhoun Letters, II," 288; "The Next President," *Connecticut Courant* (Hartford), August 19, 1823.

16. Calhoun to Colhoun, July 1, 1822, in *Calhoun Papers*, 7:197.

17. Clay to Porter, April 14, 1822, Clay to Johnston, September 10, 1824, in *Clay Papers*, 3:192, 832; Formisano, "State Development," 19; John, "Affairs of Office," 56, 58.

18. Mooney, *William Crawford*, 123, 126, 228; Gadsden to Jackson, July 30, 1823, in *Jackson Papers*, 5:286; *Adams Memoirs*, 5:89.

19. Roberts, "Public Land Disposal in Alabama," 166–74.

20. Mooney, *William Crawford*, 125; James Craine Bronaugh to AJ, January 7, 1822, in *Jackson Papers*, 5:129–30, 148; *Adams Memoirs, 5,* 482–83.

21. Clay to Hammond, August 21, 1823, Porter to Clay, September 6, 1823, in *Clay Papers,* 3:472, 486; *Adams Memoirs,* 6:110, 174–75, 184–85, 187; Calhoun to Edwards, August 20, 1822, Calhoun to Edwards, October 5, 1822, Calhoun to Southard, March 27, 1823, in *Calhoun Papers,* 7:xxxvii–xxxviii, 248, 295, 546; *Adams Memoirs,* 5:494.

22. Hecht, *John Quincy Adams,* 337–46; *Adams Memoirs,* 5:323, 496; *Adams Memoirs,* 6:26, 128–29; *Van Buren Autobiography,* 140–41; Charles Todd to Clay, May 8, 1823, in *Clay Papers,* 3:413; Jackson to Monroe, February 19, 1823, in *Jackson Papers,* 5:251.

23. Monroe to Crawford, September 7, 1822, in *Monroe Writings,* 6:297; *Adams Memoirs,* 5:479–82, 484; *Van Buren Autobiography,* 125–26.

24. Jackson to Bronaugh, January 10, 1822, Jackson to Coffee, February 15, 1824, in *Jackson Papers,* 5:136, 357.

25. Jackson to Livingston, March 24, 1823, Jackson to Overton, November 8, 1823, Jackson to Coffee, February 22, 1824, Jackson to Swartwout, March 4, 1824, Jackson to John McLean, March 22, 1824, in *Jackson Papers,* 5:265, 316, 362, 370, 379–80; Clay to Porter, February 15, 1824, in *Clay Papers,* 3:641; Remini, *Life of Jackson,* 111–13; Howe, *What Hath God Wrought,* 125–26.

26. Roberts, "Public Land Disposal in Alabama," 167–69; *Adams Memoirs,* 5:24, 303, Robert Butler to Jackson, September 19, 1821, in *Jackson Papers,* 5:101; Clay to Hammond, August 21, 1823, in *Clay Papers,* 3:472; Sterling to Calhoun, April 1822, in *Calhoun Papers,* 7:3.

27. Eaton to Jackson, February 23, 1823, in *Jackson Papers,* 5:254.

28. Allgor, *Parlor Politics,* 155–57; *Adams Memoirs,* 6:228.

29. Eaton to Jackson, February 23, 1823, Jackson to Rachel Jackson, December 7, 1823, Eaton to Rachel Jackson, December 18, 1823, Jackson to Rachel Jackson, February 6, 1824, Jackson to Rachel Jackson, March 16, 1824, in *Jackson Papers,* 5:254, 322–23, 327, 352, 375; *Van Buren Autobiography,* 513; Ratcliffe, *One-Party Presidential Contest,* 142; *Adams Memoirs,* 5:330; *Adams Memoirs,* 6:258.

30. Allgor, *Parlor Politics,* 149–52, 163–76; Eaton to Jackson, February 23, 1823, in *Jackson Papers,* 5:254; *Adams Memoirs,* 6:234; *Adams Memoirs,* 5:305, 471.

31. Jackson to Rachel Jackson, December 21, 1823, Eaton to Rachel Jackson, February 8, 1824, in *Jackson Papers,* 5:330, 353.

32. Allgor, *Parlor Politics,* 156; Pasley, *Tyranny of Printers,* 5.

33. Robbins to Clay, February 25, 1824, in *Clay Papers,* 3:661.

34. William Creighton to Clay, May 2, 1822, Warfield to Clay, December 10, 1822, in *Clay Papers,* 3:205, 336; Crawford to Tait, June 3, 1822, in Shipp, *Giant Days,* 232; Jackson to Donelson, January 18, 1824, in *Jackson Papers,* 5:339.

35. Jackson to Miller, June 9, 1823, Jackson to Calhoun, August 12, 1823, in *Jackson Papers,* 5:212, 282, 287; William Marcy to Martin Van Buren, January 11, 1824, in Mooney, *William Crawford,* 270; Francis Johnson to Clay, December 10, 1822, Johnston to Clay, October 20, 1824, in *Clay Papers,* 3:333, 869.

36. Warfield to Clay, December 10, 1822, Shaw to Clay, February 11, 1823, Clay to Hammond, February 22, 1824, Clay to Brooke, February 23, 1824, Clay to Stuart, March 24, 1824, Kentucky Circular, September 22, 1824, Johnston to Clay, September 22, 1824, Johnston to Clay, October 20, 1824, John Harvie to Clay, November 4, 1824, in *Clay Papers*, 3:336, 372, 654, 655, 676, 822, 845, 869, 872, 879; Crawford to Tait, February 16, 1823, in Shipp, *Giant Days*, 236; Eaton to Jackson, January 11, 1823, in *Jackson Papers*, 5:237; *National Gazette and Literary Register*, June 12, 1824, 1.

37. Calhoun to Fisher, August 1, 1823, in Newsome, "Correspondence of Calhoun, McDuffie, and Fisher," 482–83; Porter to Clay, January 1, 1822, [i.e., 1823], Clay to Porter, February 3, 1823, in *Clay Papers*, 3:356, 365; *Adams Memoirs*, 6:114, 227; Jackson to Gadsden, December 6, 1821, in *Jackson Papers*, 5:120–21.

38. Clay to Stuart, March 24, 1824, Johnston to Clay, October 20, 1824, in *Clay Papers*, 3:676, 869; "Extract of a Letter from a Gentleman in Cincinnati to His Correspondent in Nashville," *Nashville (TN) Gazette*, September 24, 1824; "Mr. Clay," *Nashville (TN) Gazette*, September 17, 1824; *Augusta Chronicle and Georgia Advertiser*, October 23, 1824, 2–3; Jackson to Bronaugh, January 10, 1822, Jackson to Coffee, February 17, 1823, Jackson to Calhoun, August 12, 1823, Jackson to Donelson, April 17, 1824, in *Jackson Papers*, 5:136, 249, 287, 395–96; *Adams Memoirs*, 6:114, 234, 239, 248, 254, 264.

39. *Adams Memoirs*, 6:303

40. Ratcliffe, *One-Party Presidential Contest*, 139.

41. Eaton to Jackson, February 23, 1823, in *Jackson Papers*, 5:255–56.

4. The Perpetual Campaign

1. Hecht, *John Quincy Adams*, 329–32; Nagel, *John Quincy Adams*, 269; Parsons, *Birth of Modern Politics*, 67.

2. Clay to Caesar Rodney, August 9, 1821, in *Clay Papers*, 3:107; *Adams Memoirs*, 5:304, 315; Monroe to Madison, May 10, 1822, in *Monroe Writings*, 6:286.

3. John, "Affairs of Office," 50, 57; John, *Spreading the News*, 59, 66; Calhoun to Maxcy, October 11, 1822, in *Calhoun Papers*, 7:xxxiv, 301; *Adams Memoirs*, 5:515; *Adams Memoirs*, 6:27.

4. *Adams Memoirs*, 6:61; Monroe to Ringgold, May 8, 1826, in *Monroe Writings*, 6:82.

5. *Adams Memoirs*, 6:314; Ammon, *James Monroe*, 468–69; *Adams Memoirs*, 5:451, 454.

6. Shipp, *Giant Days*, 28–29; *Adams Memoirs*, 5:342, 425–26, 478.

7. Crawford to Hall, November 20, 1821, Crawford to Tait, June 3, 1822, in Shipp, *Giant Days*, 163, 230, 232; Ammon, *James Monroe*, 494; Peterson, *Great Triumvirate*, 116; *Adams Memoirs*, 5:315; *Adams Memoirs*, 6:43, 115; Calhoun to S[amuel] Ingham, November 2, 1822, in *Calhoun Papers*, 7:327–28.

8. *Adams Memoirs*, 6:27, 56–57.

9. Crawford to Tait, September 4, 1821, in Shipp, *Giant Days*, 149.

10. Crawford to Tait, September 4, 1821; Crawford to Hall, November 20, 1821, in Shipp, *Giant Days,* 149, 160, 230; *Adams Memoirs,* 6:8, 63.

11. John, "Affairs of Office," 57; Monroe to William Wirt, September 27, 1824, in *Monroe Writings,* 6:39; *Calhoun Papers,* 7:xxxix; Skeen, "Politics of Retrenchment," 154–55; Ammon, *James Monroe,* 501–2.

12. *Adams Memoirs,* 5:361; *Adams Memoirs,* 6:42–43, 244.

13. *Adams Memoirs,* 5:478; Hay, "Calhoun and the Presidential Campaign of 1824," 36; Calhoun to Edwards, June 12, 1822, Calhoun to Edwards, August 20, 1822, Calhoun to Ingham, November 2, 1822, in *Calhoun Papers,* 7:160, 249, 327.

14. *Adams Memoirs,* 6:246, 277.

15. Moats, "President James Monroe and Foreign Affairs," 467–68; Jackson to Overton, December 5, 1823, Jackson to Lewis, December 7, 1823, in *Jackson Papers,* 5:321, 323; *Adams Memoirs,* 6:234; *Adams Memoirs,* 5:490; Anonymous to Clay, April 26, 1822, in *Clay Papers,* 3:200; Jackson to Call, June 29, 1822, Houston to Jackson, August 3, 1822, in *Jackson Papers,* 5:198, 211.

16. Coens, "Formation of the Jackson Party," 48–51; *Calhoun Papers,* 7:xxxviii; Skeen, "Politics of Retrenchment," 141–42: Jackson to William Brady and Thomas Williamson, September 27, 1823, in *Jackson Papers,* 5:299.

17. White, *Jeffersonians,* 119–22; Ammon, *James Monroe,* 470–71; "Report of the Secretary of War on the Reduction of the Army," December 14, 1818, *American State Papers: Military Affairs* 1:780; *Adams Memoirs,* 5:231, 237, 314, 316, 326; US *House Journal,* 16th Congress, 2nd session, November 22, 1820, 29; Skeen, "Politics of Retrenchment," 143–49; 37 Annals of Cong. 734, 744–56 (1855).

18. Skeen, "Politics of Retrenchment," 149–50; 37 Annals of Cong. 744–56 (1855).

19. Skeen, "Politics of Retrenchment," 151–53; Calhoun to Monroe, April 15, 1822, in *Calhoun Papers,* 7:xii–xiii, 42; Jackson to Butler, January 9, 1822, in *Jackson Papers,* 5:133.

20. *Calhoun Papers,* 7:xiii–xiv; Monroe to Madison, May 10, 1822, in *Monroe Writings,* 6:287–88; 38 Annals of Cong. 475–78 (1855).

21. Monroe to the Senate, April 13, 1822, Calhoun to Daniel Parker, May 13, 1822, in *Calhoun Papers,* 7:xiv–xix, 38, 109; Skeen, "Politics of Retrenchment," 153–54; Ammon, *James Monroe,* 500–501; Monroe to Madison, May 10, 1822, Monroe to Madison, August 25, 1822, in *Monroe Writings,* 6:288, 295; *Adams Memoirs,* 5:486–87, 514, 527; 38 Annals of Cong. 479–86, 489–502, 509–10 (1855); *Adams Memoirs,* 6:3–6, 115; Jackson to Calhoun, June 28, 1822, in *Jackson Papers,* 5:193; Crawford to Tait, June 3, 1822, in Shipp, *Giant Days,* 232.

22. Monroe to Madison, May 10, 1822, in *Monroe Writings,* 6:286–87; Ammon, *James Monroe,* 471–72; *Calhoun Papers,* 7:xxvi–xxvii.

23. Alexander Macomb to JCC, April 22, 1822, JCC to V[irgil] Maxcy, July 11, 1822, in *Calhoun Papers,* 7:xxvi, 60–61, 205; *Adams Memoirs,* 5:490; AJ to JM, July 26, 1822, in *Jackson Papers,* 5:207; Niven, *John C. Calhoun,* 79–80.

24. Farrier, "Fort Blunder," http://www.neatorama.com/2013/11/24/Fort-Blunder-The -Fort-That-America-Accidentally-Built-in-Canada/; Dobbs and Siders, "Fort Delaware

Architectural Research Project," 7; "Condition of the Military Establishment and the Fortifications," December 23, 1824, *American State Papers: Military Affairs* 2:713–14; Calhoun to Maxcy, June 9, 1822, in *Calhoun Papers*, 7:154.

25. Alexander Macomb to Calhoun, April 22, 1822, in *Calhoun Papers*, 7:xxvi–xxvii, 60; *Adams Memoirs*, 5:331–32, 490, 542.

26. Calhoun to Maxcy, May 6, 1822, Calhoun to Maxcy, June 9, 1822, in *Calhoun Papers*, 7:xxii–xxiii, xxv, 97–98, 154; Jackson to Call, June 29, 1822, in *Jackson Papers*, 5:198–99.

27. Calhoun to Charles Caldwell, November 29, 1822, in *Calhoun Papers*, 7:xlviii, 360; Shaw to Clay, April 4, 1822, Brooke to Clay, August 14, 1823, Clay to Brooke, August 28, 1823, in *Clay Papers*, 3:185, 469, 480.

28. *Adams Memoirs*, 5:203, 428–29.

29. *Adams Memoirs*, 5:431–50, 474; Ammon, *James Monroe*, 498–99; *Calhoun Papers*, 7:xxi; Peterson, *Great Triumvirate*, 122; *Adams Memoirs*, 6:217–18.

30. *Adams Memoirs*, 5:204, 231–32; Calhoun to Maxcy, June 9, 1822, in *Calhoun Papers*, 7:xlvi, 155; Shaw to Clay, April 4, 1822, John Smith to Clay, April 30, 1822, in *Clay Papers*, 3:185, 203.

31. *Adams Memoirs*, 6:43, 47–48, 61–66; Sloane to Clay, October 16, 1822, in *Clay Papers*, 3:294; Calhoun to Maxcy, April 22, 1822, in *Calhoun Papers*, 7:61.

32. Remini, *Henry Clay*, 215–18; Peterson, *Great Triumvirate*, 120–21; *Adams Memoirs*, 6:43, 49, 58–59.

33. *Adams Memoirs*, 6:8, 40–50, 54; *Adams Memoirs*, 5:452, 477, 498, 503–6, 526.

34. *Adams Memoirs*, 6:40, 66; *Adams Memoirs*, 5:537; Hecht, *John Quincy Adams*, 337–43; H. Johnson to Edwards, August 10, 1823, in Edwards, *History of Illinois*, 504; Jackson to Donelson, June 28, 1822, Jackson to Call, June 29, 1822, in *Jackson Papers*, 5:196, 198; John Smith to Clay, April 30, 1822, Cheves to Clay, November 9, 1822, in *Clay Papers*, 3:203, 315.

35. Remini, *Henry Clay*, 215–18; Clay to Brooke, January 8, 1823, in *Clay Papers*, 3:350

36. Benton to Clay, April 26, 1822, Benton to Clay, May 2, 1822, Russell to Clay, June 6, 1822, Kendall to Clay, June 20, 1822, Clay to Martin Hardin, June 23, 1823 [i.e., 1822], Clay to Kendall, June 23, 1822, Clay to Russell, July 9, 1822, Cheves to Clay, November 9, 1822, Clay to [Joseph Gales and William Seaton], November 15, 1822, Sloane to Clay, December 19, 1822, Clay to Porter, February 4, 1823, Porter to Clay, February 12, 1823, in *Clay Papers*, 3:204, 219–26, 236–40, 252–57, 314, 322–24, 341–69, 378.

37. *Adams Memoirs*, 6:8, 44, 49, 60, 116–18; *Adams Memoirs*, 5:355–56, 497, 500; Clay to Russell, April 19, 1823, in *Clay Papers*, 3:409.

38. *Adams Memoirs*, 6:54–55, 62–63, 95, 244–45, 403; Mooney, *William Crawford*, 222, 237; "From the National Gazette," *Edwardsville (IL) Spectator*, May 31, 1823; Bemis, *Adams and the Union*, 24–25; Newsome, "Correspondence of Calhoun, McDuffie, and Fisher," 500; Rochester to Clay, December 20, 1823, in *Clay Papers*, 3:547; Calhoun to Maxcy, January 20, 1823, in *Calhoun Papers*, 7:432; "Address of the Committee of Correspondence, Appointed by the Public Meeting of Citizens Friendly to the Election

of John Q. Adams as President," *National Gazette and Literary Register,* October 30, 1824; "John C. Calhoun," *Ithaca (NY) Journal,* October 29, 1823, 1.

39. Nagel, "Election of 1824: A Reconsideration," 322; "The Next President," *Connecticut Courant* (Hartford), August 19, 1823; Author of the Clay Papers, "Messrs. Adams and Clay," *Providence (RI) Gazette,* November 3, 1824.

40. Adams to Hopkinson, January 23, 1823, in *Adams Memoirs,* 6:136; Mooney, *William Crawford,* 222, 235, 237; Mason, *Slavery and Politics in the Early Republic,* 77, 199; Bolingbroke, "The Presidency," *Richmond (VA) Enquirer,* August 17, 1824.

41. Murphy, "Jackson's Rise," 268–72.

42. Mooney, *William Crawford,* 222, 274; Crawford to Tait, February 16, 1823, in Shipp, *Giant Days,* 170–71, 218, 236–37.

43. *Adams Memoirs,* 6:14; Monroe to Jackson, May 30, 1822, in *Monroe Writings,* 6:292.

44. Shaw to Clay, April 4, 1822, in *Clay Papers,* 3:185, 187, 744; Niven, *John C. Calhoun,* 97–98; *Adams Memoirs,* 5:483–84.

45. Mooney, *William Crawford,* 242–44; Ammon, *James Monroe,* 466; Ingham to Edwards, August 20, 1823, in Edwards, *History of Illinois,* 497.

46. Niven, *John C. Calhoun,* 98; *Clay Papers,* 3:187.

47. Adams to Hopkinson, January 23, 1823, in *Adams Memoirs,* 6:135; Clay to Hammond, October 29, 1823, in *Clay Papers,* 3:506.

48. *Adams Memoirs,* 6:59, 412; Clay to Porter, February 15, 1824, in *Clay Papers,* 3:641.

49. Nord, *Communities of Journalism,* 3, 81–85; *Adams Memoirs,* 6:55, 75–76; *Adams Memoirs,* 5:89.

50. Freeman, *Affairs of Honor,* xix.

51. Formisano, *The Transformation of Political Culture,* 134; Pasley, *Tyranny of Printers,* 12; *Adams Memoirs,* 5:185, 212; Shaw to Clay, April 4, 1822, "Patrick Henry" to Clay, April 21, 1822, Anonymous to Clay, April 26, 1822, Warfield to Clay, May 30, 1822, in *Clay Papers,* 3:185, 196, 200, 211; Calhoun to Maxcy, July 11, 1822, in *Calhoun Papers,* 7:206.

52. Anonymous to Clay, April 26, 1822, Warfield to Clay, May 30, 1822, in *Clay Papers,* 3:200, 211; Sellers, *Market Revolution,* 118; Hay, "Calhoun and the Presidential Campaign of 1824," 25.

53. Eaton to Jackson, January 11, 1823, Jackson to Fulton, December 21, 1823, in *Jackson Papers,* 5:237, 329, 371–72; Coens, "Formation of the Jackson Party," 26; Watson, *Liberty and Power,* 78; John, "Affairs of Office," 58; Hargreaves, *Presidency of Adams,* 28.

54. Calhoun to Ingham, November 2, 1822, in *Calhoun Papers,* 7:327; Mooney, *William Crawford,* 241, 263; Shipp, *Giant Days,* 174; Ammon, *James Monroe,* 530, 666; Hecht, *John Quincy Adams,* 383.

5. The Final Battles

1. *Adams Memoirs*, 6:415; *Van Buren Autobiography*, 196, 199.

2. Johnston to Clay, August 31, 1824, in *Clay Papers*, 3:809; Jackson to Donelson, April 17, 1824, in *Jackson Papers*, 5:396.

3. Remini, *Andrew Jackson*, 2:51–52; Ratcliffe, *One-Party Presidential Contest*, 118.

4. Brady and Williamson to Jackson, September 20, 1823, Jackson to Abram Maury, September 21, 1823, Jackson to [Calhoun?], October 4, 1823, Jackson to Coffee, October 24, 1823, in *Jackson Papers*, 5:294–98, 301, 309.

5. Jackson to Overton, January 10, 1825, in *Jackson Papers*, 6:14; Tutt to Jackson, June 24, 1823, Jackson to George Martin, July [January] 2, 1824, Jackson to Rachel Jackson, January 29, 1824, in *Jackson Papers*, 5:283, 334, 349.

6. Jackson to Coffee, February 15, 1824, Jackson to Swartwout, March 4, 1824, Jackson to Donelson, March 19, 1824, Arthur Hayne to Jackson, April 16, 1824, in *Jackson Papers*, 5:358, 370, 378, 385, 395, 463–67.

7. Jackson to Martin, July [January] 2, 1824, Jackson to Donelson, February 26, 1824, in *Jackson Papers*, 5:334, 366.

8. Jackson to George Gibson, January 29, 1822, Jackson to Jefferson, February 6, 1822, Jackson to Miller, June 9, 1823, James Jackson to Jackson, October 21, 1823, Jackson to Winfield Scott, December 11, 1823, Call to Coffee, December 14, 1823, Eaton to Rachel Jackson, December 18, 1823, Jackson to Donelson, January 14, 1824, in *Jackson Papers*, 5:139, 144, 281–82, 307–8, 326–28, 336; *Jackson Papers*, 6:212.

9. Ratcliffe, *One-Party Presidential Contest*, 122–23; Jackson to Donelson, January 21, 1824, in *Jackson Papers*, 5:344, 360; Calhoun to Maxcy, March 12, 1823, in *Calhoun Papers*, 7:515.

10. Jackson to Donelson, February 26, 1824, Jackson to Coffee, March 4, 1824, in *Jackson Papers*, 5:367, 369; Calhoun to Unknown, March 18, 1823, in *Calhoun Papers*, 7:530; B. B. Smith to Fisher, January 24, 1824, B. B. Smith to Fisher, February 7, 1824, in Newsome, "Correspondence of Calhoun, McDuffie, and Fisher," 500–503.

11. Wharton to Clay, August 13, 1823, in *Clay Papers*, 3:466–67; *Adams Memoirs*, 6:224; Eaton to Jackson, January 11, 1823, in *Jackson Papers*, 5:237.

12. *Adams Memoirs*, 5:369, 467; Jackson to Livingston, March 24, 1823, in *Jackson Papers*, 5:264–65; *Adams Memoirs*, 6:253, 289, 332–33.

13. Allgor, *Parlor Politics*, 176–77.

14. Allgor, *Parlor Politics*, 178–81; *Adams Memoirs*, 6:228–29.

15. Jackson to Butler, January 20, 1824, Jackson to Swartwout, September 27, 1824, in *Jackson Papers*, 5:341, 445; *Adams Memoirs*, 6:417.

16. Jackson to Monroe, January 16, 1824, Monroe to Jackson, January 16, 1824, Jackson to Donelson, January 18, 1824, in *Jackson Papers*, 5:338–39; *Van Buren Autobiography*, 237; Coens, "Formation of the Jackson Party," 40–46.

17. Livermore, *Twilight of Federalism*, 160–63; Jackson to Monroe, April 9, 1824, Jackson to Monroe, April 10, 1824, Jackson to Donelson, April 11, 1824, in *Jackson Papers*, 5:389–92; *Van Buren Autobiography*, 235–37; *Adams Memoirs*, 6:248, 286–87.

18. Albert Gallatin to Walter Lowrie, May 22, 1824, in Livermore, *Twilight of Federalism*, 164; Jackson to Lewis, February 22, 1824, Monroe to Jackson, February 22, 1824, Jackson to George Kremer, May 6, 1824, in *Jackson Papers*, 5:363–65, 402–3.

19. Jackson to Lewis, February 22, 1824, Jackson to Donelson, February 26, 1824, in *Jackson Papers*, 5:363, 366; *Adams Memoirs*, 6:287, 295–96, 342; *Van Buren Autobiography*, 127, 234; Livermore, *Twilight of Federalism*, 160–63.

20. George Thornton to Jackson, June 26, 1824, in *Jackson Papers*, 5:338, 422–23; Livermore, *Twilight of Federalism*, 165–66; Coens, "Formation of the Jackson Party," 43–45.

21. Jackson to Francis Preston, January 27, 1824, Jackson to Swartwout, March 25, 1824, in *Jackson Papers*, 5:347, 371–72, 381.

22. Jackson to Donelson, March 6, 1824, Jackson to Swartwout, March 25, 1824, in *Jackson Papers*, 5:373, 381; Warshauer, "Jackson and New Orleans," 79–80.

23. Jackson to Martin, July [January] 2, 1824, in *Jackson Papers*, 5:334; Clay to Brooke, May 28, 1824, in *Clay Papers*, 3:767; *Adams Memoirs*, 6:267, 275, 345.

24. Clay to Porter, April 26, 1824, in *Clay Papers*, 3:744; Heidler and Heidler, *Henry Clay*, 163.

25. Remini, *Henry Clay*, 214–15; Clay to Porter, October 22, 1822, Shaw to Clay, February 11, 1823, Clay to Brooke, August 28, 1823, in *Clay Papers*, 3:301, 372, 481; *Adams Memoirs*, 6:364, 456.

26. Remini, *Andrew Jackson* 2:1–3.

27. Jackson to Call, January 5, 1822, Jackson to Coffee, February 25, 1822, Jackson to Donelson, April 26, 1822, Jackson to Gadsden, May 2, 1822, Jackson to John Hamblen, June 29, 1822, Jackson to Coffee, May 24, 1823, Jackson to Coffee, October 24, 1823, Jackson to Donelson, March 19, 1824, in *Jackson Papers*, 5:127–28, 153, 177, 180–81, 200, 277, 310, 378.

28. Tutt to Jackson, June 12, 1824, in *Jackson Papers*, 5:414–15; *Adams Memoirs*, 6:241, 246–47, 265–66, 302–3, 360.

29. *Van Buren Autobiography*, 665; Clay to Porter, October 22, 1822, Clay to Porter, June 15, 1823, in *Clay Papers*, 3:300, 432; Mooney, *William Crawford*, 235, 281; "Mr. Clay," *Nashville (TN) Gazette*, September 17, 1824.

30. Chase, *Presidential Nominating Convention*, 12, 21–22, 26; *Adams Memoirs*, 5:60.

31. Coens, "Formation of the Jackson Party," 74–78, 88, 100; McCormick, *Second American Party System*, 23–24; Chase, *Presidential Nominating Convention*, 23, 43; Coens, "Early Jackson Party," 235–36; Sydnor, "One-Party Period," 440–43; Hayne to Jackson, April 16, 1824, in *Jackson Papers*, 5:394.

32. Chase, *Presidential Nominating Convention*, 44–45, 61; Peart, *Era of Experimentation*, 114; Mooney, *William Crawford*, 250, 254.

33. Coens, "Formation of the Jackson Party," 89, 101; *Jackson Papers*, 5:294–95, 334; Jeffrey, *State Parties*, 22–25.

34. John Elliott to General David Blackshear, September 4, 1822, in Shipp, *Giant Days*, 172–73; *Adams Memoirs*, 6:191; Clay to Porter, February 3, 1823, in *Clay Papers*, 3:365–66.

35. *Van Buren Autobiography*, 513; Niven, *Martin Van Buren*, 139; McDuffie to Unknown, November 21, 1823, McDuffie to Unknown, December 26, 1823, Miller to Fisher, January 3, 1824, in Hay, "Unpublished Calhoun Letters," 488–89, 492, 498.

36. Coens, "Formation of the Jackson Party," 86, 124, 127; Jackson to Fulton, December 21, 1823, in *Jackson Papers*, 5:328.

37. Coens, "Formation of the Jackson Party," 91–92, 101, 103, 126.

38. *Adams Memoirs*, 6:228–29, 236–37; Porter to Clay, November 17, 1823, Clay to Porter, December 11, 1823, in *Clay Papers*, 3:523, 535.

39. *Adams Memoirs*, 6:235–37, 239, 241, 245; McDuffie to Fisher, December 14, 1823, McDuffie to Unknown, January 7, 1823, in Newsome, "Correspondence of Calhoun, McDuffie, and Fisher," 485, 491; Calhoun to Swift, January 25, 1824, in Hay, "Unpublished Calhoun Letters, II," 289; Mooney, *William Crawford*, 257–58.

40. Jackson to Donelson, January 21, 1824, in *Jackson Papers*, 5:344; *Adams Memoirs*, 6:226, 235.

41. Niven, *Martin Van Buren*, 143–44; Clay to Porter, February 15, 1824, in *Clay Papers*, 3:640; Ratcliffe, *One-Party Presidential Contest*, 153.

42. Dangerfield, *Era of Good Feelings*, 5–6, 336; Larson, *Internal Improvement*, 54–55.

43. Ingalls to Clay, August 8, 1824, Brooke to Clay, October 15, 1824, Clay to Hammond, October 25, 1824, in *Clay Papers*, 3:806, 867, 870.

44. Coens, "Formation of the Jackson Party," 89, 102–6; Benton, *Thirty Years' View*, 49.

45. Jackson to Donelson, February 9, 1824, Jackson to Coffee, February 15, 1824, Jackson to Coffee, March 4, 1824, in *Jackson Papers*, 5:354, 358, 369.

46. Jackson to Coffee, March 28, 1824, in *Jackson Papers*, 5:383; Coens, "Formation of the Jackson Party," 94–108; Coens, "Early Jackson Party," 238–40; Jackson to Overton, January 10, 1825, in *Jackson Papers*, 6:13.

47. Hay, "Calhoun and the Presidential Campaign of 1824," 34; Jeffrey, *State Parties*, 26–27.

48. Peterson, *Great Triumvirate*, 117; Hay, "Calhoun and the Presidential Campaign of 1824," 36; Calhoun to Ingham, April 5, 1822, Calhoun to Rogers, June 9, 1822, Calhoun to Maxcy, January 20, 1823, Calhoun to Southard, March 19, 1823, in *Calhoun Papers*, 7:12, 155, 432, 532–33.

49. *Jackson Papers*, 5:360; Coens, "Early Jackson Party," 248–51.

50. McFarland to Jackson, August 14, 1824, in *Jackson Papers*, 5:360, 436; Chase, *Presidential Nominating Convention*, 55–57; Phillips, "Pennsylvania Origins of the Jackson Movement," 506–7.

51. McDuffie to Unknown, January 13, 1823, in Newsome, "Correspondence of Calhoun, McDuffie, and Fisher," 486; Porter to Clay, April 5, 1824, in *Clay Papers*, 3:732.

52. Calhoun to Swift, January 25, 1824, in Hay, "Unpublished Calhoun Letters, II," 289, 291; *Clay Papers*, 3:656; Hay, "Calhoun and the Presidential Campaign of 1824," 40–41.

53. *Adams Memoirs*, 6:265.

54. Calhoun to Edwards, October 5, 1822, in *Calhoun Papers*, 7:296; *Adams Memoirs*, 5:169.

55. Seager, "Politics of Compromise and Non-Compromise," 2, 7–8.

56. Heale, *Presidential Quest*, 45.

57. Remini, *Henry Clay*, 227–29; Campbell, "Internal Improvements," 132–33.

58. Larson, *Internal Improvement*, 4, 141; Campbell, "Internal Improvements," 136–37; Balogh, *Government Out of Sight*, 121–22, 130–31.

59. 41 Annals of Cong. 989–1000, 1005–42, 1053–63, 1217–91, 1295–1427, 1430–58, 1461–69, 1471 (1856); "Mr. Benton Proposed the Following Amendment to the Bill from the House of Representatives, Entitled 'A Bill to Procure the Necessary Surveys, Plans, and Estimates, upon the Subject of Roads and Canals,'" H.R. 5, 18th Cong. (1823); Root to Clay, February 9, 1824, in *Clay Papers*, 3:634.

60. *Adams Memoirs*, 6:22, 323, 418; Jackson to Monroe, July 26, 1822, Jackson to James Lanier, May 15, 1824, in *Jackson Papers*, 5:207–8, 409–10, 463–64; Mooney, *William Crawford*, 168–70; "Mr. Clay—No. 3," *Providence (RI) Gazette*, August 18, 1824.

61. Sellers, *Market Revolution*, 148–49; Ellis, "Market Revolution," 155–56.

62. Remini, *Henry Clay*, 228–33; A Bill to Amend the Several Acts for Imposing Duties on Imports, H.R. 47, 18th Congress (1824); *Jackson Papers*, 5:428; 41 Annals of Cong. 717–24, 753–56, 759–60, 765–66, 959–64, 1469–70, 1611–14, 1675–78 (1856); 42 Annals of Cong. 1697–1701, 1733–34, 1757–61, 1791–92, 1871, 1888, 1895–1900, 1903–4, 1907–12, 1962–2001, 2631–34, 2672–74, 3075–78, 3093–96, 3109–10, 3139–40 (1856).

63. *Jackson Papers*, 5:428–29; Benton, *Thirty Years' View*, 33; Remarks on tariff bill, duty on spirits, February 11, 1824, Clay to ——, February 15, 1824, in *Clay Papers*, 3:637, 639; Dangerfield, *Era of Good Feelings*, 316–19.

64. Jackson to Henry Baldwin, May 20, 1824, in *Jackson Papers*, 5:411–12, 428–29; *Jackson Papers*, 6:336, 345.

65. Jackson to Littleton Coleman, April 26, 1824, Jackson to Coffee, June 18, 1824, in *Jackson Papers*, 5:399–400, 417–18; *Van Buren Autobiography*, 239–40.

66. Jackson to Donelson, April 27, 1824, Coffee to Jackson, June 8, 1824, Eaton to Jackson, June 22, 1824, Jackson to Coffee, July 1, 1824, Jackson to [William Savin], July 4, 1824, Rachel Jackson to Latitia Chamber, August 12, 1824, in *Jackson Papers*, 5:401, 412–13, 419, 425–27, 432.

67. *Adams Memoirs*, 6:274–75, 343, 353; "Address of the Committee of Correspondence, Appointed by the Public Meeting of Citizens Friendly to the Election of John Q. Adams as President," *National Gazette and Literary Register* (Philadelphia, PA), October 30, 1824.

68. Mooney, *William Crawford*, 167; Benton, *Thirty Years' View*, 33; Silbey, *Martin Van Buren*, 39; *Van Buren Autobiography*, 241.

69. Remarks on tariff bill, duty on cotton bagging, February 16, 1824, remarks on tariff bill, duty on cotton bagging, February 17, 1824, remarks on tariff bill, duty on cotton bagging, February 25, 1824, Robbins to Clay, February 25, 1824, Brooke to Clay, July 12, 1824, in *Clay Papers,* 3:642–44, 647–51, 658–61, 737, 793.

70. *Van Buren Autobiography,* 240.

71. Peart, *Era of Experimentation,* 109, 129; Creighton to Clay, May 2, 1822, in *Clay Papers,* 3:205.

72. *Adams Memoirs,* 6:273.

73. Bemis, *Adams and Foreign Policy,* 412–25; *Adams Memoirs,* 5:217–18.

74. Bemis, *Adams and Foreign Policy,* 427–29.

75. Bemis, *Adams and Foreign Policy,* 430–35; *Adams Memoirs,* 6:321–22, 345, 427–28; "Suppression of the Slave Trade," April 30, 1824, *American State Papers: Foreign Relations* 5:315–46; US *Senate Executive Journal,* 18th Congress, 1st session, April 30 and May 21, 1824, 373–75, 380–87; Ammon, *James Monroe,* 524–27.

76. *Adams Memoirs,* 6:328–29, 348–50, 361–62, 367–68; Bemis, *Adams and Foreign Policy,* 434–35; Johnston to Clay, August 9, 1824, in *Clay Papers,* 3:807–8.

77. Bemis, *Adams and Foreign Policy,* 434.

78. Bemis, *Adams and Foreign Policy,* 416–23; *Adams Memoirs,* 5:4–9, 199, 205–9; *Adams Memoirs,* 6:342–43, 363.

79. Bemis, *Adams and Foreign Policy,* 417–18; *Adams Memoirs,* 5:10–12, 210; *Adams Memoirs,* 6:353–54.

80. "Correspondence between the Treasury, the Bank of the United States, and Other Banks, Relative to the Public Deposits," March 22, 1824, *American State Papers: Finance* 4:495; Mooney, *William Crawford,* 242–44; Friends of the 1820 Colonel Benjamin Stephenson House, "The Bank of Edwardsville," http://www.mtecpro.com/BenTheBank.asp.

81. *Adams Memoirs,* 6:296–97.

82. *Adams Memoirs,* 6:297; Jackson to Donelson, April 27, 1824, in *Jackson Papers,* 5:401.

83. Calhoun to Edwards, June 12, 1822, Calhoun to Edwards, October 5, 1822, in *Calhoun Papers,* 7:161, 295–96; *Adams Memoirs,* 5:207, 524; *Adams Memoirs,* 6:227, 262–63.

84. Mooney, *William Crawford,* 245–46; Crawford to Tait, February 16, 1823, in Shipp, *Giant Days,* 164, 236; Benton, *Thirty Years' View,* 35.

85. *Van Buren Autobiography,* 181; *Adams Memoirs,* 6:296, 298; *Jackson Papers,* 5:397–98.

86. *Van Buren Autobiography,* 181; *Adams Memoirs,* 6:299–301.

87. *Adams Memoirs,* 6:303–6.

88. 42 Annals of Cong. 2431–50, 2471–79, 2713–56 (1856); "Answer of the Secretary of the Treasury to Ninian Edwards' Charges of Financial Mismanagement," May 11, 1824, *American State Papers: Finance* 5:41–66; "Report of Committee on Ninian Edwards' Charges of Financial Mismanagement," May 25, 1824, *American State Papers: Finance* 5:69–74; Edwards, *History of Illinois,* 152–53.

89. Mooney, *William Crawford*, 242–47; Ingham to Edwards, June 5, 1824, Ingham to Edwards, July 8, 1824, in Edwards, *History of Illinois*, 499, 503; *Van Buren Autobiography*, 181–82; *Adams Memoirs*, 6:307, 309–10, 361.

90. Mooney, *William Crawford*, 240–41, 264–68; Clay to Johnston, October 2, 1824, in *Clay Papers*, 3:854.

91. Ingham to Edwards, June 5, 1824, in Edwards, *History of Illinois*, 499; 42 Annals of Cong. 2770–2916 (1856); "Report of Committee on Ninian Edwards' Charges of Financial Mismanagement," June 21, 1824, *American State Papers: Finance* 5:79–145; Shipp, *Giant Days*, 165–67; Benton, *Thirty Years' View*, 35–36; *Adams Memoirs*, 6:371, 374, 384, 389.

92. *Van Buren Autobiography*, 182; *Adams Memoirs*, 6:364, 391–93.

93. *Adams Memoirs*, 6:339–40, 367, 384–87.

94. *Adams Memoirs*, 6:389–94.

95. *Adams Memoirs*, 6:390–95.

96. *Adams Memoirs*, 6:394–95.

97. Southard to Edwards, March 6, 1823, in Edwards, *History of Illinois*, 525; Crawford to Calhoun, October 2, 1830, in Shipp, *Giant Days*, 247–48.

98. Monroe to Wirt, September 27, 1824, in *Monroe Writings*, 6:37; *Adams Memoirs*, 6:388.

99. Jackson to Donelson, April 23, 1824, in *Jackson Papers*, 5:398.

100. *Van Buren Autobiography*, 131; Silbey, *Martin Van Buren*, 39–40; Niven, *Martin Van Buren*, 117, 130–31; Calhoun to Ingham, April 5, 1822, in *Calhoun Papers*, 7:13; Hofstadter, *Idea of a Party System*, 228, 231, 251; David Woods to Clay, May 22, 1823, in *Clay Papers*, 3:420.

101. Mooney, *William Crawford*, 88, 222, 792.

102. *Van Buren Autobiography*, 183–88; *Adams Memoirs*, 6:349.

103. *Van Buren Autobiography*, 183–88.

104. Clay to Stuart, June 14, 1824, Johnston to Clay, June 27, 1824, Johnston to Clay, August 30, 1824, in *Clay Papers*, 3:776, 787, 820.

105. Johnston to Clay, June 27, 1824, Johnston to Clay, September 4, 1824, Johnston to Clay, September 11, 1824, Johnston to Clay, September 16, 1824, Clay to Johnston, September 19, 1824, Johnston to Clay, September 22, 1824, Johnston to Clay, October 3, 1824, Johnston to Clay, October 9, 1824, Ralph Lockwood to Clay, October 9, 1824, in *Clay Papers*, 3:787, 829, 836, 840–45, 856, 861, 863.

106. Johnston to Clay, August 25, 1824, Clay to Johnston, September 3, 1824, Johnston to Clay, October 9, 1824, in *Clay Papers*, 3:817, 827, 861.

107. Nagel, *John Quincy Adams*, 290–91; *Adams Memoirs*, 6:266–67, 415–16.

108. Somkin, *Unquiet Eagle*, 131–33.

109. Somkin, *Unquiet Eagle*, 135–40, 160–72; *Adams Memoirs*, 6:379.

110. Somkin, *Unquiet Eagle*, 149–51; "Resolution on Lafayette Visit," October 2, 1824, in *Clay Papers*, 3:855–56; *Adams Memoirs*, 6:419–25.

111. Jackson to Butler, January 20, 1824, Jackson to Rachel Jackson, February 6, 1824, Hayne to Jackson, April 16, 1824, Rachel Jackson to Elizabeth Kingsley, December 23, 1824, in *Jackson Papers*, 5:336, 352, 394, 456–57.

112. Remini, *Life of Jackson*, 144, 147; Jackson to Houston, August 8, 1824, in *Jackson Papers*, 5:431; Parsons, *Birth of Modern Politics*, 91–92.

113. *Adams Memoirs*, 6:356.

6. The War within the States

1. Allgor, *Parlor Politics*, 175; Adams to Hopkinson, January 23, 1823, in *Adams Memoirs*, 6:135; Eaton to Jackson, January 11, 1823, in *Jackson Papers*, 5:237; Parsons, *Birth of Modern Politics*, 88; Ratcliffe, *One-Party Presidential Contest*, 22; Robin Kolodny, "The Several Elections of 1824," 148.

2. Johnston to Clay, in *Clay Papers*, 3:809; Lewis, *American Union and Neighborhood*, 129–32; Ellis, "Market Revolution," 163–66; Hargreave s, *Presidency of Adams*, 15–16; Dangerfield, *Era of Good Feelings*, 323; Mason, *Slavery and Politics*, 184; Murphy, "Jackson's Rise," 267; Ratcliffe, *Party Spirit in a Frontier Republic*, 230; Ratcliffe, "Crisis of Commercialization," 179.

3. Holt, *Rise and Fall of the American Whig Party*, 6; Thomas Watkins to Jackson, March 13, 1822, in *Jackson Papers*, 5:156.

4. Saltman, *Voting Technology*, 55–65; Pasley, *Tyranny of Printers*, 12; Ratcliffe, *One-Party Presidential Contest*, 200.

5. McCormick, *Second American Party System*, 30; Kendall to Clay, June 20, 1822, Clay to Brooke, February 23, 1824, in *Clay Papers*, 3:237, 656; Ratcliffe, *One-Party Presidential Contest*, 197–98; Coens, "Formation of the Jackson Party," 170–83.

6. Wilentz, *Rise of American Democracy*, 250; Parsons, *Birth of Modern Politics*, 97.

7. Fisher to Edwards, April 21, 1822, in Edwards, *History of Illinois*, 522.

8. Ratcliffe, *One-Party Presidential Contest*, 118; Overton to Clay, January 16, 1822, Jackson to Coffee, March 10, 1823, Benton to Clay, July 23, 1823, in *Clay Papers*, 3:156, 258, 460.

9. McCormick, *Second American Party System*, 222–27, 288–97; Remini, *Life of Jackson*, 145–46; Jackson to Call, November 27, 1822, Houston to Jackson, January 19, 1823, Jackson to Coffee, March 10, 1823, Jackson to Fulton, April 4, 1823, Baker to Jackson, May 3, 1823, Jackson to Donelson, January 21, 1824, William Johnson to Jackson, August 16, 1824, William Johnson to Jackson, September 22, 1824, Jackson to Coffee, September 23, 1824, in *Jackson Papers*, 5:225, 241, 258–59, 268, 275, 343, 437, 441–42; "Extract of a Letter from a Gentleman in Cincinnati to His Correspondent in Nashville," *Nashville (TN) Gazette*, September 24, 1824; Ratcliffe, *One-Party Presidential Contest*, 119, 172–73; Roberts, "Public Land Disposal in Alabama," 173; Thomas Reed to Clay, August 2, 1822, Reed to Clay, September 5, 1822, John McKinley to Clay, June 3, 1823, McKinley to Clay, September 29, 1823, in *Clay Papers*, 3:267, 284, 427, 491.

10. McCormick, *Second American Party System*, 199–203; Jeffrey, *State Parties*, 21–30; Calhoun to Maxcy, March 25, 1823, in *Calhoun Papers*, 7:542; Jackson to Donelson, January 21, 1824, in *Jackson Papers*, 5:343; Coens, "Formation of the Jackson Party," 61; Ratcliffe, *One-Party Presidential Contest*, 190–95.

11. Ratcliffe, *One-Party Presidential Contest*, 192–93; Jeffrey, *State Parties*, 27–32; Mooney, *William Crawford*, 225, 252; Jno. Crowell to Edwards, April 27, 1822, in Edwards, *History of Illinois*, 523.

12. Rothbard, *Panic of 1819*, 87; Coens, "Formation of the Jackson Party," 61, 170; Ratcliffe, *One-Party Presidential Contest*, 208; *Adams Memoirs*, 6:243, 316, 353; Hayne to Jackson, September 18, 1824, in *Jackson Papers*, 5:439; Beatty to Rochester, April 18, 1822, Norvell to Clay, November 14, 1822, Godman to Clay, July 1, 1823, Clay to Porter, April 26, 1824, Johnston to Clay, September 11, 1824, in *Clay Papers*, 3:194, 321, 447, 743, 836–37; McCormick, *Second American Party System*, 134–35; McDuffie to Unknown, December 26, 1823, in Newsome, "Correspondence of Calhoun, McDuffie, and Fisher," 492.

13. Ratcliffe, *One-Party Presidential Contest*, 124–33, 164–72; Edward Ward to Jackson, August 25, 1823, Eaton to Jackson, June 22, 1824, in *Jackson Papers*, 5:290–91, 420; Phillips, "Pennsylvania Origins," 496, 500, 502; Heale, *Presidential Quest*, 60.

14. McCormick, *Second American Party System*, 124–29; Jackson to Swartwout, March 4, 1824, in *Jackson Papers*, 5:370; McDuffie to Unknown, December 26, 1823, in Newsome, "Correspondence of Calhoun, McDuffie, and Fisher," 492; Coens, "Formation of the Jackson Party," 31.

15. McCormick, *Second American Party System*, 155, 162; Watson, *Liberty and Power*, 81; McDuffie to Fisher, December 14, 1823, in Newsome, "Correspondence of Calhoun, McDuffie, and Fisher," 490.

16. Ratcliffe, *One-Party Presidential Contest*, 133, 188–89; Clay to Johnston, October 2, 1824, in *Clay Papers*, 3:855; Calhoun to Maxcy, December 15, 1822, Calhoun to Maxcy, March 13, 1823, in *Calhoun Papers*, 7:387, 518–19; Ebenezer Cummins to Jackson, August 10, 1826, in *Jackson Papers*, 6:195–96; Livermore, *Twilight of Federalism*, 83, 151–67.

17. McCormick, *Second American Party System*, 103; Ratcliffe, *One-Party Presidential Contest*, 128; Hargreaves, *Presidency of Adams*, 5–6; "Address of the Committee of Correspondence, Appointed by the Public Meeting of Citizens Friendly to the Election of John Q. Adams as President," *National Gazette and Literary Register* (Philadelphia, PA), October 30, 1824; Heale, *Presidential Quest*, 60.

18. Francis Johnson to Clay, December 10, 1822, Ingalls to Clay, June 5, 1824, Johnston to Clay, August 19, 1824, Ingalls to Clay, August 20, 1824, Shaw to Clay, October 4, 1824, Johnston to Clay, October 20, 1824, in *Clay Papers*, 3:334, 774, 816–17, 858, 869; "The Clay Meeting," *Columbian Centinel* (Boston), October 27, 1824.

19. Ratcliffe, *One-Party Contest*, 79, 103; Benson, *The Concept of Jacksonian Democracy*, 3–6.

20. Ratcliffe, *One-Party Contest*, 83–88, 100, 216; *Adams Memoirs*, 6:257–58; Rochester to Clay, June 28, 1823, McClure to Clay, July 23, 1823, Rochester to Clay, November 1, 1823, Rochester to Clay, May 29, 1824, Hammond to Clay, July 28, 1824, in *Clay Papers*,

3:445, 461, 510, 770, 801; James Tallmadge to Jackson, March 6, 1824, Jackson to Donelson, March 19, 1824, Jackson to Donelson, April 4, 1824, John Schermerhorn to Jackson, May 14, 1824, in *Jackson Papers*, 5:374–89, 406; Cole, *Van Buren*, 128–35; Niven, *Van Buren*, 154; *Van Buren Autobiography*, 113, 142.

21. Cole, *Van Buren*, 133–35; *Van Buren Autobiography*, 113; *Adams Memoirs*, 6:340, 408; Henry Storrs to Clay, September 23, 1824, Johnston to Clay, September 26, 1824, in *Clay Papers*, 3:848, 852.

22. Cole, *Van Buren*, 135–37.

23. Cole, *Van Buren*, 135–37; Calhoun to Swift, November 20, 1824, in Hay, "Unpublished Calhoun Letters, II," 293–94; Niven, *Van Buren*, 156; Porter to Clay, January 14, 1825, in *Clay Papers*, 4:17; William Brent to Clay, September 3, 1824, Clay to Johnston, October 2, 1824, Clay to Brooke, November 26, 1824, in *Clay Papers*, 3:827, 856, 888.

24. McCormick, *Second American Party System*, 37, 151, 236–40; Ratcliffe, *One-Party Presidential Contest*, 209–12; Livermore, *Twilight of Federalism*, 146.

25. McCormick, *Second American Party System*, 179, 186; *Adams Memoirs*, 6:458; Brooke to Clay, August 24, 1823, in *Clay Papers*, 3:468.

26. McCormick, *Second American Party System*, 187; *Adams Memoirs*, 6:160; Tutt to Jackson, June 24, 1823, Jackson to Coffee, March 4, 1824, in *Jackson Papers*, 5:283, 369; Coens, "Early Jackson Party," 246, 251; Brooke to Clay, August 24, 1823, Clay to Brooke, August 28, 1823, Daniel Call to Clay, June 30, 1824, Clay to Brooke, December 5, 1824, in *Clay Papers*, 3:468, 477, 790, 891.

27. McCormick, *Second American Party System*, 187; Ratcliffe, *One-Party Presidential Contest*, 195.

28. McCormick, *Second American Party System*, 177; Gutzman, "Preserving the Patrimony," 347; Hargreaves, *Presidency of Adams*, 3, 5.

29. Johnston to Clay, June 27, 1824, Clay to Henry, September 14, 1824, Clay to Brooke, November 26, 1824, in *Clay Papers*, 3:787, 838, 888–89.

30. McCormick, *Second American Party System*, 310, 313; H. Johnson to Edwards, August 10, 1823, in Edwards, *History of Illinois*, 504; Ratcliffe, *One-Party Presidential Contest*, 213–16; Thomas Robertson to Clay, July 5, 1822, Clay to Porter, April 26, 1824, Clay to Johnston, October 2, 1824, Clay to Brooke, December 22, 1824, in *Clay Papers*, 3:249, 744, 855, 900; Baker to Jackson, February 14, 1823, Baker to Jackson, May 3, 1823, David Ker to Jackson, November 23, 1824, in *Jackson Papers*, 5:247, 274, 450; Overton to Jackson, January 7, 1825, in *Jackson Papers*, 6:9.

31. Ratcliffe, *One-Party Presidential Contest*, 97; Ratcliffe, "Role of Voters and Issues in Party Formation," 868–69; Unknown to Clay, April 26, 1822, Hammond to Clay, July 1, 1822, Clay to Hammond, February 22, 1824, in *Clay Papers*, 3:200, 246, 654.

32. McCormick, *Second American Party System*, 210–15, 270–73, 304–5; Peterson, *Great Triumvirate*, 121; Ratcliffe, *One-Party Presidential Contest*, 179–84, 200; *Adams Memoirs*, 6:57; Heale, *Presidential Quest*, 61; Coens, "Formation of the Jackson Party," 178; Gabriel Johnston to Clay, May 27, 1823, in *Clay Papers*, 3:423; Hargreaves, *Presidency of Adams*, 16; *Adams Memoirs*, 5:9–10.

33. McCormick, *Second American Party System*, 278–79; Ratcliffe, *One-Party Presidential Contest*, 181–82; Coens, "Early Jackson Party," 248; Leonard, *Invention of Party Politics*, 66–72; *Adams Memoirs*, 5:9–10.

34. McCormick, *Second American Party System*, 259; Ratcliffe, *One-Party Presidential Contest*, 198; Alexander Armstrong and Samuel Potts to Clay, March 9, 1825, in *Clay Papers*, 4:97; Clay to Johnston, July 21, 1824, in *Clay Papers*, 3:799; Atwater to Jackson, June 24, 1824, Atwater to Jackson, November 1, 1824, in *Jackson Papers*, 5:421, 448.

35. Ratcliffe, *One-Party Presidential Contest*, 110–12, 173–76; Ratcliffe, "Role of Voters and Issues," 850–60; Kendall to Clay, June 20, 1822, Clay to Hammond, July 14, 1822, Clay to Brooke, May 19, 1824, in *Clay Papers*, 3:236, 260, 758; Ratcliffe, *Party Spirit*, 223–30.

36. Ratcliffe, *One-Party Presidential Contest*, 173–78; Ratcliffe, "Role of Voters and Issues," 850–61; Sloane to Clay, October 16, 1822, Clay to Brooke, May 19, 1824, in *Clay Papers*, 3:294, 758; Ratcliffe, *Party Spirit*, 223–34.

37. Clay to Hammond, October 25, 1824, Clay to Brooke, November 26, 1824, Clay to Stuart, December 6, 1824, Clay to Porter, December 7, 1824, in *Clay Papers*, 3:872, 887, 891–92.

38. Altschuler and Blumin, *Rude Republic*, 15; Ratcliffe, "Role of Voters and Issues," 853; Parsons, *Birth of Modern Politics*, 97–100.

39. Parsons, *Birth of Modern Politics*, 97–100. Donald Ratcliffe has argued that, despite Jackson's popular and electoral vote triumph, Adams was the most popular candidate nationwide. See Ratcliffe, *One-Party Presidential Contest*, 280–81 and Ratcliffe, "Popular Preferences in the Presidential Election of 1824," *Journal of the Early Republic* 34 (Spring 2014), 45–77. Ratcliffe's methodology in reaching this conclusion was flawed. He conjectured vote totals for each candidate in a theoretical popular election in New York based on the known presidential preferences of New York state legislators. Such an approach does not work, especially for a candidate like Jackson, who was unpopular with elected politicians. For instance, Jackson won the popular vote in North Carolina despite the almost unanimous support of the legislature for Crawford. Ratcliffe also failed to estimate popular vote totals in every state for all four candidates, which would be the proper way of determining the most popular candidate using his methodology. The available evidence suggests that Jackson was the most popular candidate nationwide.

40. Ratcliffe, *One-Party Presidential Contest*, 279.

41. Mooney, *William Crawford*, 248; Shipp, *Giant Days*, 163.

42. Shaw to Clay, April 4, 1822, Wharton to Clay, August 13, 1823, Clay to Brooke, February 29, 1824, Brent to Clay, September 3, 1824, in *Clay Papers*, 3:185, 466, 666–67, 828; Eaton, *Henry Clay*, 50–51.

43. Livermore, *Twilight of Federalism*, 143–44; Ratcliffe, *One-Party Presidential Contest*, 266.

44. Coens, "Formation of the Jackson Party," 158, 167.

45. Coens, "Formation of the Jackson Party," 16, 18.

46. Coens, "Formation of the Jackson Party," 29, 55, 67; Parsons, *Birth of Modern Politics,* 97; Ratcliffe, *One-Party Presidential Contest,* 265; Peart, *Era of Experimentation,* 110–11.

47. Ratcliffe, *One-Party Presidential Contest,* 275–76; Wilentz, *Rise of American Democracy,* 251–53; Coens, "Formation of the Jackson Party," 26–28; Parsons, *Birth of Modern Politics,* 91–94; Ellis, "Market Revolution," 167.

48. Shaw to Clay, April 4, 1822, Unknown to Clay, April 26, 1822, Sloane to Clay, October 16, 1822, Miner to Clay, November 16, 1822, Woods to Clay, May 22, 1823, McClure to Clay, July 23, 1823, in *Clay Papers,* 3:185, 200, 294, 325, 419, 462; Eaton to Jackson, November 11, 1823, in *Jackson Papers,* 5:235–36.

7. Kingmaking behind Closed Doors

1. *Van Buren Autobiography,* 145; Cole, *Martin Van Buren,* 137; Ratcliffe, *One-Party Presidential Contest,* 216, 226.

2. Clay to Leigh, December 22, 1824, in *Clay Papers,* 3:901; Clay to Blair, January 8, 1824 [i.e., 1825], in *Clay Papers,* 4:9.

3. Clay to Blair, January 8, 1824 [i.e., 1825] in *Clay Papers,* 4:9.

4. Clay to James Erwin, December 13, 1824, Clay to Leigh, December 22, 1824, in *Clay Papers,* 3:895, 901; *Adams Memoirs,* 6:478; Thomas Cobb to a constituent, January 15, 1825, in Shipp, *Giant Days,* 179–80.

5. *Van Buren Autobiography,* 149–50; *Adams Memoirs,* 6:474, 478; Jackson to Coffee, December 27, 1824, in *Jackson Papers,* 5:459; John Crittenden to Clay, February 15, 1825, in *Clay Papers,* 4:67–68; Eaton to Overton, February 7, 1825, in *Jackson Papers,* 6:27.

6. Jackson to Overton, December 19, 1824, Rachel Jackson to Kingsley, December 23, 1824, in *Jackson Papers,* 5:455–56.

7. Eaton to Overton, February 7, 1825, in *Jackson Papers,* 6:25–26.

8. Jackson to Lewis, December 27, 1824, in *Jackson Papers,* 5:459; Jackson to Tutt, January 9, 1825, Tutt to Jackson, January 9, 1825, Jackson to Coffee, January 23, 1825, Jackson to Lewis, January 29, 1825, in *Jackson Papers,* 6:12–13, 18, 23–25.

9. *Adams Memoirs,* 5:303; *Adams Memoirs,* 6:438–63; Allgor, *Parlor Politics,* 186–87.

10. *Adams Memoirs,* 6:444, 451, 459–63, 475.

11. *Adams Memoirs,* 6:441–42.

12. *Adams Memoirs,* 6:448, 451, 470–71, 480; Porter to Clay, January 14, 1825, in *Clay Papers,* 4:18.

13. Ratcliffe, *One-Party Presidential Contest,* 240; *Adams Memoirs,* 6:443–44, 472, 476, 495.

14. McCormick, *Second American Party System,* 305; *Adams Memoirs,* 6:443, 473, 475; Ratcliffe, *One-Party Presidential Contest,* 245–46.

15. *Adams Memoirs,* 5:58.

16. Clay to Blair, January 8, 1824 [i.e., 1825], Kendall to Clay, January 21, 1825, in *Clay Papers,* 4:9–10, 35; Clay to Hammond, October 25, 1824, in *Clay Papers,* 3:871.

17. *Adams Memoirs*, 6:440–58.

18. *Adams Memoirs*, 6:464–65.

19. *Adams Memoirs*, 6:467–69; William Barry to Clay, January 10, 1825, in *Clay Papers*, 4:11; Skowronek, *Politics Presidents Make*, 116; *Jackson Papers*, 6:19; Brown, "Election of 1824–1825," 400.

20. Remini, *Henry Clay*, 259; Peterson, *Great Triumvirate*, 127; Ratcliffe, *One-Party Presidential Contest*, 241.

21. *Adams Memoirs*, 6:478, 483; Clay to Blair, January 29, 1825, Clay to Brooke, February 4, 1825, in *Clay Papers*, 4:47, 55.

22. Jackson to Lewis, January 24, 1825, Jackson to Lewis, January 29, 1825, in *Jackson Papers*, 6:20, 22–23; Crawford to Jefferson, January 31, 1825, in Mooney, *William Crawford*, 247; Clay to Blair, January 29, 1825, Kendall to Clay, February 9, 1825, in *Clay Papers*, 4:47, 77.

23. *Jackson Papers*, 6:24.

24. Eaton to Overton, February 7, 1825, in *Jackson Papers*, 6:26; Clay to Gales and Seaton, January 30, 1825, in *Clay Papers*, 4:48, 53–54; 1 Reg. Deb. 440–44, 463–86 (1825).

25. Kremer to Clay, c. February 3, 1825, Clay to Erwin, February 24, 1825, John Binns to Clay, February 27, 1825, in *Clay Papers*, 4:52, 54, 82, 85; Eaton to Overton, February 7, 1825, in *Jackson Papers*, 6:26; *Adams Memoirs*, 6:497.

26. *Adams Memoirs*, 6:496–97, 509; Kremer to Jackson, March 18, 1825, James Buchanan to Jackson, August 10, 1827, in *Jackson Papers*, 6:48, 374; Klein, *James Buchanan*, 49–52.

27. Jackson to Coffee, January 6, 1825, Jackson to Lewis, February 7, 1825, Jackson to Swartwout, May 16, 1825, Jackson to Carter Beverley, June 5, 1827, in *Jackson Papers*, 6:8, 25, 70–71, 331.

28. Eaton to Overton, February 7, 1825, Jackson to the Public, July 18, 1827, in *Jackson Papers*, 6:26, 364–65; US House Journal, 18th Congress, 2nd Session, February 4, 1825, 204; 1 Reg. Deb. 463–86 (1825).

29. *Jackson Papers*, 6:24; *Clay Papers*, 4:54; 1 Reg. Deb. 522–25 (1825).

30. *Adams Memoirs*, 6:480–90.

31. Livermore, *Twilight of Federalism*, 139–57, 167–68; *Adams Memoirs*, 6:291, 312–13.

32. Livermore, *Twilight of Federalism*, 134, 152; *Adams Memoirs*, 6:315, 352, 364.

33. *Adams Memoirs*, 6:442, 469, 474, 483; Livermore, *Twilight of Federalism*, 159.

34. Livermore, *Twilight of Federalism*, 140, 173–77; *Adams Memoirs*, 6:492.

35. Livermore, *Twilight of Federalism*, 173–77; *Adams Memoirs*, 6:493–501.

36. *Adams Memoirs*, 6:471–72.

37. Eaton to Overton, February 7, 1825, in *Jackson Papers*, 6:26–27.

38. *Clay Papers*, 4:63; US House Journal, 18th Congress, 2nd session, February 9, 1825, 220–22; Livermore, *Twilight of Federalism*, 176–80.

39. *Van Buren Autobiography*, 150–52.

40. Livermore, *Twilight of Federalism*, 178, 180; *Van Buren Autobiography*, 151.

41. *Van Buren Autobiography,* 151–52; *Adams Memoirs,* 6:493; Ratcliffe, *One-Party Presidential Contest,* 250.

42. John Adams to Adams, February 18, 1825, in *Adams Memoirs,* 6:501, 505; Clay to Brooke, February 10, 1825, [Daniel Drake] to Clay, February 20, 1825, in *Clay Papers,* 4:62, 80.

43. Shipp, *Giant Days,* 183–84.

44. Jackson to Overton, February 10, 1825, Jackson to Swartwout et al., February 10, 1825, in *Jackson Papers,* 6:28–29; Coens, "Formation of the Jackson Party," 206, 220; Crittenden to Clay, February 15, 1825, in *Clay Papers,* 4:67.

45. Eaton to Overton, February 7, 1825, John Pemberton to Jackson, February 15, 1825, Jackson to Lewis, February 20, 1825, in *Jackson Papers,* 6:27, 30, 36–37.

46. Clay to Wharton, February 5, 1825, "Address to the People of the Congressional District Composed of the Counties of Fayette, Woodford, and Clarke in Kentucky," March 28, 1825, in *Clay Papers,* 4:59, 154, 156.

47. *Adams Memoirs,* 6:493; Watson, *Jackson vs. Clay,* 65; Benton, *Thirty Years' View,* 47.

48. Clay to Brooke, February 4, 1825, in *Clay Papers,* 4:56; *Adams Memoirs,* 6:506, 508.

49. Clay to James Brown, January 23, 1825, Clay to Brooke, February 4, 1825, Crittenden to Clay, February 15, 1825, Clay to Brooke, February 18, 1825, in *Clay Papers,* 4:39, 56, 68–69, 73; *Adams Memoirs,* 6:508, 513.

50. Peterson, *Great Triumvirate,* 129–30; Clay to Brooke, February 18, 1825, Creighton to Clay, February 19, 1825, in *Clay Papers,* 4:73, 76.

51. Jackson to Lewis, February 14, 1825, Jackson to Coffee, February 19, 1825, Jackson to Lewis, February 20, 1825, Jackson to Wilson, February 20, 1825, Baker to Jackson, March 21, 1825, in *Jackson Papers,* 6:29–30, 36–38, 49; Benton, *Thirty Years' View,* 48; Blair to Clay, March 7, 1825, in *Clay Papers,* 4:91.

52. Jackson to Lewis, February 20, 1825, Kendall to Jackson, August 27, 1827, in *Jackson Papers,* 6:37, 376, 381–82; *Adams Memoirs,* 6:522; Blair to Clay, February 11, 1825, in *Clay Papers,* 4:66.

53. Shipp, *Giant Days,* 194; *Van Buren Autobiography,* 150, 666–67.

54. Calhoun to Swift, March 10, 1825, in Hay, "Unpublished Calhoun Letters, II," 295; *Adams Memoirs,* 6:495, 506–7; *Van Buren Autobiography,* 666–67.

55. Watson, *Liberty and Power,* 81; Wilentz, *Rise of American Democracy,* 255; Heidler and Heidler, *Henry Clay,* 203; Bemis, *Adams and the Union,* 58; Dangerfield, *Awakening of American Nationalism,* 225; Remini, *Henry Clay,* 258, 270; Howe, *What Hath God Wrought,* 209; Hargreaves, *Presidency of Adams,* 47.

56. *Jackson Papers,* 6:38.

Epilogue

1. *Adams Memoirs,* 6:518; Jackson to Swartwout, March 6, 1825, in *Jackson Papers,* 6:47.

2. Calhoun to Swift, September 2, 1825, in Hay, "Unpublished Calhoun Letters, II," 297.

3. Crawford to Calhoun, October 2, 1830, in Shipp, *Giant Days*, 241; Mooney, *William Crawford*, 301–2.

4. Shipp, *Giant Days*, 190–91.

5. *Adams Memoirs*, 6:486; Ammon, *James Monroe*, 543.

6. Ammon, *James Monroe*, 533–56.

7. Ammon, *James Monroe*, 535–58; *Adams Memoirs*, 6:287–89; Monroe to Jefferson, December 11, 1824, Monroe to Madison, December 13, 1824, Monroe to Jackson, July 3, 1825, in *Monroe Writings*, 6:53, 57–58.

8. Calhoun to Thompson, November 10, 1824, in Hay, "Unpublished Calhoun Letters, II," 292; *Adams Memoirs*, 5:366–73; Crawford to Calhoun, October 2, 1830, Crawford to John Williams, March 1, 1831, in Shipp, *Giant Days*, 208, 248; Ammon, *James Monroe*, 567–68.

9. Livermore, *Twilight of Federalism*, 187–90.

10. Barry to Clay, January 10, 1825, Kendall to Clay, February 9, 1825, Kendall to Clay, March 23, 1825, in *Clay Papers*, 4:12, 79, 134.

11. Jackson to Kremer, May 6, 1824, in *Jackson Papers*, 5:403; Jackson to Lee, October 7, 1825, in *Jackson Papers*, 6:104.

12. Baldwin to Jackson, April 11, 1825, Henry Banks to Jackson, February 10, 1826, in *Jackson Papers*, 6:58, 138.

13. *Van Buren Autobiography*, 193; Hargreaves, *Presidency of Adams*, 15.

14. Waldstreicher, "Nationalization and Racialization of American Politics," 47; Hofstadter, *Idea of a Party System*, 209; McCormick, *Second American Party System*, 13; Skowronek, *Politics Presidents Make*, 61–154; Benton, *Thirty Years' View*, 47–48; *Adams Memoirs*, 6:478; Calhoun to Swift, September 2, 1825, in Hay, "Unpublished Calhoun Letters, II," 297.

15. *Adams Memoirs*, 6:499; *Jackson Papers*, 6:24; McFarland to Jackson, August 14, 1824, in *Jackson Papers*, 5:436; Ratcliffe, "Role of Voters and Issues," 870.

16. McDonald, *States' Rights*, vii, 4–5; Dangerfield, *Era of Good Feelings*, 237; John, "Affairs of Office," 55; Balogh, *Government Out of Sight*, 381, 121–22, 131, 136; Coens, "Formation of the Jackson Party," 282–83.

17. Watson, *Liberty and Power*, 94; Smith, "First Straw?," 30–31; McCormick, *Second American Party System*, 29.

18. Dangerfield, *Era of Good Feelings*, 115; McCormick, *Presidential Game*, 116.

19. Chase, *Presidential Nominating Convention*, 18; Bowers, "Caucus to Convention," 293; *Adams Memoirs*, 6:191.

20. Coens, "Formation of the Jackson Party," 186–97; Coens, "Early Jackson Party," 246–53; Ratcliffe, *One-Party Presidential Contest*, 198; Howe, *What Hath God Wrought*, 210.

BIBLIOGRAPHY

Primary Sources

Adams, Charles Francis, ed. *Memoirs of John Quincy Adams: Comprising Portions of his Diary from 1795 to 1848*. Vol. 5. Philadelphia: J. B. Lippincott, 1875.

———. *Memoirs of John Quincy Adams: Comprising Portions of his Diary from 1795 to 1848*. Vol. 6. New York: AMS Press, 1970.

"Answer of the Secretary of the Treasury to Ninian Edwards' Charges of Financial Mismanagement." May 11, 1824. *American State Papers: Finance* 5:41–66.

Augusta Chronicle and Georgia Advertiser. "If it should be demonstrated . . ." October 23, 1824.

———. "To the Editor of the Chronicle and Advertiser." April 30, 1823.

———. "Voice of Maine!" February 6, 1823.

Author of the Clay Papers. "Messrs. Adams and Clay." *Providence (RI) Gazette*. November 3, 1824.

Baltimore Patriot and Mercantile Advertiser. "Alabama." January 15, 1824.

Benton, Thomas H. *Thirty Years' View, or A History of the Working of the American Government for Thirty Years, from 1820 to 1850*. New York: D. Appleton, 1854.

Bolingbroke. "The Presidency." *Richmond Enquirer*. August 17, 1824.

City Gazette (Charleston, SC). "Nomination of Mr. Crawford." December 20, 1823.

Columbian Centinel (Boston). "The Clay Meeting." October 27, 1824.

Columbian Centinel (Boston). "Voice of Maine." January 21, 1824.

"Condition of the Military Establishment and the Fortifications." December 23, 1824. *American State Papers: Military Affairs* 2:698–728.

Connecticut Courant (Hartford). "The Next President." August 19, 1823.

"Correspondence between the Treasury, the Bank of the United States, and Other Banks, Relative to the Public Deposits." March 22, 1824. *American State Papers: Finance* 4:495.

Delaware Gazette and State Journal (Wilmington). "The Caucus." February 20, 1824.

Eastern Argus (Portland, ME). "Presidential Election." January 28, 1823.

Easton (MD) Gazette. "Another State Nomination." December 21, 1822.

Edwards, Ninian W. *History of Illinois, from 1778 to 1833 and Life and Times of Ninian Edwards*. Springfield: Illinois State Journal Company, 1870.

Edwardsville (IL) Spectator. "From the National Gazette." May 31, 1823.

Essex Register (Salem, MA). "The Presidency." February 1, 1823.

Ferguson, E. James, ed. *Selected Writings of Albert Gallatin.* Indianapolis: Bobbs-Merrill, 1967.

Fitzpatrick, John C., ed. *The Autobiography of Martin Van Buren.* Vol. 2. Washington, DC: Government Printing Office, 1920.

Hamilton, Stanislaus Murray, ed. *The Writings of James Monroe.* Vol. 6. Putnam, 1902; reprint, Lexington, KY: Elibron Classics, 2007.

Hay, Thomas Robson. "John C. Calhoun and the Presidential Campaign of 1824: Some Unpublished Calhoun Letters." *American Historical Review* 40, no. 1 (1934): 82–96.

———. "John C. Calhoun and the Presidential Campaign of 1824: Some Unpublished Calhoun Letters, II." *American Historical Review* 40, no. 2 (1935): 287–300.

Hemphill, W. Edwin, ed. *The Papers of John C. Calhoun.* Vol. 5, *1820–1821.* Columbia: University of South Carolina Press, 1971.

———. *The Papers of John C. Calhoun.* Vol. 6, *1821–1822.* Columbia: University of South Carolina Press, 1972.

———. *The Papers of John C. Calhoun.* Vol. 7, *1822–1823.* Columbia: University of South Carolina Press, 1973.

———. *The Papers of John C. Calhoun.* Vol. 8, *1823–1824.* Columbia: University of South Carolina Press, 1975.

Hopkins, James F., and Mary W. M. Hargreaves, eds. *The Papers of Henry Clay.* Vol. 3, *The Presidential Candidate, 1821–1824.* Lexington: University of Kentucky Press, 1963.

Hopkins, James F., Mary W. M. Hargreaves, Wayne Cutler, and Burton Milward, eds. *The Papers of Henry Clay.* Vol. 4, *Secretary of State, 1825.* Lexington: University of Kentucky Press, 1972.

Ithaca (NY) Journal. "John C. Calhoun." October 29, 1823.

Independent Chronicle and Boston Patriot. "Rhode Island Nomination." January 24, 1824.

Moser, Harold D., J. Clint Clifft, and Wyatt C. Wells, eds. *The Papers of Andrew Jackson.* Vol. 6, *1825–1828.* Knoxville: University of Tennessee Press, 2002.

Moser, Harold D., David R. Hoth, and George H. Hoemann, eds. *The Papers of Andrew Jackson.* Vol. 5, *1821–1824.* Knoxville: University of Tennessee Press, 1996.

Nashville (TN) Gazette. "Extract of a Letter from a Gentleman in Cincinnati to His Correspondent in Nashville." September 24, 1824.

———. "Mr. Clay." September 17, 1824.

National Gazette and Literary Register (Philadelphia, PA). "A writer in one of the Cincinnati papers . . ." June 12, 1824.

———. "Address of the Committee of Correspondence, Appointed by the Public Meeting of Citizens Friendly to the Election of John Q. Adams as President." October 30, 1824.

Newsome, A. R. "Correspondence of John C. Calhoun, George McDuffie, and Charles Fisher, Relating to the Presidential Campaign of 1824." *North Carolina Historical Review* 7, no. 4 (1930): 477–504.

Painesville (OH) Telegraph. "Our readers need not be told . . ." February 19, 1824.

Portsmouth (NH) Journal of Literature and Politics "New Expedition." February 8, 1823.

Providence (RI) Gazette "Mr. Clay—No. 3." August 18, 1824.

"Report of Committee on Ninian Edwards' Charges of Financial Mismanagement." May 25, 1824. *American State Papers: Finance* 5:69–74.

"Report of Committee on Ninian Edwards' Charges of Financial Mismanagement." June 21, 1824. *American State Papers: Finance* 5:79–145.

"Report of the Secretary of War on the Reduction of the Army." December 14, 1818. *American State Papers: Military Affairs* 1:779–82.

Rhode Island American (Providence). "Election of President." February 18, 1825.

———. "Presidential Election." February 22, 1825.

Shipp, J. E. D. *Giant Days, or the Life and Times of William H. Crawford.* Americus, GA: Southern Printers, 1909.

Somerville, Henry V. "To the Voters of the Fifth Electoral District Composed of Baltimore County." *Baltimore Patriot,* July 21, 1824.

"Suppression of the Slave Trade." April 30, 1824. *American State Papers: Foreign Relations* 5:315–46.

Virginius. "For the Enquirer." *Richmond Enquirer,* November 7, 1820.

Secondary Sources

Allgor, Catherine. *Parlor Politics: In Which the Ladies of Washington Help Build a City and a Government.* Charlottesville: University of Virginia Press, 2001.

Altschuler, Glenn C., and Stuart M. Blumin. *Rude Republic: Americans and Their Politics in the Nineteenth Century.* Princeton, NJ: Princeton University Press, 2000.

Ammon, Harry. *James Monroe: The Quest for National Identity.* Charlottesville: University of Virginia Press, 1990.

Appleby, Joyce. *Inheriting the Revolution: The First Generation of Americans.* Cambridge, MA: Belknap Press of Harvard University Press, 2000.

Ashworth, John. *Slavery, Capitalism, and Politics in the Antebellum Republic.* Vol. 1, *Commerce and Compromise, 1820–1850.* New York: Cambridge University Press, 1995.

Balogh, Brian. *A Government Out of Sight: The Mystery of National Authority in Nineteenth-Century America.* New York: Cambridge University Press, 2009.

Bemis, Samuel Flagg. *John Quincy Adams and the Foundations of American Foreign Policy.* Random House, 1949; reprint, Norwalk, CT: Easton Press, 1987.

———. *John Quincy Adams and the Union.* Alfred A. Knopf, 1956; reprint, Norwalk, CT: Easton Press, 1956, 1984.

Benson, Lee. *The Concept of Jacksonian Democracy: New York as a Test Case.* Princeton, NJ: Princeton University Press, 1961.

Bowers, Douglas E. "From Caucus to Convention in Pennsylvania Politics, 1790–1830." *Pennsylvania History: A Journal of Mid-Atlantic Studies* 56, no. 4 (1989): 276–98.

Brown, Everett S. "The Presidential Election of 1824–1825." *Political Science Quarterly* 40, no. 3 (1925): 384–403.

Brown, Samuel Gilman. *The Life of Rufus Choate.* Boston: Little Brown, 1870.

Campbell, Stephen. "Internal Improvements." In *A Companion to the Era of Andrew Jackson,* edited by Sean Patrick Adams, 130–53. Malden, MA: Wiley-Blackwell, 2013.

Chase, James S. *Emergence of the Presidential Nominating Convention 1789–1832.* Champaign: University of Illinois Press, 1973.

Coens, Thomas. "The Early Jackson Party: A Force for Democratization?" In *A Companion to the Era of Andrew Jackson,* edited by Sean Patrick Adams, 231–59. Malden, MA: Wiley-Blackwell, 2013.

———. "The Formation of the Jackson Party, 1822–1825." PhD diss., Harvard University, 2004.

Cohen, Kenneth. "'Sport for Grown Children': American Political Cartoons, 1790–1850." *International Journal of the History of Sport* 28, nos. 8–9 (2011): 1301–18.

Cole, Donald B. *Martin Van Buren and the American Political System.* Princeton University Press, 1984; reprint, Norwalk, CT: Easton Press, 1984.

———. *Vindicating Andrew Jackson: The 1828 Election and the Rise of the Two-Party System.* Lawrence: University Press of Kansas, 2009.

Crenson, Matthew A. *The Federal Machine: Beginnings of Bureaucracy in Jacksonian America.* Baltimore: Johns Hopkins University Press, 1975.

Dangerfield, George. *The Awakening of American Nationalism: 1815–1828.* New York: Harper & Rowe, 1965.

———. *The Era of Good Feelings.* London: Methuen, 1953.

Dobbs, Kelli W., and Rebecca J. Siders. "Fort Delaware Architectural Research Project." Center for Historic Architecture and Design, School of Urban Affairs and Public Policy, University of Delaware. Published 1999. https://udspace.udel.edu/handle/19716/1598.

Farrier, John. "Fort Blunder: The Fort That America Accidentally Built in Canada." Neatorama. Published November 24, 2013. http://www.neatorama.com/2013/11/24/Fort -Blunder-The-Fort-That-America-Accidentally-Built-in-Canada/.

Dubin, Michael J. *United States Presidential Elections, 1788–1860: The Official Results by County and State.* Jefferson, NC: McFarland, 2002.

Eaton, Clement. *Henry Clay and the Art of American Politics.* Glenview, IL: Scott, Foresman, 1957.

Ellis, Richard E. "The Market Revolution and the Transformation of American Politics, 1801–1837." In *The Market Revolution in America: Social, Political, and Religious Expressions, 1800–1880,* edited by Melvyn Stokes and Stephen Conway, 149–76. Charlottesville: University Press of Virginia, 1999.

Farrier, John. "Fort Blunder: The Fort That America Accidentally Built in Canada." Neatorama. Published November 24, 2013. http://www.neatorama.com/2013/11/24/Fort -Blunder-The-Fort-That-America-Accidentally-Built-in-Canada/.

Fink, William B. "Stephen Van Rensselaer and the House Election of 1825." *New York History* 32, no. 3 (1951): 323–30.

Formisano, Ronald P. "Deferential-Participant Politics: The Early Republic's Political Culture, 1789–1840." *American Political Science Review* 68, no. 2 (1974): 473–87.

———. "State Development in the Early Republic: Substance and Structure, 1780–1840." In *Contesting Democracy: Substance and Structure in American Political History, 1775–2000,* edited by Byron E. Shafer and Anthony J. Badger, 7–35. Lawrence: University of Kansas Press, 2001.

———. *The Transformation of Political Culture: Massachusetts Parties, 1790s–1840s.* New York: Oxford University Press, 1983.

Freehling, William W. *The Road to Disunion*. Vol. 1, *Secessionists at Bay, 1776–1854*. New York: Oxford University Press, 1990.

Freeman, Joanne B. *Affairs of Honor: National Politics in the New Republic*. New Haven, CT: Yale University Press, 2002.

Friends of the 1820 Colonel Benjamin Stephenson House. "The Bank of Edwardsville." Friends of the 1820 Colonel Benjamin Stephenson House. Accessed September 21, 2021. http://www.mtecpro.com/BenTheBank.asp.

Gutzman, Kevin R. "Preserving the Patrimony: William Branch Giles and Virginia versus the Federal Tariff." *Virginia Magazine of History and Biography* 104, no. 3 (1996): 341–72.

Hailperin, Herman. "Pro-Jackson Sentiment in Pennsylvania, 1820–1828." *Pennsylvania Magazine of History and Biography* 50, no. 3 (1926): 193–240.

Hammond, Bray. *Banks and Politics in America: From the Revolution to the Civil War*. Princeton, NJ: Princeton University Press, 1957.

Hargreaves, Mary W. M. *The Presidency of John Quincy Adams*. Lawrence: University Press of Kansas, 1985.

Haworth, Peter Daniel. "James Madison and James Monroe Historiography: A Tale of Two Divergent Bodies of Scholarship." In *A Companion to James Madison and James Monroe*, edited by Stuart Leibiger, 521–39. Malden, MA: Wiley-Blackwell, 2013.

Hay, Robert P. "The Case for Andrew Jackson in 1824: Eaton's 'Wyoming Letters.'" *Tennessee Historical Quarterly* 29, no. 2 (1970): 139–51.

Hay, Thomas Robson. "John C. Calhoun and the Presidential Campaign of 1824." *North Carolina Historical Review* 12, no. 1 (1935): 20–44.

Heale, M. J. *The Presidential Quest: Candidates and Images in American Political Culture, 1787–1852*. New York: Longman, 1982.

Hecht, Marie B. *John Quincy Adams: A Personal History of an Independent Man*. New York: Macmillan Company, 1972.

Heidler, David S., and Jeanne T. Heidler. *Henry Clay: The Essential American*. New York: Random House, 2010.

Hickey, Donald R. *The War of 1812: A Forgotten Conflict*. Champaign: University of Illinois Press, 1990.

Hofstadter, Richard. *The Idea of a Party System: The Rise of Legitimate Opposition in the United States, 1780–1840*. Berkeley: University of California Press, 1969.

Holt, Michael, *The Rise and Fall of the American Whig Party: Jacksonian Politics and the Onset of the Civil War*. New York: Oxford University Press, 1999.

Howe, Daniel Walker. *The Political Culture of the American Whigs*. Chicago: University of Chicago Press, 1979.

———. *What Hath God Wrought: The Transformation of America, 1815–1848*. New York: Oxford University Press, 2007.

Jeffrey, Thomas E. *State Parties and National Politics: North Carolina, 1815–1861*. Athens: University of Georgia Press, 1989.

Jenkins, Jeffrey A., and Brian R. Sala. "The Spatial Theory of Voting and the Presidential Election of 1824." *American Journal of Political Science* 42, no. 4 (1998): 1157–79.

John, Richard R. "Affairs of Office: The Executive Departments, the Election of 1828, and the Making of the Democratic Party." In *The Democratic Experiment: New Directions in*

American Political History, edited by Meg Jacobs, William J. Novak, and Julian E. Zelizer, 50–84. Princeton, NJ: Princeton University Press, 2003.

———. *Spreading the News: The American Postal System from Franklin to Morse*. Cambridge, MA: Harvard University Press, 1995.

Key, V. O., Jr. "A Theory of Critical Elections." *Journal of Politics* 17, no. 1 (1955): 3–18.

Klein, Philip Shriver. *President James Buchanan: A Biography*. Pennsylvania State University Press, 1962; reprint, Norwalk, CT: Easton Press, 1987.

Kolodny, Robin. "The Several Elections of 1824." *Congress and the Presidency* 23, no. 2 (1996): 139–64.

Kresson, W. P. *James Monroe*. University of North Carolina Press, 1946, 1974; reprint, Norwalk, CT: Easton Press, 1986.

Larson, John Lauritz. *Internal Improvement: National Public Works and the Promise of Popular Government in the Early United States*. Chapel Hill: University of North Carolina Press, 2001.

Leonard, Gerald. *The Invention of Party Politics: Federalism, Popular Sovereignty, and Constitutional Development in Jacksonian Illinois*. Chapel Hill: University of North Carolina Press, 2002.

Leutscher, George D. *Early Political Machinery in the United States*. Philadelphia: Kessinger, 1903.

Lewis, James E., Jr. *The American Union and the Problem of Neighborhood: The United States and the Collapse of the Spanish Empire, 1783–1829*. Chapel Hill: University of North Carolina Press, 1998.

Livermore, Shaw, Jr. *The Twilight of Federalism: The Disintegration of the Federalist Party, 1815–1830*. New York: Gordian Press, 1972.

Madonna, G. Terry, and Michael Young. "The First Political Poll." *Politically Uncorrected*. Published June 18, 2002. https://www.fandm.edu/uploads/files/271296109834777015 -the-first-political-poll-6-18-2002.pdf.

Mason, Matthew. *Slavery and Politics in the Early Republic*. Chapel Hill: University of North Carolina Press, 2006.

May, Ernest R. *The Making of the Monroe Doctrine*. Cambridge, MA: Harvard University Press, 1975.

Mayhew, David R. *Electoral Realignments: A Critique of an American Genre*. New Haven, CT: Yale University Press, 2002.

McCormick, Richard P. "New Perspectives on Jacksonian Politics." *American Historical Review* 65, no. 2 (1960): 288–301.

———. *The Presidential Game: The Origins of American Presidential Politics*. New York: Oxford University Press, 1982.

———. *The Second American Party System: Party Formation in the Jacksonian Era*. Chapel Hill: University of North Carolina Press, 1966.

McDonald, Forrest. *States' Rights and the Union: Imperium in Imperio, 1776–1876*. Lawrence: University Press of Kansas, 2000.

McManus, Michael J. "President James Monroe's Domestic Policies, 1817–1825: 'To Advance the Best Interests of Our Union.'" In *A Companion to James Madison and James Monroe*, edited by Stuart Leibiger, 438–55. Malden, MA: Wiley-Blackwell, 2013.

Meyers, Marvin. *The Jacksonian Persuasion: Politics and Belief.* Stanford, CA: Stanford University Press, 1957.

Moats, Sandra. "President James Monroe and Foreign Affairs, 1817–1825: An Enduring Legacy." In *A Companion to James Madison and James Monroe,* edited by Stuart Leibiger, 456–71. Malden, MA: Wiley-Blackwell, 2013.

Mooney, Chase C. *William H. Crawford, 1772–1834.* Lexington: University Press of Kentucky, 1974.

Morgan, William G. "The Decline of the Congressional Nominating Caucus." *Tennessee Historical Quarterly* 24, no. 3 (1965): 245–55.

———. "The Origin and the Development of the Congressional Nominating Caucus." *Proceedings of the American Philosophical Society* 113, no. 2 (1969): 184–96.

Morse, John T, Jr. *John Quincy Adams.* Boston: Houghton, Mifflin, 1898.

Murphy, Brian Phillips. "The Market Revolution." In *A Companion to the Era of Andrew Jackson,* edited by Sean Patrick Adams, 95–110. Malden, MA: Wiley-Blackwell, 2013.

Murphy, Sharon Ann. "The Myth and Reality of Andrew Jackson's Rise in the Election of 1824." In *A Companion to the Era of Andrew Jackson,* edited by Sean Patrick Adams, 260–79. Malden, MA: Wiley-Blackwell, 2013.

Nagel, Paul C. "The Election of 1824: A Reconsideration Based on Newspaper Opinion." *Journal of Southern History* 26, no. 3 (1960): 315–29.

———. *John Quincy Adams: A Public Life, a Private Life.* New York: Alfred A. Knopf, 1997.

Newsome, Albert Ray. *The Presidential Election of 1824 in North Carolina.* Chapel Hill: University of North Carolina Press, 1939.

Niven, John. *John C. Calhoun and the Price of Union: A Biography.* Baton Rouge: Louisiana State University Press, 1988.

———. *Martin Van Buren: The Romantic Age of American Politics.* Oxford University Press, 1983; reprint, Norwalk, CT: Easton Press, 1986.

Nord, David Paul. *Communities of Journalism: A History of American Newspapers and Their Readers.* Champaign, IL: University of Illinois Press, 2006.

Opal, J. M. *Avenging the People: Andrew Jackson, the Rule of Law, and the American Nation.* New York: Oxford University Press, 2017.

Parsons, Lynn Hudson. *The Birth of Modern Politics: Andrew Jackson, John Quincy Adams, and the Election of 1828.* New York: Oxford University Press, 2009.

Pasley, Jeffrey L. *"The Tyranny of Printers": Newspaper Politics in the Early American Republic.* Charlottesville: University of Virginia Press, 2001.

Peart, Daniel. *Era of Experimentation: American Political Practices in the Early Republic.* Charlottesville: University of Virginia Press, 2014.

Pessen, Edward. *Jacksonian America: Society, Personality, and Politics.* Champaign, IL: University of Illinois Press, 1969.

Peterson, Merrill D. *The Great Triumvirate: Webster, Clay, and Calhoun.* New York: Oxford University Press, 1987.

Phillips, Kim T. "The Pennsylvania Origins of the Jackson Movement." *Political Science Quarterly* 91, no. 3 (1976): 489–508.

Pocock, J. G. A. "The Classical Theory of Deference." *American Historical Review* 81, no. 3 (1976): 516–23.

Ratcliffe, Donald J. "The Crisis of Commercialization: National Political Alignments and the Market Revolution, 1819–1844." In *The Market Revolution in America: Social, Political, and Religious Expressions, 1800–1880,* edited by Melvyn Stokes and Stephen Conway, 177–201. Charlottesville: University Press of Virginia, 1999.

———. *The One-Party Presidential Contest: Adams, Jackson, and 1824's Five-Horse Race.* Lawrence: University Press of Kansas, 2015.

———. *Party Spirit in a Frontier Republic: Democratic Politics in Ohio, 1793–1821.* Columbus: Ohio State University Press, 1998.

———. *The Politics of Long Division: The Birth of the Second Party System in Ohio, 1818–1828.* Columbus: Ohio State University Press, 2000.

———. "Popular Preferences in the Presidential Election of 1824." *Journal of the Early Republic* 34, no. 1 (2014): 45–77.

———. "The Role of Voters and Issues in Party Formation: Ohio, 1824." *Journal of American History* 59, no. 4 (1973): 847–70.

Remini, Robert V. *Andrew Jackson.* Vol. 2, *The Course of American Freedom, 1822–1832.* Baltimore: The Johns Hopkins University Press, 1981.

———. *Henry Clay: Statesman for the Union.* New York: W. W. Norton, 1991.

———. *The Life of Andrew Jackson.* Harper and Row, 1988; reprint, Norwalk, CT: Easton Press, 1997.

Reynolds, David S. *Waking Giant: America in the Age of Jackson.* New York: Harper Perennial, 2009.

Richards, Leonard L. *The Slave Power: The Free North and Southern Domination, 1780–1860.* Baton Rouge: Louisiana State University Press, 2000.

Roberts, Frances C. "Politics and Public Land Disposal in Alabama's Formative Period." *Alabama Review* 21 (1969): 153–74.

Robertson, Andrew W. "Voting Rites and Voting Acts: Electioneering Ritual, 1790–1820." In *Beyond the Founders: New Approaches to the Political History of the Early American Republic,* edited by Jeffrey L. Pasley, Andrew W. Robertson, and David Waldstreicher, 57–78. Chapel Hill: University of North Carolina Press, 2004.

Rothbard, Murray N. *The Panic of 1819: Reactions and Politics.* Auburn, AL: Ludwig Von Mises Institute, 2007.

Saltman, Roy G. *The History and Politics of Voting Technology: In Quest of Integrity and Public Confidence.* New York: Palgrave Macmillan, 2006.

Seager, Robert, II. "Henry Clay and the Politics of Compromise and Non-Compromise." *Register of the Kentucky Historical Society* 85, no. 1 (1987): 1–28.

Sellers, Charles. *The Market Revolution: Jacksonian America, 1815–1846.* New York: Oxford University Press, 1991.

Silbey, Joel H. *Martin Van Buren and the Emergence of American Popular Politics.* Lanham, MD: Rowman & Littlefield, 2002.

Skeen, C. Edward. "Calhoun, Crawford, and the Politics of Retrenchment." *South Carolina Historical Magazine* 73, no. 3 (1972): 141–55.

Skowronek, Stephen. *The Politics Presidents Make: Leadership from John Adams to Bill Clinton.* Cambridge, MA: Belknap Press of Harvard University Press, 1997.

Smith, Tom W. "The First Straw? A Study of the Origin of Election Polls." *Public Opinion Quarterly* 54, no. 1 (1990): 21–36.

Somkin, Fred. *Unquiet Eagle: Memory and Desire in the Idea of American Freedom, 1815–1860.* New York: Cornell University Press, 1967.

Starr, Paul. *The Creation of the Media: Political Origins of Modern Communications.* New York: Basic Books, 2004.

Stenberg, Richard R. "Jackson, Buchanan, and the 'Corrupt Bargain' Calumny." *Pennsylvania Magazine of History and Biography* 58, no. 1 (1934): 61–85.

Sydnor, Charles S. "The One-Party Period of American History." *American Historical Review* 51, no. 3 (1946): 439–51.

Torre, Jose R. "Financial Panics in the Early American Republic." In *A Companion to the Era of Andrew Jackson,* edited by Sean Patrick Adams, 435–53. Malden, MA: Wiley-Blackwell, 2013.

Waldstreicher, David. *In the Midst of Perpetual Fetes: The Making of American Nationalism, 1776–1820.* Chapel Hill: University of North Carolina Press, 1997.

———. "The Nationalization and Racialization of American Politics: Before, Beneath, and Between Parties, 1790–1840." In *Contesting Democracy: Substance and Structure in American Political History, 1775–2000,* edited by Byron E. Shafer and Anthony J. Badger, 37–63. Lawrence: University of Kansas Press, 2001.

Ward, John William. *Andrew Jackson: Symbol for an Age.* New York: Oxford University Press, 1953.

Warshauer, Matthew. "Andrew Jackson and the Legacy of the Battle of New Orleans." In *A Companion to the Era of Andrew Jackson,* edited by Sean Patrick Adams, 79–92. Malden, MA: Wiley-Blackwell, 2013.

Watson, Harry L. *Andrew Jackson vs. Henry Clay: Democracy and Development in Antebellum America.* Boston: Bedford/St. Martin's, 1998.

———. *Liberty and Power: The Politics of Jacksonian America.* New York: Hill and Wang, 1990.

Watts, Steven. *The Republic Reborn: War and the Making of Liberal America, 1790–1820.* Baltimore: Johns Hopkins University Press, 1987.

White, Leonard D. *The Jeffersonians: A Study in Administrative History, 1801–1829.* New York: Macmillan, 1951.

Wilentz, Sean. *The Rise of American Democracy: Jefferson to Lincoln.* New York: W. W. Norton, 2005.

Wiltse, Charles M. *John C. Calhoun, Nationalist, 1782–1828.* Indianapolis, IN: Bobbs-Merrill, 1944.

INDEX

A.B. controversy, 100–101, 141–50; cabinet debates over, 143–44, 148; congressional investigation, 101, 141–47; effect on presidential race, 101, 142, 149–50; letters, 100–101

Adams, John, 16, 18, 49, 99, 153, 172, 176, 213

Adams, John Quincy, 14–19; campaign organization, 44–45; campaign strategy, 4, 18, 153; and congressional caucus, 121, 122; as diplomat, 18–19, 140; early political career, 15–16; and election results, 186; and Federalists, 15–16, 81, 100; and Ghent letters controversy, 95–98; inauguration of 1825, 221; insider deal-making, 6, 196, 197–98, 199–200, 207–8, 209–10, 219; and internal improvements, 133, 196; negative attacks against, 17, 98, 99, 100, 104; newspaper network, 52, 53, 56; party commemorating Battle of New Orleans, 111–13; and patronage, 70–71; qualifications for presidency, 17–18, 19; relationship with Calhoun, 86–87; relationship with Clay, 198; relationship with Crawford, 83–86, 148, 223; relationship with Monroe, 14–15; and retrenchment, 93; as secretary of state, 18, 138; and slavery, 99, 140–41;

and social politicking, 74–75, 111–13, 153; state nominations, 65; and tariff legislation, 136, 196; and treaty negotiations, 18, 138–39

Adams, Louisa, 74–75

Adamsites, 44–45, 78, 136, 174, 181, 192, 195, 200, 201, 210, 216, 227–28

Adams-Onís Treaty, 18, 24

Africa, 139, 140

Alabama, 62, 69–70, 72, 167

Albany, New York, 71

Albany Regency, 12, 43, 71, 123, 173, 229

Alien and Sedition Acts, 175

Allgor, Catherine, 73

alliances, political. *See* political alliances

American Colonization Society, 140

American System, 131–32, 173, 179–80, 189, 191, 198, 200, 201, 205–6, 216, 219, 220, 228–29

antipartisanship, 7, 16, 187

antislavery, 5, 25, 64, 93, 140–41, 154, 158, 179–80, 181, 189

Argus of Western America, 51

Arkansas Territory, 197, 198, 208

army reduction, 5, 20, 89–90

Augusta, Georgia, 99

Aurora (Philadelphia), 152

Balch, Alfred, 227

ballots, 35, 40, 64, 158, 162–63

Baltimore, Maryland, 170–71

Baltimore American, 39

Baltimore Morning Chronicle, 123

Bank of Edwardsville, 141

Bank of the United States (BUS), 12, 22, 44, 45, 57, 103, 177, 179, 180, 181, 182, 224

Baptists, 25, 75, 169, 171, 181

Barbour, James, 105, 123

Barbour, Philip, 94

Battle of New Orleans, 28–29, 30, 47, 57, 112, 155, 178

Benton, Thomas Hart, 47, 109, 125, 215, 217

Bill to amend the several acts for imposing Duties on Imports (1824), 134–35

Bill to procure the necessary Surveys, Plans, and Estimates, upon the subject of Roads and Canals (General Survey Bill, 1824), 132–33

biographies. *See* candidate biographies

Boston, Massachusetts, 153

Brooke, Francis, 46–47, 93, 137

Brown, Jacob, 196

Brown's Hotel, 74

Buchanan, James, 204

Burr, Aaron, 119

cabinet, 68–69, 82–83

cabinet debates, 5, 82–83, 85–86; over A.B. controversy, 143–44, 148; over Albany Postmaster, 71; over officer appointment process, 90; over retrenchment, 90, 91–92; over slave trade convention, 139

Calhoun, John C., 19–23; and army reduction, 89–90; campaign collapse, 127–29; campaign organization, 45–46; campaign strategy, 4, 6, 21–22; and congressional caucus, 121; early political career, 19, 21; and election aftermath, 224–25; as nationalist, 21–22; negative attacks against, 22–23, 98, 99, 104; newspaper network, 53–54, 56; and patronage, 70; qualifications for presidency, 19, 21–22; relationship with Adams, 86–87; relationship with Crawford, 83–86, 130, 148, 225; relationship with Jackson, 225; relationship with Monroe, 19–21; relationship with "Radicals," 21; and retrenchment, 90–92; as secretary of war, 19, 21; state nominations, 64–65; and vice presidential race, 129–30, 183–84, 209; and War of 1812, 21, 22

Calhounites, 38, 45–46, 54, 70, 76, 84, 88, 111, 121, 122, 127–28, 143, 203, 205, 216, 226, 227, 228

Call, Richard, 47

Cambreleng, C. C., 123

campaign literature, 37–39

campaign organizations, 2, 3, 37, 41–48; Adams's, 44–45; Calhoun's, 45–46; Clay's, 46–47; Crawford's, 43–44; Jackson's, 47–48

Canada, 21, 96, 140

candidate biographies, 3, 32, 37, 38–39

Carmel Academy, 84

cartoons. *See* political cartoons

Castlereagh, Lord, 138–39

Charleston, South Carolina, 155

Chesapeake and Delaware Canal, 201

Cheves, Langdon, 12, 97

Chile, 71

Choate, Rufus, 19

Cincinnati, Ohio, 181

City Gazette (Washington, D.C.), 56

Clark, John, 37, 84

Clay, Henry, 23–27; and American System, 131–32, 216; appointed secretary of state,

215–17; campaign organization, 46–47; campaign strategy, 4, 26–27, 151–53; and congressional caucus, 121, 122; early political career, 23, 25; and election aftermath, 222; and election results, 184–85; and Ghent letters controversy, 95–98; and health issues, 117; as House Speaker, 23, 131; and internal improvement bill, 132–33; as issues candidate, 25, 137–38, 152–53, 185; and Missouri Compromise, 25–26; negative attacks against, 26, 98, 99, 104; newspaper network, 57–58, 152–53; and patronage, 71–72; qualifications for presidency, 25; relationship with Adams, 198; relationship with Crawford, 198; relationship with Jackson, 24, 198–99, 202; relationship with Monroe, 24; state nominations, 63–64; and tariff legislation, 133–35, 137

Clayites, 46–47, 173, 174, 178, 181, 228

Clinton, DeWitt, 5, 29, 64, 78, 173, 196–97

Clintonians, 71, 93, 174, 196–97, 227

coalitions, political. See political alliances

Cobb, Thomas W., 88

Cocke, John, 109

Coffee, John, 47

Colombia, 70

Columbian Observer (Philadelphia), 38, 54, 55, 57, 100, 110, 114, 126, 202, 214

Columbus, Ohio, 63, 180

Commercial Treaty, French-American (1822), 18

Compensation Act, 24

Congress, U.S., 5, 13, 26, 29, 35, 53, 71, 88–92, 102, 103, 123–24, 133–34, 139, 143–47, 158, 224

congressional caucus, 1–2, 121–26, 187–88, 230; arguments against, 119–20; arguments for, 120; history of, 119–20

congressional factions, 4, 5, 46, 61, 80

Connecticut, 21, 65, 172

Constitution, U.S., 35, 119–20, 125, 183, 215

conventions, delegate nominating, 2, 110, 128–29, 179, 180, 230–31. See also specific conventions by city

Cook, Daniel P., 197, 205, 225

correspondence, 2, 3, 37, 48–51, 55

corrupt bargain, 6, 202, 217–20

corruption, political, 5, 59, 79–80, 102–5, 106, 125, 149–50, 158, 186–90, 206, 232

Crawford, William H., 10–14; and army reduction, 90; and BUS, 12, 44, 177, 179–80; campaign organization, 43–44; campaign strategy, 4, 13, 150; and congressional caucus, 2, 13, 62, 107, 119–20, 124, 230; early political career, 10–11; in 1816 Republican caucus, 10, 43, 119; and election aftermath, 222–23; and election results, 184; as front-runner, 5, 6, 13–14, 20, 41, 62, 69, 78, 83–84, 105, 175, 184; in Georgia politics, 10–11, 43, 222–23; illness, 105, 116–17, 145–46, 150, 193; and internal improvements, 124, 133; negative attacks against, 12, 14, 98, 99–100, 103–4, 125, 151; newspaper network, 52–53, 56; and Panic of 1819, 11–12, 44, 88, 101, 145; and patronage, 69–70; qualifications for presidency, 11; relationship with Adams, 83–86, 223; relationship with Calhoun, 83–86, 149, 225; relationship with Monroe, 10, 11, 15, 83, 85–86, 223; relationship with "Radicals," 12–13, 83, 85; and retrenchment, 88, 90, 94–95, 170; state nominations, 65; and tariff legislation, 136; as treasury secretary, 11

Crawfordites, 21, 43–44, 65, 84–85, 88, 118–19, 124, 136, 139–40, 143–44, 147, 216, 223–24, 226, 227, 228

Creeks, 163

Cunningham, William, 49

Dallas, George M., 45, 128–29

declension, national, 5, 31, 154, 155, 188

defense spending. *See* fortifications program

Delaware, 16, 35, 172, 175

Democratic Gazette, 86

Democratic Party, 2, 227, 228

Democratic Press (Philadelphia), 113

democratization of presidential elections, 1, 2–3, 34–35, 63, 64, 75–76, 103, 125, 162, 185, 229–31

Democrats (as alternate name for Republicans). *See* Republican Party

Dickinson, Charles, 109

Drayton, William, 114

Duralde, Martin, 178

Eaton, John, 38, 47, 54, 65–66, 73, 74, 75, 80, 107–8, 109, 111, 126, 135, 194, 204, 209, 214

Edwards, Ninian, 141–49, 197

electioneering, 3, 35–36, 42, 59, 69, 73, 74–75, 76, 101–2, 106

election results, 162–63, 164–66, 182–90. *See also* regional contests; *specific states*

elections, congressional, 225, 229

elections, presidential: of 1800, 10, 16, 119, 172; of 1816, 10, 16; of 1820, 16, 231; of 1828, 6, 103, 104, 220, 223, 224, 226, 228, 231, 232; of 1832, 103, 223; of 1836, 103; of 1840, 103, 232; of 1844, 103, 222; of 1872, 232; of 1876, 232; of 1948, 232; of 1981, 232; of 2016, 232

elections, state, 1, 35, 84, 128, 148, 180, 225, 229

electors, 1–2, 158–62, 229

Embargo Act, 15

Episcopalians, 75

Era of Good Feelings, 34

Erie Canal, 46, 64

Erwin, Andrew, 109

Europe, 28, 38, 74, 113, 154

Family Party, Philadelphia, 45, 110, 127, 128

Federalist Party, 16–17, 113, 158; decline of, 6, 16, 60–61, 184, 225; and House election, 207–8, 210–11, 225; pro-Federalist as Republican epithet, 99–100, 114–15; proscription of by Republicans, 16–17, 115; and Republican candidates, 17, 115, 127, 206–7

Florida, 18, 20, 29–30

Floyd, John, 143

fortifications program, 21, 88, 90–92

Forts, U.S.: Calhoun, 92; Delaware, 91; Gaines, 91–92; Monroe, 92; Morgan, 91–92; Rouse's Point, 91

France, 154

franchise laws. *See* voting laws

Franklin Gazette (Philadelphia), 39, 86

Fredericktown Political Examiner, 60

Gadsden, James, 89

Gaillard, John, 209

Gales, William, 53

Gallatin, Albert, 28, 114, 124–25

Gazette (Nashville), 220

Gazette (Washington, D.C.), 215

Geneva, Switzerland, 125

Georgia, 10, 35, 43, 65, 175

Ghent Treaty letters, 95–98, 143

Gouverneur, Nicholas, 91

Gouverneur, Samuel, 45, 54, 91

government spending, debates over, 5, 13, 83, 88–89, 90–92. *See also* retrenchment

Grant, Ulysses S., 232

Great Britain, 18, 81

Greeley, Horace, 232

Hamilton, Alexander, 16
Harrisburg convention, 128–29
Harrisburg Pennsylvanian, 40
Harrison, William Henry, 232
Hartford Convention, 126
Hay, George, 151, 176
Hayne, Robert, 77
Heale, M. J., 6
Holmes, John, 71
Holt, Michael, 6
House election of 1825, 6, 208–13; and
    Adams/Clay alliance, 199–202; Adams'
    strategy for, 192, 195–96; Calhoun's role
    in, 205–6; Clay's role in, 191–92; Craw-
    ford's strategy for, 192, 193–94; Federalist
    role in, 207–8; Jackson's strategy for, 192,
    194–95; post-election reaction, 213–15,
    225
House Speaker, 23, 93; race for, 5, 93–94
Houston, Samuel, 31
Huntingdon convention, 110, 128

Illinois, 64, 142–43, 167, 172, 179–80
Indiana, 167, 179
Ingham, Samuel, 123, 145, 146, 203–4, 205
internal improvements, 12, 25, 132, 158, 201

Jackson, Andrew, 27–33; campaign organi-
    zation, 47–48, 130; campaign strategy, 4,
    31–33, 155–56; and congressional caucus,
    121–22, 125–26; early political career,
    27–28; and election aftermath, 225–26;
    and election results, 186–89; as gover-
    nor of Florida, 20, 29–30; health issues,
    117–18; and internal improvements
    bill, 133; negative attacks against, 30,
    116; newspaper network, 54, 55, 57; and
    patronage, 71–72; as political outsider, 5,
    6, 27–28, 30, 31–32, 48, 54, 57, 74, 104–5,

186–87; and pro-Federalist letters, 113–16,
    127; qualifications for presidency, 30;
    relationship with cabinet secretaries,
    87, 105, 225; relationship with Clay,
    201–2; relationship with Eaton, 109; and
    Seminole War, 29; as senator, 108–9; state
    nominations, 62–63; and tariff legisla-
    tion, 135–36; use of corruption issue, 5–6,
    30–31, 32–33, 38, 80, 105, 126, 186–88,
    189–90, 202, 220, 232; and War of 1812,
    28–29, 155, 178
Jackson, Rachel, 74, 75, 110, 195
Jacksonian era, 1–2, 4–5, 7, 59, 61, 68, 82, 104,
    163, 220, 228–29
Jacksonians, 47–48, 128–29, 201–2, 204,
    216, 217, 227; opposition to congressional
    caucus, 121–22, 125–26, 227–28, 230–31
Jefferson, Thomas, 2, 9, 10, 14, 16, 18, 22, 49,
    114, 119, 120, 124, 151, 184, 202; endorse-
    ment of Crawford, 11, 151
Johnson, Richard Mentor, 123, 125
Johnston, Josiah, 152–53

Kendall, Amos, 51–52, 63
Kentucky, 63–64, 179
Kentucky Reporter, 39
King, Rufus, 16, 71
Kremer, George, 203–5, 216

Lafayette, Marquis de, 153–55, 188, 195
Land Office, 69, 70
Lane, Samuel, 223–24
Lansing, Joseph, 71
legislatures, state, 65–66
Letcher, Robert P., 199
Letters of Wyoming, 38, 126, 155, 220
Lewis, William B., 107–8
Lexington, Kentucky, 25
Litchfield Law School, 21

Livingston, Edward, 143, 147

Lockwood, Ralph Ingersoll, 152

Louisiana, 35, 64, 140, 167, 172, 178

Louisiana Purchase, 18, 98

Lowndes, William, 64, 93

Lowrie, Walter, 114

Macon, Nathaniel, 123, 124, 183

Madison, James, 14, 18, 22, 71, 119, 120, 176

Maine, 65, 172

Mangum, Willie P., 104

Maryland, 64–65, 66, 170–71, 172

Massachusetts, 65, 172

McArthur, Duncan, 143

McDuffie, George, 203–5

McLane, Lewis, 193, 208, 209, 210

Meigs, Return J., 71

Methodists, 75, 169, 171

Mexico, 142

Mid-Atlantic, 5, 6, 16, 157, 161, 166, 171, 182, 211; Adams's campaign in, 44, 173, 183, 195–97; Calhoun's campaign in, 22, 45, 67; Clay's campaign in, 27, 152–53, 185; Crawford's campaign in, 124, 170–71, 177; and internal improvements, 132–33; Jackson's campaign in, 110, 130, 167, 170–71, 183, 186, 197, 226; and protective tariffs, 133–34, 136

Milledgeville, Georgia, 69

Mississippi, 167

Mississippi River, 28, 95–96, 97

Missouri, 25–26, 64, 179

Missouri Compromise, 5, 25–26, 34, 64, 140, 158

Mix, Elijah, 92

Monroe, James: and anti-partisanship, 16, 45–46; and 1816 nomination, 10, 119; and fortifications program, 21, 90, 91–92; and Jackson's pro-Federalist letters, 113–15;

and officer appointment process, 89–90; relationship with Adams, 14–15, 221; relationship with Calhoun, 19–20; relationship with Clay, 24; relationship with Crawford, 10, 11, 15, 83, 85–86, 148–49, 223; relationship with Crawfordites, 83, 86, 223–24; relationship with Jefferson, 151; and retrenchment, 90–92; and War of 1812, 21

Monrovian Era, 217

mudslinging, 58, 102–3, 231–32

Murfreesboro, Tennessee, 108

Nashville, Tennessee, 47

Nashville Gazette, 39, 118

Nashville Junto, 47

Nashville Republican, 55

Nashville Whig, 136

national bank. *See* Bank of the United States

National Intelligencer, 53, 56, 96, 97, 101, 114, 131, 139–40, 143, 203

nationalism, 189–90

National Journal, 56, 140

National Republican (Cincinnati), 119

National Road, 169, 181, 201

Native Americans, 29, 72, 151, 163

Netherlands, 18

New England, 5, 16, 66, 157, 159, 164, 182, 211, 224; Adams's campaign in, 15, 18, 27, 39, 40, 44–45, 87, 98, 140, 153, 172, 173, 175, 186, 195, 209–10; Clay's campaign in, 162, 178, 185, 188; Crawford's campaign in, 121, 126, 172, 177; and Ghent letters controversy, 96; and internal improvements, 132, 201; Jackson's campaign in, 162; and protective tariffs, 134

New Hampshire, 65, 172

New Jersey, 66, 170, 178

New Orleans, 21, 29

newspaper networks, 2, 3, 56–58, 152–53

newspapers, 3, 37, 51–55. *See also specific newspapers by name and location*

newspaper "wars," 5, 58, 95–101

New York, 35, 172–74

New York City, 152

Niles, Hezekiah, 25

nomination, presidential: by congressional caucus (*see* congressional caucus); by state legislatures, 4, 61, 62–65, 230

North, 67, 158, 196–97; Adams's campaign in, 15, 18, 86–87, 111, 118, 140–41, 186; Calhoun's campaign in, 4, 21, 22, 45, 86–87, 127; Crawford's campaign in, 118, 124, 141; Jackson's campaign in, 42; and Missouri Compromise, 26, 93, 99; and protective tariffs, 99, 136; and Revolutionary War pensions, 92–93

North Carolina, 35, 167–68; Calhoun's campaign in, 66, 127; Jackson's campaign in, 110–11, 127

Northwest, 5, 157, 160, 165, 212; Adams's campaign in, 45, 186; Clay's campaign in, 178–82; Crawford's campaign in, 12, 44, 177; Jackson's campaign in, 130, 167, 183; and protective tariffs, 134, 137

officer appointment process, 89–90

Ohio, 44, 63–64, 180–81

organizations. *See* campaign organizations

Owen, George, 143

pamphlets, 37–39

Panic of 1819, 5, 11–12, 34, 88, 101, 157–58

Parsons, Lynn Hudson, 7

party (political), 150, 227, 228–29

party (social gathering), 2, 4, 61, 73–76; commemorating Battle of New Orleans, 111–13

Pasley, Jeffrey, 75

Patriot (New York), 54, 130, 152

patronage, 2, 4, 13, 20, 61, 68–73

Peart, Daniel, 7

Pennsylvania, 66, 169; Calhoun's campaign in, 64, 127–29; Jackson's campaign in, 110, 128–29, 135

People's Ticket (New Jersey), 170

People's Ticket (North Carolina), 110–11, 127, 167–68

Philadelphia, Pennsylvania, 45, 110, 127, 128, 152

Pickering, Timothy, 206–7

Pittsburgh, Pennsylvania, 169

Plumer, William, 200

political alliances, 65–66, 227–28; between Adams and Clay, 227–28; between Adams and Jackson, 111–12; between Crawford and Adams, 118, 123; between Crawford and Clay, 118–19, 123; rumored between politicians, 78–79, 112–13, 193; state-to-state, 4, 61, 66–67, 127. *See also* Virginia/New York axis

political buttons, 3, 37

political cartoons, 3, 37, 39

polls, 3, 37, 40, 230

Pope family, 142

Porter, Peter, 46

Post Office Act of 1792, 51

Post Office Department, 68–69, 71

Presbyterians, 75, 169, 171, 181

protective tariff, 12, 25, 133–34, 158

Prussia, 18

public meetings (political), 2, 162, 170, 180, 230–31

quasi-war with France (1798), 99–100

"Radicals," 12–13, 21, 83, 85, 88, 92, 94, 105, 198, 226

Raleigh, North Carolina, 168

Raleigh Star, 130

Randolph, John, of Roanoke, 104, 143

Ratcliffe, Donald, 7

Reagan, Ronald, 232

regional contests, 5–6, 157; Mid-Atlantic, 161, 166, 169–71, 172–74; New England, 159, 164, 172; Northwest, 44, 160, 165, 167, 177, 178–82; South, 159, 164, 167–69, 172, 175–77; Southwest, 160, 163, 165, 167

regionalism, 157–58

Republican and Congressional Examiner, 56, 95, 100, 143

Republican factions, 17, 46, 48, 120, 173, 180

republicanism, 36, 55, 59, 106, 158

Republican Party, 68, 226–27; and factionalism, 17, 42, 48, 60–61, 65–66, 71, 73, 75–76, 93, 106, 120, 150, 162, 184

retrenchment, 88–89, 94

Revolutionary War pensions, 5, 92–93

Rhode Island, 35, 65, 172

Richmond, Virginia, 99, 176

Richmond Inquirer, 43, 176

Richmond Junto, 12, 43

Ritchie, Thomas, 43, 46, 49, 176

Root, Erastus, 133

rumors, political, 4, 61, 76–79

Russell, Jonathan, 95–98

Russia, 18

Russo-American Treaty, 18

Salisbury Western Carolinian, 168

Sanford, Nathan, 183–84

Scott, John, 198, 225

Scott, Winfield, 109

Seaton, Joseph, 53

secretary of state as "stepping-stone" to presidency, 2, 14, 199, 200, 206, 217, 230

Seminole War, 24, 29, 47, 163

Shulze, John, 128

Simpson, Stephen, 54, 55, 57, 100, 110, 122, 128, 214

slavery, 26, 64, 140–41, 158

slave trade convention (1824), 138–40

Smith, Samuel, 123

Smith, William, 77

South, 5, 16, 67, 99, 157–58, 159, 164, 196, 211; Adams's campaign in, 15, 79, 118, 140–41, 172, 185, 186; Calhoun's campaign in, 4, 9, 22, 45, 84, 87; Clay's campaign in, 27, 137, 152; Crawford's campaign in, 13, 79, 84, 118, 169, 175, 177; and internal improvements, 132–33, 201; Jackson's campaign in, 167, 169, 171, 183, 186, 188, 226; and Missouri Compromise, 26; and protective tariffs, 134–35, 136–37; and Revolutionary War pensions, 92

Southard, Samuel, 147, 148, 149, 221

South Carolina, 21, 35, 64, 66, 77, 168–69

Southern Patriot, 104

Southwest, 5, 157, 160, 165, 212; Adams's campaign in, 167, 185, 186; Clay's campaign in, 163, 167; Crawford's campaign in, 177; Jackson's campaign in, 32, 130, 163, 167, 188; and protective tariffs, 134–35

Spain, 18

Spanish-American republics, 24

State Department, 14, 16, 24, 52, 96, 194, 199–200, 204, 215–17, 219

Statesman, 103

states' rights, 22, 228

state-to-state political alliances, 4, 61, 66–67, 127

Stephenson, Benjamin, 141–42

Storrs, Henry, 66

Story, Joseph, 218

straw polls. *See* polls

Supreme Court, 70, 218
Swift, Joseph, 92

Tallmadge, James, 25
Taney, Roger B., 188
tariff. *See* protective tariff
Taylor, John (of Caroline), 123
Taylor, John W., 93–94, 122–23, 143
Tennessee, 62, 167
Thompson, Smith, 71
tickets. *See* ballots
Tilden, Samuel, 232
Tompkins, Daniel, 71
Towson, Nathan, 89
Treasury Department, 68–69, 83, 85, 101
Treaty of Ghent, 18, 24, 95–98, 198
Trimble, David, 88
Truman, Harry, 232
Trump, Donald, 232
turnout, voter, 158–62, 182–83, 231

United Kingdom. *See* Great Britain

Van Buren, Martin, 77, 94, 121, 183, 196,
    223, 229, 232; and A.B. controversy,
    144, 146–47; and Adams, 226–27; and
    Calhoun, 224–25; and Clay, 118; and con-
    gressional caucus, 123–24; and "corrupt
    bargain" charges, 217, 218; and Crawford's
    campaign, 43, 125, 150–51; and House
    election, 193–94, 210, 212; and Jackson, 31;
    and Monroe, 20; and New York's legisla-
    tive election, 173–75; and patronage, 71
Vandeventer, Christopher, 92
Van Rensselaer, Solomon, 71
Van Rensselaer, Stephen, 208, 210–12
Vermont, 35, 172
vice presidential race of 1824, 183–84
Virginia, 35, 65, 175–77

Virginia dynasty, 13, 99, 230
Virginia/New York axis, 1–2, 12, 27, 43, 46,
    66–67, 127, 150, 173, 184, 230
Virginia Resolutions, 176
"Virginius," 1
voters: black, 35; Dutch, 173, 181, 188;
    English, 170; Federalist, 168, 169, 171,
    173; German, 169; Irish, 169, 188; mid-
    Atlantic, 169–71, 172–73; militiamen,
    168; New England, 172; New England
    émigrés, 15, 44, 167, 173, 181; northwest-
    ern, 179, 180–81; religious, 169, 171,
    181; Scots-Irish, 169, 181, 188; southern,
    167–69, 176–77; southwestern, 163; urban,
    171, 188; women, 35; young, 169
voting laws, 35, 158–62

Walsh, Robert, 15
War Department, 21, 70, 83, 88, 89, 92
Warfield, Henry, 208, 210
War of 1812, 5, 11, 16, 18, 21, 24, 28–29, 34, 88,
    126, 140
Washington, D.C., 73, 108
Washington, George, 18, 27, 102, 114, 154,
    155
Watkins, Thomas, 109
Webster, Daniel, 136, 143, 207–8, 209–10,
    225
Weed, Thurlow, 174
West, 16, 67, 77, 158, 173, 181, 227; and A.B.
    controversy, 100–101, 141–42, 145, 147;
    Adams's campaign in, 15, 111, 197–98;
    Calhoun's campaign in, 22, 42; Clay's
    campaign in, 25, 26–27, 40, 46, 57, 97, 98,
    163, 167; and "corrupt bargain" charges,
    201–2, 214–19; Crawford's campaign in,
    43, 118; and Ghent letters controversy,
    95–96, 97, 98; and House election,
    194–95, 197–202, 209–10, 225;

West (*continued*)
    and internal improvements, 132–33,
    200–201; Jackson's campaign in, 32, 78,
    163, 167, 171, 187, 191–92, 194–95, 226; and
    Revolutionary war pensions, 92
Wheeling, Virginia, 142

Whig Party, 2, 217, 227, 228
Williams, John, 107–8
Wilson, John, 133
Wirt, William, 71, 85, 148, 221

Yale University, 21